# Editing Audio
# in Pro Tools®

## Skill Pack

Michael White

**THOMSON**
——————★—————— TM
**COURSE TECHNOLOGY**

Professional ■ Technical ■ Reference

# Editing Audio in Pro Tools®
## Skill Pack

**Publisher and General Manager, Thomson Course Technology PTR:** Stacy L. Hiquet

**Associate Director of Marketing:** Sarah O'Donnell

**Manager of Editorial Services:** Heather Talbot

**Marketing Manager:** Mark Hughes

**Acquisitions Editor:** Orren Merton

**Marketing Assistant:** Adena Flitt

**Project Editor/Development Editor:** Cathleen D. Snyder

**Technical Reviewer:** Scot Gresham-Lancaster

**PTR Editorial Services Coordinator:** Erin Johnson

**Copy Editor:** Kim Cofer

**Interior Layout:** Shawn Morningstar

**Cover Designer:** Mike Tanamachi

**CD-ROM Producer:** Brandon Penticuff

**Indexer:** Katherine Stimson

**Proofreader:** Kim V. Benbow

**Assistant Writer:** John Valencia

Digidesign and Pro Tools are registered trademarks of Avid Technologies, Inc. in the United States. All other trademarks are the property of their respective owners.

*Important:* Thomson Course Technology PTR cannot provide software support. Please contact the appropriate software manufacturer's technical support line or Web site for assistance.

Thomson Course Technology PTR and the author have attempted throughout this book to distinguish proprietary trademarks from descriptive terms by following the capitalization style used by the manufacturer.

Information contained in this book has been obtained by Thomson Course Technology PTR from sources believed to be reliable. However, because of the possibility of human or mechanical error by our sources, Thomson Course Technology PTR, or others, the Publisher does not guarantee the accuracy, adequacy, or completeness of any information and is not responsible for any errors or omissions or the results obtained from use of such information. Readers should be particularly aware of the fact that the Internet is an ever-changing entity. Some facts may have changed since this book went to press.

Educational facilities, companies, and organizations interested in multiple copies or licensing of this book should contact the Publisher for quantity discount information. Training manuals, CD-ROMs, and portions of this book are also available individually or can be tailored for specific needs.

ISBN-10: 1-59863-281-7
ISBN-13: 978-1-59863-281-1
Library of Congress Catalog Card Number: 2006927127
Printed in the United States of America
07 08 09 10 11 TW 10 9 8 7 6 5 4 3 2 1

**THOMSON**

★

**COURSE TECHNOLOGY**

Professional ■ Technical ■ Reference

Thomson Course Technology PTR, a division of Thomson Learning Inc. 25 Thomson Place Boston, MA 02210

http://www.courseptr.com

*I would like to dedicate this book to my wife, Mary Leck, whose undying belief in me has enabled me to accomplish things I never thought or dreamed possible.*

# Acknowledgments

First and foremost, I would like to thank Orren Merton for believing in me and supporting me when he had no rational reason to do so. This book would not have been possible without his guidance and encouragement. I would also like to thank Mark Garvey, who very graciously met with me out of a very busy travel schedule and offered me the chance to write this book in the first place. Special thanks to Brian Cline for giving me a song to build this book upon. I really must thank John Valencia, my writing assistant for this project, for his hard work and dedication, which helped me finish the project when I didn't think I could. I would also like to thank Cathleen Snyder for picking up the ball and carrying me to the finish line. On the music front, I would like to thank R. A. Neuman and Michael Minkowitz for their programming and sampling work; and Gabe Wilhelm, Phil Bogard, and Joe Cutrell for donating their music skills. Although they were not directly part of the writing of this book, Udo Hoppenworth, John Jansen, and Fred Ditman have been such a big part of supporting my teaching career and this venture that they at least deserve this modest mention. There are so many other people involved in the process who I have never met or communicated with directly that I would like to thank for their work in bringing this book to fruition. Bravo!!! But mostly, I want to thank my wife and life partner, Mary, for her love and support in helping me take on and finish this project, knowing that it would make our life a bit more difficult.

# About the Author

**Michael White** received his B.A. in music production and engineering in 1986. He started his career by working his way through the highly acclaimed world-class Right Track Recording Studios in New York City, and eventually through the prestigious home of Jimi Hendrix's Electric Lady Studios. Learning the art of engineering from the top engineers in the world, Michael honed his craft and took the leap to freelance engineer in the early nineties, where he has worked with many of the top recording artists in the industry. Michael has worked on half a dozen Whitney Houston albums, as well as the likes of James Taylor, the Rolling Stones, David Byrne and the Talking Heads, David Bowie, 3 Doors Down, and many others.

Michael's unique ability to communicate recording concepts and teach them to others led him to Solid State Logic, the largest and perhaps most prominent recording console manufacturer in the world, where he contracted his services to help develop, teach, and support the award-winning SL 9000 J Series console for many of the most prestigious recording studios in the United States. His desire to maintain a career in recording arts in a rapidly changing industry eventually led him to learn emerging technologies that helped broaden his experience to the post-production world, where he worked for the Outdoor Life Network and Sirius Satellite Radio. Michael's talents eventually led him to education as a career path. He currently contracts teaching services to the SAE Institute in New York City. He resides in New York City and continues to work as a professional recording engineer for music, film, and post-production.

# Table of Contents

# Introduction

The genesis of *Editing Audio in Pro Tools: Skill Pack* stems from my firm belief that editing audio is actually quite simple, only *we* make it complicated! A little bit of knowledge and insight can go a long way to changing one's perception of how "good" an application is. Through my own experience and years of teaching the art of engineering, it has also become my belief that most often, the best way to learn anything is by applying it in a real-life situation. If you were learning how to ride a bicycle, you could read books on biking techniques; break down the different parts of the bicycle, how they work, how to adjust them, and how to fine-tune and lubricate them; and train all you want on a stationary bike, but when you get out on the road on a real bicycle, you will still stumble and fall. Until you gain the necessary skills from real-life experience, you will never really learn how to ride your bike. If you learn by experience rather than reading, then this book is for you. Pro Tools is your bike, and it is from this perspective that I present to you this book, *Editing Audio in Pro Tools: Skill Pack.*

You will be given a song, disassembled, and throughout the course of the book, we will create a completed song using all of the editing tools available. Each tool will also provide a technique, method, or engineering skill to further enrich the learning experience. This is critical because it will add perspective to the use of the program and teach you some fundamental engineering and production skills.

My engineering experience dates back to the mid '80s, when all records were recorded entirely in the analog realm. I will not wax poetic about the wonders of analog tape—digital is the recording medium for the vast majority of all the music today, it's here to stay, and there is no logical reason to go back in time. That being said, the basic engineering skills I learned during that era have not fundamentally changed. The tools are more refined, the methods are streamlined, and the options are limited only by one's imagination. This, however, requires a little bit of discipline. Just because you have the ability to take a performance, chop it up, and fix the timing pitch and timbre until it is "perfect," that doesn't mean you should. This knowledge can only come through experience and listening. As we progress with the exercises in the book, I will try to provide you with as many tips, tricks, insights, explanations, and also the origins of any technique, tool, or skill that I have found to be particularly useful. Remember, Pro Tools, originally called Sound Designer, was initially a program created for editing audio and marketed to professional engineers. Therefore, learning the way professional engineers make records will go a long way to helping you *know* Pro Tools, not just understand it.

With this in mind, I have tried to simulate as best as I can the real-world process of editing a song as it would be presented to you by a producer, artist, songwriter, or record company. We will start by editing our basic tracks and continue through the process of overdubbing, compiling multiple takes, and fixing timing pitch and performance issues. By using as many of the editing tools as possible, we will end the book with a produced song ready to be mixed. (Sorry, that topic is covered in a different *Skill Pack* book!)

So buckle your chinstrap, boot up your Pro Tools system, and let's take it for a ride!

# What You'll Find in This Book

What you will find in this book is an interactive and hands-on method for learning the art of editing audio in Pro Tools. Rather than just discussing the available features and options within the program (in other words, giving you a manual), I am offering something a step deeper that will not just show you how a feature works, but when and where you might actually want to use it, including the real-world application of editing a demo song. Some of the many things you might gain from following the book are:

- A fundamental understanding of the design and philosophy of editing audio in Pro Tools
- Real-world practical application of editing techniques
- Ease and flow of operation and navigation when editing audio
- How to avoid common pitfalls and mistakes
- Increased workflow capability

# Whom This Book Is For

Upon taking up the challenge of writing this book, I came across one fundamental issue. The readers of this book come from a wide variety of differing experience and skill levels. Some of you may be engineers looking to refine your editing skills in Pro Tools. Others, with little or no engineering experience at all, might be looking to unveil the dark, mysterious world of editing audio. You may be a songwriter or musician trying to find a simple guide to teach you how to use this insane application that the salesman in your local music store somehow convinced you to buy. Perhaps you are switching to Pro Tools from another recording application and you want to adapt your skills to a new platform. Or maybe you're even a producer, looking to understand the application on a deeper level to improve your editing skills without requiring the services of an engineer.

All in all, this is quite a large group to satisfy....

To be successful in this endeavor, it was necessary to provide valuable information to all potential readers so that no one person would feel left out or slighted. I also felt it was critically important to find the one need that ties all of the aforementioned people together, the one goal that brings you here to this book in the first place. That goal, of course, is making better music. I am sure that no person would buy a program with the reputation and capabilities of Pro Tools because they were looking to make their music worse! I share with you this fundamental desire. I have spent the better part of the last 20-plus years helping producers, artists, songwriters, and composers make their music better. I hope I can do the same for you! If you fit into one of these categories or you find that you are drawn to this book for whatever reason, then perhaps this book is for you.

Is it possible to satisfy every buyer of this book, given the differing backgrounds? The answer of course is no, it is not entirely possible. What I can promise, however, is that if you follow this book from beginning to end, and go through each exercise and process with an open mind and a thirst for learning this program, you will know a whole lot more about how to edit audio in Pro Tools and how records are made than you did before buying this book.

The very first thing I teach my students, above all else, is to have fun with the process. I'm sure that very few people got into the process of making music because they were looking for a boring, tedious way to eat up their valuable time. The most important thing you can do to learn Pro Tools is to have a little fun with the audio, and in the process of having fun, you'll be amazed at what you can learn.

## How This Book Is Organized

This book is organized into six chapters. The information included in each chapter is grouped in such a way that it logically leads you from the basics of editing audio to an in-depth study of the more sophisticated and powerful features available in Pro Tools. Although each chapter has its own logical flow, so too does the book itself flow from chapter to chapter.

- ■ Chapter 1, "Getting Started," prepares you to start the book exercises. The structure of the book is detailed, as well as proper methods for copying files from the CD-ROM. The always-important preference settings will be set to alleviate any confusion with the exercises.

- ■ Chapter 2, "Working with the Edit Modes," lays out the most fundamental part of Pro Tools. Each exercise details the practical function and usage of the four Edit modes.

- ■ Chapter 3, "The Edit Tools," details the function and practical application of each tool and all its variations. You will gain an in-depth understanding of the fundamental philosophy behind each tool.

- ■ Chapter 4, "Integrating the Edit Modes and Edit Tools," opens the door to the real power of editing audio in Pro Tools. Each edit tool is matched with each Edit mode to display the limitless options available to the informed user.

- ■ Chapter 5, "Grouping," discusses the two kinds of grouping, track and region. These two forms of grouping greatly enhance your workflow by multiplying your editing work over many tracks or regions.

- ■ Chapter 6, "Looping, Tempo, and Timing (Beat Detective)," offers a vast palate of automated editing features, beyond the obvious cut, copy, and paste options. This chapter shows you how to adapt and extract tempo and groove information to and from your music to expand the capabilities of your editing work.

Because of the vast number of features and options available, it may not be possible to remember or understand fully every feature discussed in the book. For this reason, the book will allow you to freely move to any exercise within any chapter to review any feature or option in the book without having to start from the beginning. This is accomplished through the use of session templates and will be discussed in detail in Chapter 1. Enjoy!

# 1

# Getting Started

**W**elcome to *Editing Audio in Pro Tools*! Before you begin editing your song, it is very important to review a few of the particulars as they relate to the structure of this book. First, we need to ensure that we are in fact speaking the same language as you proceed with the book. This chapter starts with a "How To" section that looks at software compatibility issues, Mac versus PC issues, the ergonomic structure of the book, and the usage of Pro Tools conventions, such as playlists and templates.

Next you will load in files from the CD-ROM, review any precautions regarding hard drive compatibility, and set up the template session. Finally, you will calibrate your preference settings to make certain your program settings will match those of the book. So bear with me for a few minutes, and the rest of the book will be a breeze!

## How to Use This Book

To understand how to use this book, you first need to understand the fundamental design of the "Skill Pack." Skill Packs focus on a particular skill set within an audio application—in this case, editing audio in Pro Tools. They encompass a range of skills from the root elements of the subject matter to the advanced techniques used by today's professionals.

You can approach this book in one of two basic ways. You can start each chapter from the beginning and follow each exercise through to the end of the book. This method will give you an in-depth look at the design of the Pro Tools editing system. Alternatively, you might want to focus on a particular editing feature within a chapter, without having to start from the beginning. This is made possible by the use of session templates, which are explained in more detail later in this chapter. In that respect, the book is designed to be a reference source. The editing techniques and methods used in this book are universal and may be adapted to future software revisions. Unless, of course, Pro Tools decides to scrap entirely the most successful and popular editing system yet designed. With this in mind, it is important to first lay down the ergonomic structure of the book, look at some compatibility issues, and delve into some of the useful features included with Pro Tools that will make the learning process easy and fun.

## Compatibility

This book is compatible with all supported HD, LE, and M-Powered versions of Pro Tools. Whether you are using an HD, LE, or M-Powered interface has no bearing whatsoever on your ability to use this book. The focus will be primarily software-based rather than hardware-based. Given that the software for each of the systems (HD, LE, or M-Powered) varies based on its processing capabilities (HD, for example, uses processing chip sets on separate PCI cards to handle all of the audio processing), I will only use features from the basic software package for the exercises in the book. Should I cover a topic including a feature only offered in an HD system, for example, I will discuss its application or use, but not make it a part of finishing the exercise. Many features, such as Beat Detective, are offered in HD as a multi-channel version, but only as mono in the LE version. In such a case, I will obviously use the mono version so all readers can apply the techniques.

## Optional Upgrades

Pro Tools now provides upgrade packages that include additional plug-ins, software synthesizers, advanced editing features, higher sample rates, and so on. For a few extra dollars, these bundled features can improve your editing palette and greatly expand the capabilities of your system. Most of these upgrade features, however, are extensions of the techniques you will learn in this book, do not affect the features at all, or are tools that are beyond the scope of editing audio.

As of this writing, the upgrade packages are the Music Production Toolkit, which includes expanded track count, multi-track Beat Detective, SoundReplacer, and the DINR intelligent noise reduction plug-in; and the DV Toolkit 2, which is focused primarily on post-production for film and video. It includes the previously mentioned features from the Music Production Toolkit, and also includes VocALign, a time alignment tool; DigiBase, a file management tool; and DigiTranslator, an import and export utility for OMF, AAF, and MXF files.

## Mac versus PC

This book is both Mac- and PC-compatible. Given that Pro Tools software operates equally for both Mac and PC, the book should seem transparent of platform as you work through the exercises. There are no differences in terms of menu layout, display characteristics, or available features. The keyboard layout is the only obvious difference and is addressed in more detail in the following section. Although I am primarily a Mac user, I have attempted to be as unbiased as possible with regard to platform because this is a book about editing audio in Pro Tools, rather than a debate about who makes the most kick-ass computer system. Each platform has its inherent strengths and flaws. Where necessary, I will break down any differences as they relate to each platform, but only within the context of this book.

I will assume that your software has already been installed and functions properly. Because software upgrades and operating systems are changing so rapidly, it is beyond the scope of this book to walk you through installing your software. See the Read Me folder included with your install disc first, or log on to Digidesign's website at www.digidesign.com for the latest system requirements and installation procedures.

## Debugging Your Software

Debugging software can be the most frustrating problem you can have after installing the software, especially for new users who are still learning the program and who are not certain whether it is the software that is not working or whether it is them. I cannot give you the answers to debugging your setup because that could encompass an entire book's worth of material all on its own! I will, however, give you a few tips to help steer you in the right direction:

- **Make sure you are on the recommended operating system version.** Many of the problems I have seen with Pro Tools software are a result of being over- or under-upgraded with the operating system. Given the number of different computers, specifications, operating systems, and new technologies being introduced seemingly every day, it is difficult for a software manufacturer to bring its whole product line up to these new specifications as they are released. Be patient, and check with the Digidesign website (www.digidesign.com) before upgrading your operating system. Once you get your operating system and software stable, do not upgrade until you need to.

- **Write down error numbers as problems occur.** These numbers are generated for a reason! Digidesign has created a system of checks and balances with the design of its software to help you get to the root cause of an existing problem with your system. Digidesign has two forms of online help for all users at no extra charge—the Answerbase and the User Conference.

- **Use Digidesign's Answerbase.** The Answerbase is an online search engine that answers most error message problems. You can access it through www.digidesign.com by clicking on Support and selecting Support Search. Once there, simply type in the error message number, select Answerbase, and click the Search button, and you will receive a list of the most recent solutions to your problem. If you receive no responses to your query, try to simplify your request information. For example, instead of typing Error-9031, try typing in just 9031. You may find that you have more leads to investigate.

- **Use Digidesign's User Conference.** If you cannot find the solution to your problem on the Answerbase, you may want to investigate the User Conference. Again, go to www.digidesign.com, select Support, and then select Support Forum. A short description of the User Conference will pop up with a link to Digidesign User Conference. Click on the link, and you can create a user profile. If you have already created a user profile, then sign in. If not, select New User and fill in the appropriate information, and you will have a user profile at no charge to you! You do not need to create a user profile to browse any of the posts; however, you *will* need one if you want to submit a post. The posts are broken down

3

into categories as they relate to different software and hardware. For example, you can select from categories such as HD Systems, LE Systems, M-Powered Systems, Control Surfaces, and so on. Subcategories will designate either the Mac or Windows platform. Find the category that most closely matches your setup and hack away! The User Conference is moderated by Digidesign tech support, and they will help to address technical issues as they come about. I have personally found this to be a valuable resource for information and debugging solutions.

## Shortcuts and Menus

The shortcuts for Mac and PC are feature-equal; that is, the same shortcuts exist for both Mac and PC. The differences lay in the modifier keys used to enable the shortcut. The main modifier key for Mac is the Command key. On a PC, it is the Ctrl key. The Option key in Mac will either duplicate or perform an opposing function, depending on the usage. The same functions on a PC can be performed by selecting the Alt key. The Control key (Mac) and the Start key (PC), sometimes called the *clutch key*, will perform a variety of functions throughout the system when performing copy functions, toggling through parameter settings with dialog boxes, and much, much more.

In this book, all shortcuts will be conveyed in both Mac (Control, Option, Command) and PC (Ctrl, Start, Alt) formats. All shortcut commands will be ***bold and italicized***. For example, to create new tracks you would ***press Command+Shift+N*** (Mac) or ***Ctrl+Shift+N*** (PC). Furthermore, any actions required for those tasks such as ***click, click/drag, grab, move, press, hit, select***, and so on will also be bold and italicized.

All menu and icon selections will be in **bold** type. For example, I may ask you to ***open*** the **File** menu and ***select*** **Save Session As (File/Save Session As)**. Or I may ask you to ***select*** the **TC/E** tool to perform a certain task. However, I may also discuss the uses of the TC/E tool without asking you to use it. In such a case, the tool or menu selection will be written in normal text. My hope is that using these conventions will help to alleviate any confusion as to the requested action. After all, time is money....

## Session Templates

I have carefully organized this book to allow it to be used in two basic ways:

- You can follow the book chapter by chapter from beginning to end.
- You can start from a specific chapter or any particular point within any chapter to focus on a particular skill.

Starting from the beginning of any chapter or any exercise within a chapter is made possible by the use of session templates. Templates allow a basic setup or start point to be achieved simply by booting up Pro Tools and opening the template for the chapter you wish to start from. This feature will allow you to revisit the book at a later date and review a particular feature covered in a chapter without having to start the whole process again from the beginning of the book. I will discuss this in more detail in the "Using Session Templates" section later in this chapter.

If you want to start from the beginning of the book and go all the way through to the end, you will need to use the templates at the start of each chapter. This will allow you to reset your system with the exercises dedicated to that chapter's subject matter. For example, you've finished Chapter 3, "The Edit Tools," and you are now ready to embark on Chapter 4, "Integrating the Edit Modes and Edit Tools." *Select* **Close Session** from the **File** menu and then *select* **Open Session** from the **File** menu. *Find* and *select* the Chapter 4 Start template, and begin Chapter 4 with all of the edits from previous chapters already performed correctly for you.

## Screenshots

I will make use of screenshots to help display, as accurately as possible, the feature or task you are trying to accomplish. The screenshots will be focused mostly on the editing techniques being employed for creation of the song. The purpose is for clarification and to verify that you are using the correct tool or feature. For basic utilitarian functions, such as Save Session, Cut, Copy, Paste, and so on, I won't include screenshots so as not to clog the book with redundant images.

The screenshots were created from version 7.1 software. If you are using a previous version of the software and are attempting to complete the exercises, you will find that your screen will look slightly different in some screenshots, exactly the same in others, and completely different in screenshots showing menu selections. If you are using a later version of the software, you may find that you have additional selections and features that are unaccounted for.

## Loading Files from the CD-ROM

Before you start the editing exercises for your song, you will first need to load the files in from the CD-ROM. Place the CD-ROM included with this book into your CD drive. If the CD-ROM does not automatically load up, *double-click* on the **disk image** in the Mac Finder or Windows Explorer to view the contents. *Double-click* on the link for your computer type, **Start.osx** (Mac) or **Start.exe** (PC), and preview the License agreement. If acceptable, *select* **I agree**. *Click* once on the **Chapter Files** link at the bottom of the screen, and you will be given a list of chapters. (See Figure 1.1.) *Select* **Chapter 1-2**. This will open your default browser and give you access to the chapter files.

Each chapter has a separate folder. Each folder contains within it an Audio Files folder, a Fade Files folder, a folder for Region Groups, and Pro Tools Session icons for each exercise. These session icons will allow you, as mentioned earlier in this chapter, to start from any point in the chapter.

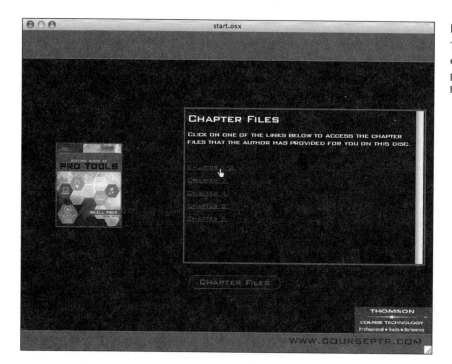

**Figure 1.1**

This figure shows the contents of the CD-ROM provided with this book.

## Copying the Files to Your Hard Drive

Copying files to your hard drive may seem to be a simple matter, but before you begin dragging and dropping, there are a few important things to consider. Where will the files be copied to? Is the disk formatted properly for audio? How much space is available on the drive? What is the best way to organize your files?

Once all of these factors are considered and acted upon, you will find that your sessions run smoother, your files will be easier to access, and your file management will be easier.

### The Destination Drive

Pro Tools recommends that a hard drive, whether it's internal or external, be dedicated to audio. Recording to a drive that contains your operating system is not recommended and may cause problems with proper storage of your audio files. It may also negatively affect proper functioning of your operating system. If you cannot dedicate an entire drive to audio, you might consider partitioning your internal drive. Although this is not recommended by Digidesign either, it will at least separate your audio from your operating system.

Copying your audio files to your boot drive is like throwing your favorite marbles into a big barrel full of rocks and pebbles. Sure, you know where your marbles are, but how hard is it going to be to get them all out when you need them? And if those rocks and pebbles are constantly being added and taken away, how long do you think it will take before your marbles start disappearing? So, before you lose your marbles, consider exactly where you want to keep them.

Pro Tools also recommends that audio drives be formatted to a Mac OS Extended format (also known as HFS+) for Mac systems and either FAT32 or NTFS format for Windows systems. Windows users may want to consider using the NTFS format instead of FAT32 due to partitioning limitations and the ability of NTFS-formatted drives to be restored by a data recovery service should your hard drive crash. Although drives that are formatted for Mac can be accessed on a PC and vice versa, Pro Tools designates these drives as "transfer" drives. This prohibits Pro Tools sessions from being recorded to or played back from the foreign drive format. Pro Tools files from a transfer drive must be copied to a properly formatted drive for the operating system you are working on. If you are considering reformatting or partitioning your drives, please refer to the Digidesign website (www.digidesign.com) regarding hard drive formatting and maintenance requirements.

## Disk Space

The CD-ROM contains approximately 600 MB of files. Be sure that you have enough hard drive space to accommodate copying all of the files. Alternatively, you can copy the folders for each chapter one at a time as you complete each chapter's work. This may allow you to free up the additional space needed at a later time if your drive is close to full. Please note that if you wish to start from any chapter other than Chapters 1 and 2, you will need to copy all of the previous chapters' folders, in addition to the chapter you are starting from, in order to properly load that chapter's session template. This is necessary because each chapter's work will use audio files from the previous chapter(s) in addition to the new files for that chapter.

It is not possible to load session templates or play back Pro Tools sessions directly from a CD-ROM drive. CD-ROM drives are not designed to gather and buffer audio data files and play them back in the manner that is necessary for many audio tracks to be heard simultaneously. Hard drives are designed for just this purpose. All files must be copied to a suitably formatted drive. See "The Destination Drive" section earlier in this chapter.

## Copy the Files

At this point, you can *right-click* to **Save As** or *drag/drop* the **Chapter 1-2** folder onto your hard drive. You can copy all of the files from the CD-ROM, if you wish, by returning to the Chapter Files menu from the CD-ROM. Follow the same procedure as with Chapter 1-2. Otherwise, you can copy chapter by chapter as you wind your way through the book. Keep in mind that each subsequent chapter requires the files from the previous chapter(s) to work.

Should your internal boot drive be the only one available, try to avoid the easy drag and drop to the Macintosh Finder or Windows Explorer, and copy them to the root level of your drive. Because you will be loading sessions primarily from the Pro Tools Workspace window (see the sidebar

"The Workspace Window" later in the chapter), you will find that the Mac Finder or Windows Explorer is not as easily accessible as if you copy the files to the root level of your drive. This is simply because you will have to dig through extra folders and subfolders to get to your Finder or Explorer window.

The Pro Tools Workspace window is accessed from the Window menu and is primarily a platform for data file management. Files can be copied, deleted, previewed, analyzed, and loaded in from this window. Although it may seem awkward at first, a lot of valuable resources are available to you from this window. Throughout the course of this book, I will go into more detail about the features of the Workspace.

**The Workspace Window**

The Workspace in Pro Tools provides a variety of features well beyond the capabilities of a simple Open Session selection from the File menu. The Workspace allows you to designate available hard drives as playback drives, record drives, or transfer drives. This allows you to separate your valuable sample libraries (playback or transfer) to be write-protected from erasure, or to designate them as a record volume to save your recordings (Record). You can also preview audio files and view their file type, bit depth, file size, and so on. Any available removable drive that is in the Pro Tools Workspace can only be unmounted from the Workspace menu for it to be removed from the operating system, even if the drive is not being used in the current session.

## Using Session Templates

Session template icons have been created for each chapter. Simply double-clicking on the session icon will load the session into Pro Tools. The only difference between a regular session icon and a session template icon is that the template will not be written over when you save. Should you try to save your session, Pro Tools will automatically create a copy of the session template in a regular session file format. This prevents the starting point from being overwritten should you accidentally corrupt the exercise content.

Unfortunately, there is no immediate way of visually distinguishing a template session file from a standard session file. If you are on a Windows system, *locate* the **Chapter 1–2 Start** session file from your Explorer, *right-click*, and *select* **Properties**. If the Read Only box is checked, you have a template. If not, then *select* the **Read Only** box to designate it as a template. It is not necessary to designate the session file as Read Only, except that the session file may be written over when saving. On Mac systems, *click* once on the session icon, *press Command+I*, and open the **General** selection. If the Stationary Pad box is selected, then your session is a template. If not, then *select* the **Stationary Pad** box (see Figure 1.2). The exact process for loading your session will be covered in the "Setting Up Your Session" section later in this chapter and also at the beginning of each subsequent chapter.

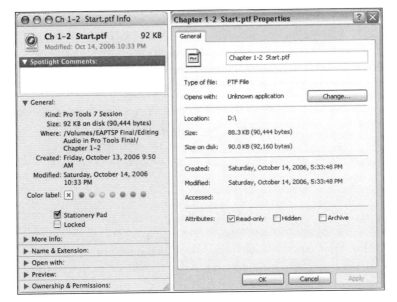

**Figure 1.2**

A session template for both Mac and PC. Notice the Stationary Pad and Read-Only boxes are selected in both, indicating they are both session templates.

If you are following the book and you find that you are struggling with a particular exercise or have corrupted the region placement, you can close your current session by selecting Close Session from the File menu, and then open the session template closest to the exercise you wish to redo. This will reset the exercises and guarantee that you will be starting with the correct edits for the upcoming exercises.

I suggest that you try to finish each exercise within each chapter without using the session templates to reset your start point, unless, of course, you corrupt the exercises. Although some of the exercises may at first seem mundane, there is always a little nugget of knowledge contained within. Should you struggle with an exercise, try your best to figure out the problem. I find that I often learn more from failing at first than from succeeding at first. If you are willing to stay the course until you get it right, you will not only learn how to use the editing tool or technique, but you may also learn how *not* to use the editing tool or technique. In my own experience, whenever things went wrong in a recording session, it would force me to find a solution to the problem and, more importantly, it would teach me a valuable lesson on how to avoid the same problem or situation in the future.

## Verifying Your Preference Settings

Okay, you're in the home stretch—just one last little bit of important business left before you dig into some audio files. That business is, of course, the preference settings. To make the exercises run smoothly, you need to take a few minutes to verify that we are in fact operating with the same settings and preferences. This will hopefully prevent any confusion due to a preference setting or two that may change the way a given tool or technique works. I will make notes to refer back to this section at the beginning of each chapter. If you continue from one chapter into the next, you will not need to verify your settings. If you work on other projects between chapters, you may find that you change certain settings to suit your needs. You will need to change those settings back to the book's standard to avoid any confusion or potential problems.

The first issue with preferences is that some of the preference settings in Pro Tools are not stored as part of the session file when you are saving your project. This can be confusing at times, and even annoying, as you may recall changing a setting that seemingly, for no apparent reason, reverts to its old setting unannounced. We will start by setting up your session and clarifying some of these enigmatic little features.

## Setting Up Your Session

To start, you will first need to load in the Chapter 1-2 Start template. If you have not already done so, copy the contents of the CD-ROM onto an appropriate hard drive (as described earlier in this chapter). Remember, if you are limited in available hard drive space, you can copy only the Chapter 1–2 folder from the CD-ROM.

1. Once the files are copied, boot up Pro Tools, and *select* Workspace from the Window menu. This will open up a window that will show you all of your available drives.

2. Select the drive you copied your files to by *double-clicking* on the drive icon or *single-clicking* on the arrow directly to the left of the drive icon.

3. Locate and open the folder you just copied and *double-click* on the Chapter 1-2 Start session icon. Upon opening the new session, you may be confronted by a dialog box or two. The first will be a warning, telling you that the original disk allocation cannot be used for this session (see Figure 1.3).

   When an audio track is created, it is assigned to a specific hard drive. This will be the destination for newly recorded or created audio files from this track. Because the original destination hard drive (my hard drive) is not available, Pro Tools will automatically assign a new one. Typically, this will be the hard drive you copied the files to from the CD-ROM (a.k.a. your hard drive). This is merely a formality, and selecting either Yes or No will still boot the session. If you select Yes, you will see a text document showing the new destination assignments for each track.

4. Mac users will be confronted with a dialog box notifying you that the booted session is a template and prompting you to either edit stationery (edit the template session) or create a new session (see Figure 1.4). *Select* New Session with a *single click*. You will be prompted to rename the session.

   Windows users must *select* Save As from the File menu to go straight to the New Session dialog box.

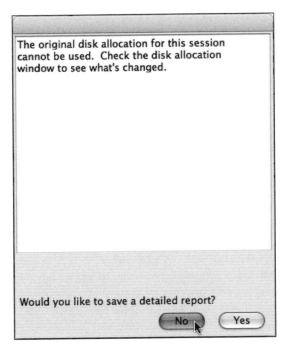

**Figure 1.3**

When booting a session copied to a new hard drive, you will often encounter an Original Disk Allocation warning.

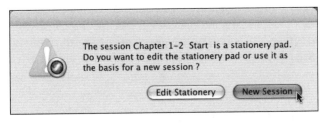

**Figure 1.4**

Upon booting the Chapter 1-2 Start session template, you will be prompted to edit stationery or create a new session.

5.  Rename it anything you like and then *select* **Save**. The session will, by default, be saved to the same folder you booted the template session from. If you wish to store it elsewhere, you will need to select the new destination before selecting Save.

    You may also receive a warning, as shown in Figure 1.5, stating that there are missing files. The Automatically Find & Relink option will be selected by default. If it is not, then *select* it and *hit* **OK**. The session will boot up, and you can begin to set up your settings and preferences.

    Pro Tools creates a unique identification number whenever a file is created and keeps track of where the file is stored. When audio files are copied to a new destination, Pro Tools will want to reacquaint itself with the new location of the files so it can access them.

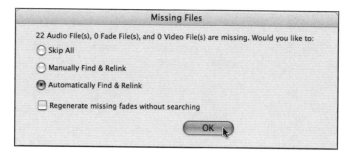

**Figure 1.5**

The Missing Files dialog box that appears when audio files are copied to a new destination.

6. Finally, if you are using a hardware setup other than an Mbox, you will be confronted with yet another dialog box that will inform you that the original hardware is not available. It will then ask you whether you would like to boot up the session using your hardware setup. *Select* OK, and the session will boot up. This is once again a formality and will not create any additional problems because the total number of available tracks, inputs, or outputs on every other Pro Tools–certified hardware is at least the same. Unfortunately, there is no way to avoid all these extra formalities, and you may be required to wind your way through them every time you start a new chapter. Soon enough, though, you will find yourself breezing through them without pause.

7. If you are returning to the book exercises from any chapter other than Chapter 1–2, to reset your preferences, boot up Pro Tools and *select* **Show Workspace** from the **Window** menu (if the Workspace is not already open). Locate and open the folder for the latest saved session file you worked on, and *double-click* on the appropriate **session** file icon to boot your session.

## Edit Menu Preferences

1. If your session does not have the Edit window displayed, *select* **Edit** from the **Window** menu.

2. You will start in the top-left corner. *Set* the **Edit** mode to **Grid**, and then set the **Grabber** tool to **Time** mode. If you are not sure which mode is selected, *click/hold* the **Grabber** tool to *select* **Time** mode, as shown in Figure 1.6.

**Figure 1.6**

Grid mode is the Edit mode selection, and the Grabber tool is set to Time.

3. In the top-center of the Edit window, *set* the **Main Counter Time** to be **Bars:Beats** and the **Sub Counter** to be **Mins:Sec** (see Figure 1.7).

**Figure 1.7**
The Main and Sub Counter displays at the top-center of the Edit window.

4. *Select* **View/Edit Window/None** (see Figure 1.8).

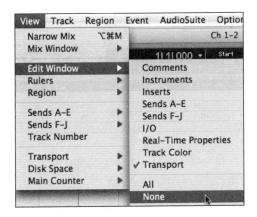

**Figure 1.8**
The View menu sets the viewing options for the Tracks section of the Edit window.

5. *Select* **View/Rulers** and verify that only the following items are checked: **Minutes:Seconds**, **Markers**, and **Tempo**. Note: The grayed out Bars:Beats in this menu cannot be changed because it is the Main Counter selection (see Figure 1.9).

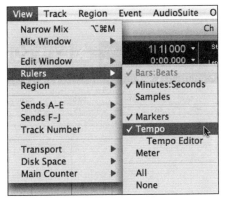

**Figure 1.9**
The Ruler display is set to show Minutes:Seconds, Markers, and Tempo.

6. The Ruler bar items you have selected can now be reordered by *click/dragging* the **Ruler bar** item you want to relocate and moving it to the desired location (see Figure 1.10).

7. On the black bar between the Edit tools and the Ruler bars is a series of options that can greatly affect any editing task you are trying to perform. *Make sure* that only **Link Timeline and Edit Selection** is selected, as shown in Figure 1.11.

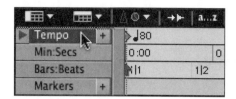

**Figure 1.10**

The Tempo display in the Ruler bar is dragged to the top of the Ruler bar section. Notice the narrow checkered line above the Tempo bar, indicating the position it will be moved to.

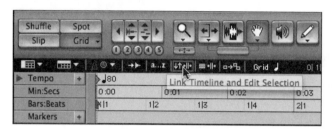

**Figure 1.11**

Notice that the Link Timeline and Edit Selection is the only item selected from this row.

## Transport Preferences

1. If the Transport window is not displayed, *select* **Window/Transport** so that it shows up on the screen. Now *select* **View/Transport** and *verify* that **MIDI Controls** and **Expanded** are selected, as shown in Figure 1.12.

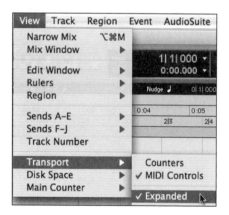

**Figure 1.12**

The View window controls what items are shown when the Transport window is displayed.

Your Transport window should look like Figure 1.13. Note that the Transport Online selection in the top-left corner is turned off, and Conductor and Metronome (Click) are turned on.

**Figure 1.13**

The Transport window—notice what items are selected and deselected.

2. *Select* the **Options** menu and verify that **Loop Playback** is deselected and **Scrolling** is set to **None** (see Figure 1.14).

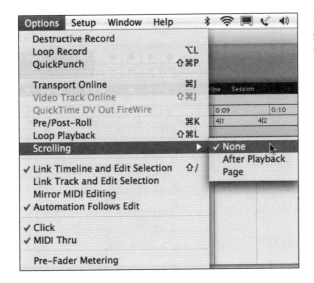

**Figure 1.14**

Scrolling options for the Edit window can be selected here.

**Scrolling Options**

Many people enjoy the use of the scrolling features in Pro Tools. I find that scrolling of whatever flavor is great when recording or mixing, but is often better turned off when editing, especially if you're doing very detailed editing. This becomes obvious as soon as you zoom in to work on a detailed edit. The screen will scroll your display upon previewing, just as you are moving your cursor in to refine the work. It's very frustrating! Unfortunately, as of this writing, Digidesign has not yet defined a shortcut to toggle this feature on and off.

## Setup Menu

Most of the settings you have just configured will restore with a simple session save. The following settings will stay set from session to session until you change them manually. I will circle and explain the most important of these features so that you are aware of their functions in the program.

*Select* I/O from the **Setup** menu, and verify that you are using the default names for the Input, Output, Insert, and Bus selections at the top of this menu.

*Select* **Input**, **Output**, **Insert**, and **Bus** one at a time, and then *click* on the **Default** button near the bottom-right of the window. This allows you to restore the factory names for all available inputs, outputs, inserts, and buses. If you have carefully set up a naming scheme for your own particular setup, you can store those settings by selecting Export Settings. Once they are saved, you can load in the default settings and later return to your personal setup by selecting Import Settings. You will need to do this for each selection: input, output, insert, and bus (see Figure 1.15). When you are finished, be sure to **select OK** to store your new setup.

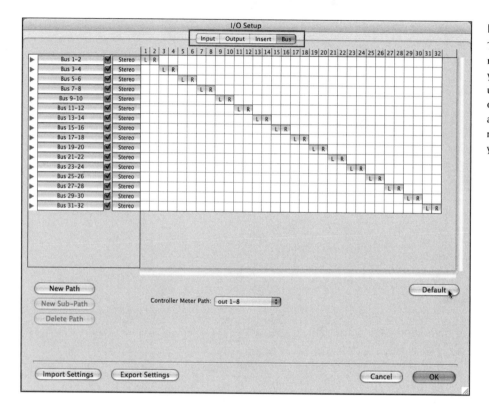

**Figure 1.15**

The I/O Setup menu allows you to configure the input, output, insert, and bus assignments to suit your needs.

Alternatively, you may wish to leave these settings as they are. Just be aware that certain selections in the book may not match your naming scheme.

From the Setup menu, **select Preferences**, and then **select Display**. The Display preferences will affect how information is displayed in the Edit and Mix windows. Match the settings in your setup to the ones in Figure 1.16.

Before closing the Preferences window, **select Operation**. The Operation preferences will affect the general operation of the system (see Figure 1.17). If selected, Timeline Insertion Follows Playback is a feature that makes the transport operate as a tape machine would. In other words, if you hit the spacebar to play the track starting from bar 1 beat 1, and then 15 bars later press the spacebar to stop the transport, your cursor will now remain at bar 15. In the same scenario with

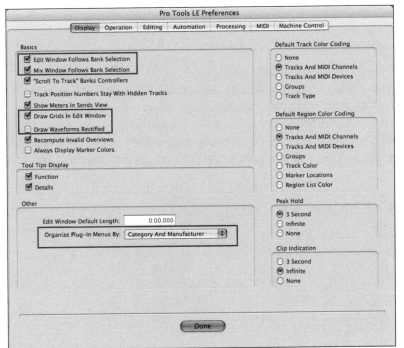

**Figure 1.16**
The Preferences menu allows you to select Display preferences for the Edit window that are detailed features not covered in the View menu.

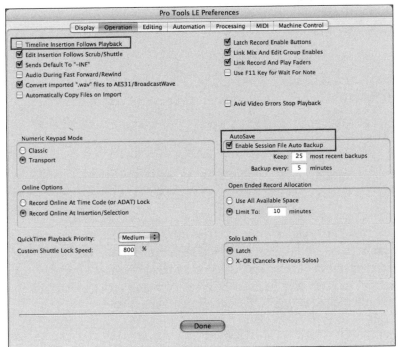

**Figure 1.17**
The Operation preferences window.

this feature deselected, your cursor would return to bar 1 beat 1. I find that the latter (deselected) works best for most editing work because you will typically want to return immediately after stopping to the region you are editing to refine your edit.

Now *select* Editing from the **Preferences** menu (see Figure 1.18). These features affect the way regions are handled when editing. Region List Follows Edit Selection and Edit Selection Follows Region List are simple settings that allow a selected region in the Regions list to be highlighted in the Edit window (if the selected region is being used in the Edit window), and it also allows a selected region in the Edit window to be highlighted in the Regions list. The Regions list is located on the right-hand side of the Edit window and is accessed by selecting the double-arrow at the bottom of the window.

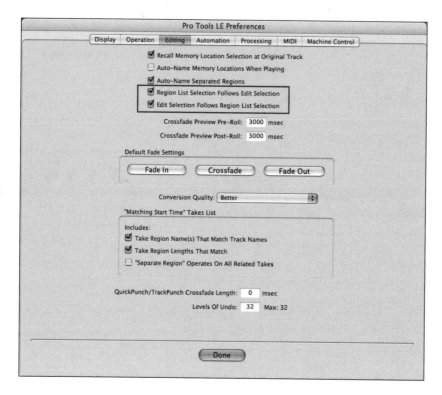

**Figure 1.18**

The Editing preferences window.

Finally, you will need to set up your TC/E Plug-In settings. *Select* Processing from the **Preferences** menu, and you can then select the plug-in that will be assigned to the TC/E tool in the Edit window. Time compression/expansion plug-ins from other manufacturers, if you own any, may show up on this list in bold text to indicate that they may be assigned to the TC/E tool. For the purposes of this book, you will use the Digidesign TC/E plug-in (see Figure 1.19).

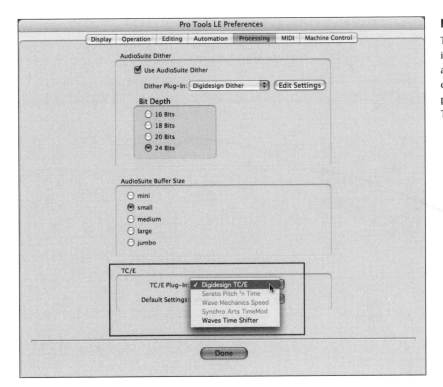

**Figure 1.19**

The Processing selection in the Preferences dialog allows you to define how certain files will be processed, such as the TC/E tool.

*Close* the **Preferences** window by *selecting* **Done** at the bottom of the window. You can now set up your TC/E tool settings. From the **Audiosuite** menu, *select* **Other/Time Compression Expansion**. *Click/drag* the **slider** for the **Accuracy** setting all the way to the left until you get a reading of —5, as shown in Figure 1.20. Now *select* the **double-arrow** near the top on the left, where it says "factory default," and *select* **Save Settings As**. *Type* **Sound** and *select* **Save**.

Before closing the TC/E plug-in, *click/drag* the **Accuracy** setting all the way to the right to read +5. Again, *select* the **double-arrow** as just described, and *name* this setting **Rhythm**. If you return to the Setups/Preferences/Processing window, you will now be able to use these preset settings you've just stored with the TC/E tool by selecting the setting that is most appropriate for the task you are performing (see Figure 1.21).

*Select Command+S* (Mac) or *Control+S* (PC) to save your work. You are now ready to begin Chapter 2. If you begin Chapter 2 at another time, you will be prompted to locate and boot the session file you just saved.

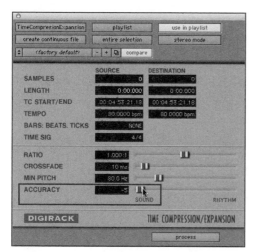

**Figure 1.20**

The Time Compression/Expansion or TC/E Audiosuite plug-in.

**Figure 1.21**

The TC/E section of the Processing window under Setups/Preferences.

## TC/E Settings

The TC/E tool settings can be optimized for a variety of sounds. For example, you may want to lower the Minimum Pitch setting when you are working with basses or raise it if you are stretching a flute note. You may need to raise the Crossfade setting when you are working with grainier-sounding instruments, such as strings, acoustic guitars, or reed instruments, to minimize artifacts. After optimizing a setting, be sure to save the setting for future use. It may not be perfect for the next sound, but it may get you within tweak range.

The purpose of this section is not to cramp your style; rather, it is to minimize the number of variables that may lead you astray. If you feel confident enough with the preferences set the way you like to work, by all means, go for it. If you get confused while working on the exercises, or the features are not acting as described in the book, you can refer back to this chapter to review and reset your preferences at any time.

With this last bit of business behind you, let's get started! The artist is late, the record company is calling every five minutes, you're already over budget, and the deadline was last week!

# 2 Working with the Edit Modes

The Edit modes are the foundation for editing audio and MIDI data in Pro Tools. Every tool you use, every editing task you perform, be it audio or MIDI, will be fundamentally affected by the Edit mode you are using. Understanding each mode and the different ways each one can be utilized will simplify and greatly expand your understanding of the program.

Even if you are already familiar with the function of the Edit modes, it is worth a review of their function and design. No matter how much I think I know about Pro Tools, I've always managed to find something new about it with every user I meet and every student I teach. Perhaps it's a new way to use an Edit mode, a subtle aspect of the mode I never considered, or a whole new horizon of possibilities with a seemingly unrelated feature.

## Setting Up Chapter 2

If you have not already done so, **boot** **Pro Tools** and *select* **Show Workspace** from the **Window** menu. If you are continuing from Chapter 1, you can go straight to "Navigating the Edit Modes." If your session from Chapter 1 is not currently booted up, then locate the Chapter 1–2 folder you have already copied to your hard drive from the CD-ROM. Once located, open the folder and *double-click* on the **session** file you saved from the "Setting Up Your Seesion" section in Chapter 1. If you have not set up your preference settings from Chapter 1, then return to the "Setting Up Your Session" section of Chapter 1 and follow the instructions to the end of the chapter before continuing with Chapter 2.

If you have not copied the files for Chapter 1–2, then you must return to the "Loading Files from the CD-ROM" section in Chapter 1 to avoid any confusion with the process. Follow the instructions to the end of Chapter 1 before returning to Chapter 2.

# Navigating the Edit Modes

Even when editing at the most basic level in Pro Tools, you will find that the Edit modes need to be changed quite frequently in order to facilitate whatever task you have at hand. As you become more familiar with the way each of these modes acts and interacts, this will become a simple and seamless part of the flow of your work. Before you begin learning how the Edit modes work, you must investigate the many ways you can select or change the Edit modes. Let's start with some matter-of-fact information.

The Edit modes are located in the top-left corner of the Edit window, as shown in Figure 2.1. There are four basic Edit modes: Shuffle, Slip, Spot, and Grid. You will note that the Grid selection has a small down arrow to the right of the button's name. Whenever you see this little down arrow next to any button or feature, you will find more than one way to use that particular feature or display item. With a simple click and hold on the down arrow, you will open up a list of available features or values.

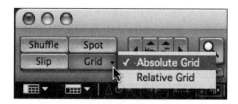

**Figure 2.1**

The Edit modes in the Edit window. Notice that there is more than one way to use Grid mode.

The Edit modes can be changed using four different methods:

■ Position the cursor over the desired Edit mode and click.

■ Use the small open quote key ( ` ) located directly above the Tab key on both the Mac and the PC. Hitting this key will allow you to cycle through the Edit modes.

■ Use Function keys F1 through F4 on both Mac and PC keyboards. Note that pressing the F4 key more than once will toggle between Absolute and Relative Grid mode. Laptop users may have to hold the Fn key at the bottom left of the keyboard to access the Function key set.

■ Use the Option+1–4 keys on a Mac or Alt+1–4 keys on a PC. Note that pressing the Option (Mac) or Alt (PC) and the number 4 key more than once will toggle between Absolute and Relative Grid modes. (This option is mapped to the alphanumeric number 1–4 keys located directly above your QWERTY keys.)

Try using all of the above-mentioned techniques. It is very important to actually put your fingers on the computer and dabble a little. This will aid greatly in the memorization process that is such a large part of using shortcuts effectively. I will ask you to use different methods for each of the exercises to help aid this process.

**Shortcuts and Numeric Keys**

Pro Tools creates a distinction between the alphanumeric number keys, located above your QWERTY keys, and the numeric keypad to the right of your alphanumeric key set. For example: Selecting Option+alphanumeric 1 (Mac) or Alt+alphanumeric 1 (PC) will switch the Edit mode to Shuffle. Selecting Option+numeric keypad 1 (Mac) or Alt+numeric keypad 1 (PC) will open up the Time Operations dialog box. Laptop users, both Mac and PC, have access to the numeric keypad shortcuts by holding the Fn key at the bottom-left of the keyboard and selecting the numeric keypad number that is superimposed, on most laptop keyboards, starting with the letter J. (J=1, K=2, L=3, and so on.)

## Using the Edit Modes

Now that you know how to navigate the Edit modes, let's get to the heart of how they work. As I stated previously, there are four Edit modes: Shuffle, Slip, Spot, and Grid. Each Edit mode performs a unique and useful function in the Edit window. You will primarily work with the Grabber tool and moving regions in this chapter to emphasize the fundamental design of each Edit mode. After you learn the Edit tools in more detail in Chapter 3, all of the Edit tools will be tied together with the Edit modes in Chapter 4 to bring everything full circle.

As you go through each Edit mode, I will direct you to the exercise track located at the top of your Track list in the Edit window for practice or to the audio tracks to perform actual edits for the song. You will use the Memory Locations window to navigate your way around the Edit window from exercise to exercise. If your Memory Locations window is not displayed, click on the Window menu and select Memory Locations. Check to make sure the Grabber tool is also selected using Time mode. You can display the available options by click/holding on the small down arrow at the bottom of the Grabber tool button and selecting Time mode, as shown in Figure 2.2.

**Figure 2.2**
The Grabber tool set to Time mode.

## Spot Mode

Spot mode allows users to place audio regions at any specified location by simply typing in that location number. Regions can be placed on any specified bar:beat, minute:second, or sample number location. HD users have the additional luxury of typing in frame numbers for video synchronization. Spot mode is most often used when dragging and dropping audio files onto tracks or for relocating audio regions that have been moved or displaced.

In practical day-to-day editing work, Spot mode is usually selected for a given task, and then the user immediately switches back to one of the other Edit modes. The reason for this is simple: Spot mode's only function is to locate or relocate audio files, which, of course, limits its ability to perform any other function. For example, if you wanted to delete a region by selecting it and hitting the Delete key, all you would get is the Spot dialog box asking where you want it moved. Unfortunately, the Trash or Recycle Bin is not an option.

### Exercise 2.1.1 The Spot Dialog Box

Spot mode and the Spot Dialog box are inextricably intertwined. In fact, Spot mode will only function through the Spot Dialog box. To see how this works, let's begin by moving some regions around using Spot mode.

1. If Spot mode is not selected, *move* your cursor over the **Spot** button located in the top-left of the **Edit** window and *click* on it.

2. From the **Memory Locations** window, *select* **Ex 2.1.1**.

3. Now open the Regions list by *clicking* on the **double arrow** at the bottom right-hand portion of the **Edit** window, as shown in Figure 2.3, and start the first exercise.

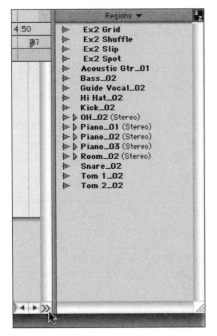

**Figure 2.3**

The Regions list can be opened or closed by selecting the double arrow at the bottom-right of the Edit window.

4. At the top of the Regions list you will see an audio region labeled "Ex2 Spot." *Click/drag* this **region** and *drop* it anywhere onto the **Exercise track**. Upon releasing the region, you will notice that a dialog box opens up. Oddly enough, it is called the Spot Dialog box (see Figure 2.4).

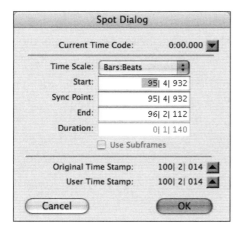

**Figure 2.4**

The Spot dialog box.

As you can see in Figure 2.4, the Spot Dialog box offers many features to help you locate your regions precisely where you want them to be. You can enter a value for the start point, end point, or Sync Point. You will note that the Start time in the dialog box has a numerical value that directly corresponds to the exact place you "dropped" the region on the audio track. The Time Scale can be changed to display Bars:Beats, Min:Secs, or Samples. The Spot Dialog box will automatically default to the same display setting as the Main Counter display at the top-center of the Edit window.

The Sync Point is a user-defined place within the audio region that can act as a reference point to be lined up to another event, region, bar, and beat number or video frame that may be displaying an exploding car, for example. Chapter 6, "Looping, Tempo, and Timing (Beat Detective)" looks at Sync Points in more detail.

As complements to these options, two Time Stamp options are available, an original time stamp and a user time stamp. The original time stamp is automatically created when the region is record-ed or created by edit. This exact location point, to sample accuracy, is stored with the audio file. The arrows to the right of the original time stamp and user time stamp numbers will move the Time Stamp position to the selected reference point for the start, end, or Sync Point of the region.

### Exercise 2.1.2 Spotting Regions

Should you accidentally move a region away from its original position, the original time stamp will get you back home. Simply switch to Spot mode, click on your misplaced region with the Grabber tool, click on the arrow to the right of the original time stamp number, and hit OK. Your region will now be moved back to its original time stamp position! Let's investigate this a little further in the next exercise.

1. If you have not exited the Spot Dialog box, close it now by *clicking* on the **OK** button.

2. *Select* **Ex 2.12** from the **Memory Locations** window.

3. Now *drag/drop* the **Ex2 Spot** region from the **Regions** list onto the exercise track.

4. *Type* in **991000** as a start point and *click* on the **OK** button to accept the new placement. Notice the region start has moved to bar 99, beat 1, tick 000.

5. *Click* on the **region** once again with the **Grabber** tool and *select* the **up arrow** next to the original time stamp. The original time stamp number is now moved into the start time field, as shown in Figure 2.5.

6. *Click* **OK**, and the region will now be moved to its original start point.

**Figure 2.5**

The original time stamp number has been moved to the Start time field.

7. You can also enter the region end as the point of reference. *Click* on the **region** once with the **Grabber** tool and *select* the **End** point bar number. *Type* in **991000**, *click* **OK**, and you will now find the region end has been lined up to bar 99, beat 1, tick 000.

8. Now that you have moved your region to a more "musical" location, a user time stamp can be created by simply *selecting* **Time Stamp** from the **Regions** list menu on the right side of the Edit window. You can access this menu by clicking on the down arrow at the head of the Regions list.

9. *Click* on the **up arrow** next to **Current Selection**, as shown in Figure 2.6, and *click* **OK**. You now have a user time stamp stored with the region for future reference.

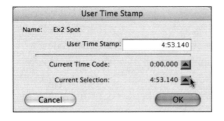

**Figure 2.6**

The User Time Stamp dialog box. Clicking on the highlighted up arrow will move the Current Selection time to the User Time Stamp field.

**Regions and Audio Files**

The terms "region" and "audio file" are tossed around with great frequency on all nondestructive editing systems, such as Pro Tools. And although they may seem to be the same thing, there is an important distinction. A region is a graphic display of an audio file or any part of an audio file. It is this graphic representation that allows you to edit audio visually so the computer can translate your requests into sound.

An audio file, however, is the actual file stored on your hard drive. It is the real-world data stream of ones and zeros that can be used whenever and wherever you want. The beauty of the region is that it is a nondestructive representation of your audio file that can be bounced around, cut, copied, pasted, and deleted without affecting the original audio file. In Pro Tools, a region that is a whole audio file is displayed in the Regions list in bold type. A region that is a piece or part of that audio file is displayed in normal text.

Spot mode is very handy when you know the specific destination of the selected region. The majority of the time, however, you will likely need to use visual cues to set the placement of your regions against other regions. Slip mode is perfectly suited for just this way of working.

# Slip Mode

Slip mode is the mode of choice when a region must be moved or edited at a point other than a specific bar:beat or timecode number. Slip mode's resolution will depend on how far you are zoomed in or out. If you are zoomed in to sample accuracy, your edits or moves will be performed with sample accuracy. If you are zoomed out to display the whole song, you will only be able to edit or move regions around to a general location.

When you are editing music that has not been cut to a click track, you will find yourself working almost exclusively in Slip mode. However, even music cut to a click will deviate off of the exact tempo. If performed well, this is called "feel" or "groove." If performed poorly, this is called a headache, because you now have the unenviable task of somehow making this train wreck of a performance sound like something!

### Exercise 2.2.1 Slip Mode

Slip mode is perhaps the easiest of the Edit modes to understand because there is no mystery in its application. It goes where you go without any restrictions. The following exercise will best convey this fact.

1.  *Select* Slip mode by *pressing* the F2 key at the top of your keyboard, and investigate the ins and outs of Slip mode. (Laptop users may need to hold the Fn key at the bottom-left of their keyboard before selecting F2.)

27

2. *Select* **Ex 2.2.1** from the **Memory Locations** window to start Exercise 2.2.1.

3. *Click/drag* the region called **Ex2 Slip** from the **Regions** list and *move* **it** around on your exercise track. You will notice that the region will move wherever you desire to place it without restriction.

4. *Move* the region slightly after the first **Spot** region and *release* the **mouse button**. Your region will land exactly where you dropped it.

## Exercise 2.2.2 The Event Edit Area

Directly to the right of the Main Counter located at the top and center of the Edit window are three very useful sets of numbers: Start, End, and Length (see Figure 2.7). This is called the Event Edit area.

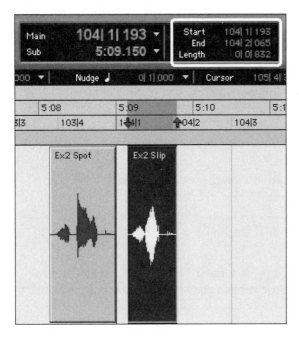

**Figure 2.7**

The Event Edit area shows the Start, End, and Length of selected regions

1. *Click/drag* your **region** once again and *move* **it** around while looking at the Start and End fields of the Event Edit area. You will notice that these numbers change as you move the region.

2. See whether you can *place* the **region** as close as you can to Bar 104, Beat 2, Tick 000 and *release* the **mouse button**.

You may have found it difficult or impossible to get it precisely on Bar 104, Beat 2, Tick 000. This would require a bit of zooming to enable the level of resolution necessary to make this type of edit work. Although there are more efficient ways of performing this particular task, most notably Spot mode, the point of the exercise is to show you how these numbers can be useful when moving regions to a general location until you can zoom in to more accurately place them.

### Exercise 2.2.3 Overlapping Regions

Because Slip mode is the simplest of the Edit modes, I think this is a good place to discuss a bit of region logic as it relates to moving regions in Slip mode. In the previous exercises you moved regions around and next to each other but not on top of one another. In Pro Tools this is called "overlap." This exercise contains a few shortcuts, features, and tips that will help you through any confusion.

1. *Select* Ex 2.2.3 from the **Memory Locations** window, and you will see a single region placed on the exercise track.

2. From the **View** menu, *select* **Region** and verify that **Overlap** is selected. If not, select it as shown in Figure 2.8.

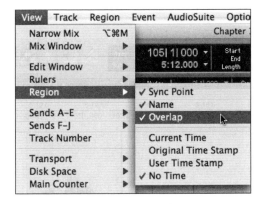

**Figure 2.8**

Overlap is selected from the View menu.

3. Open the Regions list by *hitting* the **double arrow** at the bottom-right of the **Edit** window, and **drag/drop** the **Ex2 Slip** region onto the exercise track.

4. *Place* the **region** partially over the top of the **Ex2 Spot** region on the exercise track, as shown in Figure 2.9.

5. Now *drag* the **Ex2 Shuffle** region, from the **Regions** list, partially over the top of the **Ex2 Slip** region. A quick look at the top-left corner of the two regions you have just placed will show a fold that indicates that the region is overlapping another region.

6. *Select* Clear from the **Edit** menu to remove the region. You can also *hit* the **Delete** key (Mac) or **Backspace** key (PC) on your keyboard to achieve the same effect. Notice how the overlapped region is also deleted.

29

**Figure 2.9**
The placement of the Ex2 Slip region on the exercise track.

7.  *Select Command+Z* (Mac) or *Ctrl+Z* (PC) to undo this clear, and then *select* the **Ex2 Slip** region by *clicking* on **it** once.

8.  From the **Region** menu, *select* **Bring to Front** and notice how the Ex2 Slip region is now placed on top of the surrounding regions, as shown in Figure 2.10.

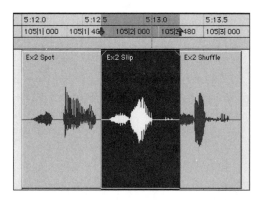

**Figure 2.10**
The Ex2 Slip region has been pulled on top of the surrounding regions on the exercise track.

9.  From the **Region** menu, now *select* **Send to Back** and notice how the Ex2 Slip region is now placed behind the surrounding regions.

These few simple guidelines for dealing with audio regions are the foundation that underlies all of your editing work. Understanding these concepts will aid you greatly in making your editing experience a bit less of a mystery. It is also important to note that these region editing techniques will work equally well in Grid mode and in Slip mode.

## Grid Mode

Grid mode is used whenever a region or edit needs to be placed on a defined bar:beat or min:secs location. Unlike Slip mode, which allows regions to be moved around to sample accuracy, Grid mode relies on a user-defined grid value to determine the placement of the region. When moved, the region start will be locked to the defined grid value. The grid value is located below the Edit tools on a black bar above the Timeline bar, as shown in Figure 2.11. The green number directly to the right of the Grid label defines the currently selected standard and resolution of the Grid value setting as a numerical value.

**Figure 2.11**

The location of the Grid value pop-up.

The Grid value has two settings: the Grid Standard and the Grid Resolution. The Grid Standard can be defined in terms of bars:beats, min:secs, samples, or regions/markers. HD users have the additional benefit of feet:frames and timecode as standards. Once a standard is selected, the menu offers a variety of levels of resolution based on the standard set.

Each standard has its benefits based on the needs of the work you are trying to accomplish. Bars:beats works well for songs recorded to a defined tempo, but is less useful when placing sound effects to video frames, where the timecode standard is more suitable. Mins:secs is a useful standard when the program material must have a defined length, such as music for advertising on TV or radio. Let's take a look at this process in more detail.

### Exercise 2.3.1 Setting the Grid Value

1. *Select* Ex 2.3.1 from the **Memory Locations** window.

2. *Select* **Grid** mode by *pressing* the **F4** key at the top of your keyboard.

3. *Select* the **down arrow** directly to the right of the **Grid** value, as shown in Figure 2.12. The pop-up will allow you to set your standard and resolution.

4. *Set* the **standard** to Mins:Secs.

5. *Click* on the **Grid value** down arrow again to set the grid resolution of 1 Second. Look at the grid lines displayed in the Edit window and notice how they no longer have any connection to the Kick and Snare tracks.

6. Now *select* the **Grid value** down arrow again and set the grid standard back to Bars:Beats and the resolution to 1/4 Note. You will need to select the Grid value twice, once to set the standard and again to select the resolution. Notice that the grid lines now relate to the individual hits of the Kick and Snare tracks.

Now that you have defined your grid value, it is time to look at the ways you can use Grid mode. There are two variations of Grid mode: Absolute Grid and Relative Grid. Let's start by taking a closer look at Absolute Grid mode.

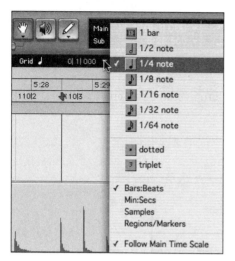

**Figure 2.12**

The grid resolutions available when the selected standard is set to Bars:Beats.

## Exercise 2.3.2 Absolute Grid Mode

Absolute Grid mode forces regions that are moved to lock or *snap* to the defined Grid value line. This has the obvious advantage of allowing regions to be laid into a song precisely on a bar or beat.

1. *Select* Ex 2.3.2 from the **Memory Locations** window.

2. Check that the Edit mode is set to Absolute Grid by *click/holding* on the **Grid** button in the top-left corner of the **Edit** window and *selecting* **Absolute Grid**, as shown in Figure 2.13. Absolute Grid mode is just that, *absolute*. Move a region, and the region start will lock to the defined grid resolution.

**Figure 2.13**

Grid mode set to Absolute Grid.

3. Go to the Regions list and *drag* out the region named **Ex2 Grid** onto the exercise track. Notice as you drag the region around how it snaps to the nearest grid line.

4. *Drop* this **region** somewhere after the **Ex2 Slip** region.

5. Go to the Grid value and now *change* the **resolution** to 1/8 note.

6. *Grab* and *drag* the Ex2 Grid region and move it around again. Notice that region now snaps to the 1/8-note grid lines.

### The Grid Line Display

If grid lines are not displayed on the exercise track as shown in Figure 2.17, you will need to select the Setup menu and Preferences. At the top of this menu, select Display, and make sure the Draw Grids in Edit Window box is selected. Select Done, and your grid lines are back! Alternatively, select the Bars:Beats header to the far left of the Timeline bar, below the Edit modes. Selecting this will quickly toggle back and forth between grids and no grids.

Now that you have explored the world of Absolute Grid mode, let's take a look at Relative Grid mode.

## Exercise 2.3.3 Relative Grid Mode

Relative Grid mode allows regions to be moved by Grid value increments while maintaining their *relative* distance from the nearest grid line. This is useful when the region starts before or after a grid line due to a grace note or a lead-in note that does not start exactly on a grid line. In Relative Grid mode, this region can be moved freely, without affecting its timing in relation to the rest of the track.

1. *Select* Ex 2.3.3 from the **Memory Locations** window.
2. Select Relative Grid mode by *holding* the **Option** key (Mac) or **Alt** key (PC) and *hitting* the alphanumeric number *4* key until Rel Grid is displayed in the button.
3. Change the grid value back to 1/4 note by *clicking* on the **down arrow** next to the Grid value field and *selecting* 1/4 Note.
4. *Grab* the Ex2 Spot region and move it to the left or right on the exercise track. Notice how the region moves by 1/4-note increments and snaps to unmarked areas between the grid lines.
5. *Drop* this **region** back where you started and try this same exercise with the Ex2 Slip region.

Relative Grid mode is perfect for moving regions that are locked to the session's tempo but, due to the performance, the region start is not edited exactly to a grid line. This allows the performance to remain locked to the tempo of the song as it is being moved to its new start point. For example, you may find that a bass part's region starts before the downbeat of the verse section because of a slide or grace note before the downbeat. If you use Absolute Grid mode, the bass's relationship to the tempo of the song will be changed, assuming that the region start is not cut exactly on a grid line. Using Relative Grid mode will allow you to shift the performance without losing the bass's timing to the track.

# Shuffle Mode

Shuffle mode allows regions to be moved in a variety of ways that are not covered by Slip, Grid, or Spot mode. Regions moved in Shuffle mode will snap automatically to the nearest region boundary. If there is no other region on the track, your region will snap to the beginning of the audio track. A thin black line will appear to show you what region boundary your region will snap to. Moved regions can be snapped to the front or the back end of a region. There is no way to overlap regions when moving them in Shuffle mode. In fact, Shuffle mode has the unique ability to displace or move regions by the length of the region you are moving.

Imagine having four poker cards on a table in front of you side by side, with no space between each card. The cards cannot overlap, so if you add a fifth card between the first and second cards, you will need to move cards 2, 3, and 4 to the right by one card width to accommodate the fifth card. This is how Shuffle mode works when you are moving regions.

If you now remove the second card and slide cards 3, 4, and 5 to the left to fill the void left by card 2, you will have experienced the effects of Shuffle mode when moving or deleting a region that is between a group of other regions. Let's get to the exercises to remove any confusion.

**Shuffle Mode Rules to Remember When Moving Regions**

As with all Edit modes, there are rules to the design and function of Shuffle mode. Shuffle mode is so unique and somewhat disguised in its purpose, however, that it deserves a closer look to fully grasp its use:

■ Moved regions snap to the nearest region boundary, start or end, or to the beginning of the track.

■ You cannot overlap regions in Shuffle mode.

■ All regions *after* your move will be shifted forward or backward by the length of the region you are moving unless they are locked.

■ If a region is moved *before* a locked region, the locked region will also protect any subsequent regions from being moved.

## Exercise 2.4.1 Shuffle Mode

1. From the **Memory Locations** window, *select* Ex 2.4.1.

2. Select Shuffle mode by *hitting Option+alphanumeric 1* (Mac) or *Alt+alphanumeric 1* (PC). As you can see, you have three regions back to back to back.

3. *Click/drag* the **Ex2 Shuffle** region from the **Regions list** and place it *after* the three regions you see displayed. *Release* your **mouse button**. Notice that the region snaps to the end of the last region.

4. Now *grab* the **Ex2 Shuffle** region and move it to your left until you see a black line appear at the end of the Ex2 Slip region.

5. *Release* the **mouse button**. Notice how the Ex2 Grid region has shifted to the right, and the space between the regions is maintained (see Figure 2.14).

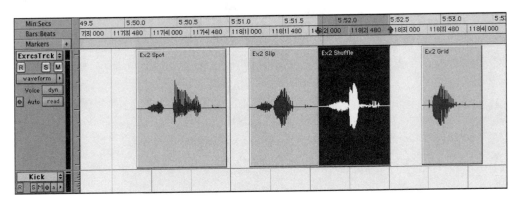

**Figure 2.14**

The Ex2 Grid region moves to the right when the Ex2 Shuffle region is placed before it.

6. Now *select* the **Ex2 Shuffle** region and *move* it back to the end of the Ex2 Grid region. Notice that the Ex2 Grid region moves back to the left because the Ex2 Shuffle region has been removed.

Shuffle mode exhibits some unique characteristics that can be incredibly useful for tasks such as editing a voiceover for a TV or radio commercial, in which the total length is of utmost importance. It also has some very useful applications for editing audio in music, which you will see in the following section.

# Laying In Your Basic Tracks

Now that you have a basic feel for the Edit modes and how they work, you can start laying in your basic tracks and apply them in a more real-world situation. Here's the deal: The basic tracks have been recorded, and you have been hired to do all of the editing work for the song. As the overdubs start pouring in from the recording studio, your job will be to integrate these overdubs into the master session ASAP! The studio will be waiting for your work to be completed in order to move on to the next overdub, so time is of the essence. Because the budget is low, the overdubs rushed, and the engineers on the project have less experience using Pro Tools, you will need to use every editing tool and available feature in the book to get through the project. So let's get busy!

## Exercise 2.5.1 The Drums

1. In the **Memory Locations** window, *select* the memory location called **Ex 2.5.1**. Your Edit window should look just like Figure 2.15.

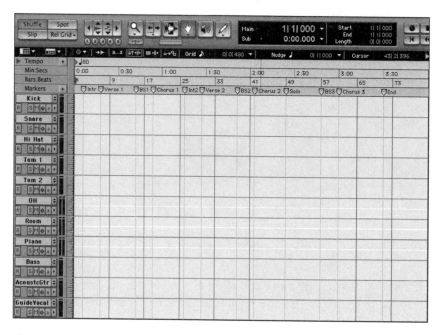

**Figure 2.15**

The Edit window for the basic tracks with no regions displayed.

2. Take a deep breath and scream at the top of your lungs, "Where are the audio files? Trained monkeys could do better work than this!"

3. Now that you've got that out of your system, it's time start sorting out this mess. Anyway, look on the bright side—maybe you're getting paid by the hour....

   As you can see, the tracks are named, memory locations are created, and the audio files exist in the Regions list, but they are not on the tracks. Let's start by matching up the audio files with the tracks using the Edit modes.

   In situations like this, Spot mode will usually save the day. As you may recall, the original time stamp in Spot mode will tell you the exact start time for each region.

   A quick glance at the Regions list will tell you that you have a single region for each of the tracks, but you have three Piano regions and only one track available for the piano. This one may require a little investigation.

4. ***Select Option+3*** (Mac) or ***Alt+3*** (PC) to change the Edit mode to Spot. ***Click/drag*** the **Kick_02** region onto the Kick track, as shown in Figure 2.16. As you can see in this figure, there is an outline of the region on the track display; this exact placement will be entered in the Start time field in the Spot Dialog box when you release the click. Should you drag the file onto the wrong track, you will have to either select Undo from the Edit menu or switch to another Edit mode in order to move it to the correct track.

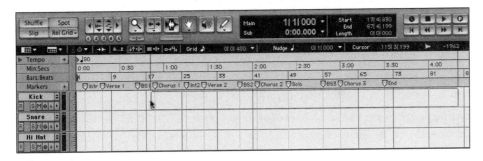

**Figure 2.16**

The Kick_02 region being dragged onto a track. The outline of the region on the track display will indicate its destination.

5. ***Release*** the **mouse button** and look at the original time stamp location near the bottom of the Spot Dialog box. It looks like your file was recorded from bar 1 beat 1 (see Figure 2.17).

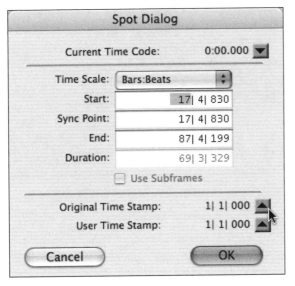

**Figure 2.17**

The Spot Dialog box for the Kick_02 region. The original time stamp gives you the original location of the region.

6. ***Click*** on the **up arrow** next to the Original Time Stamp field. It should now appear in the Start Time box.

37

7. *Click* OK. The region should now appear on the Kick track from the beginning of the session.

8. Follow the same procedure with the Snare_02 audio file on the Snare track.

   At this point it might seem easy enough to "Spot" all of your regions for the drums, but because you already know their location, take a look at a few easier ways you can move these files.

9. Change the Edit mode to Slip mode by *hitting* the *small open quote* key ( ` ) located above the Tab key on your keyboard until the Slip button is highlighted.

10. *Click/drag* Hi Hat_02 from the **Regions** list all the way to the beginning of the Hi Hat track. See? Easy! No extra buttons to hit, no up arrows, no nonsense!

11. Now that you're feeling it a little, try to lay in more than one region at a time. *Click* once on the **Tom 1_02** region in the **Regions** list. It should now be highlighted.

12. While *holding* the *Shift* key, *click* once on **Tom 2_02**. *Release* the *Shift* key. Both of the tom tracks should now be highlighted.

13. *Click/drag* on either **Tom** region and drop them at the beginning of the track. They will be bundled together, as shown in Figure 2.18.

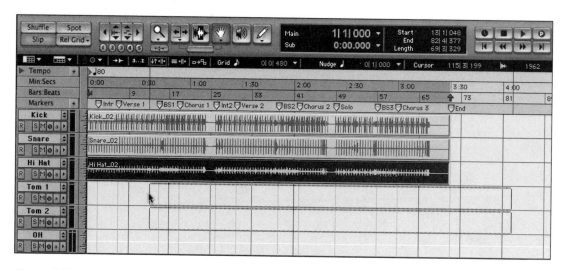

**Figure 2.18**

Regions may be dragged in bundles onto the audio tracks.

14. Now change the Edit mode to **Shuffle** *using* the *small open quote* key ( ` ).

15. *Click* once on the **OH_02** region in the **Regions** list to select it.

16. *Hold* the *Command* key (Mac) or the *Ctrl* key (PC) and single *click* on the **Room_02** region from the **Regions** list. *Release* the *Command* or *Ctrl* key. You have now selected the OH and Room regions while bypassing all of the Piano regions that are between them on the Regions list.

17. *Click/drag* the **two regions** from the **Regions** list onto the OH and Room audio tracks. You will notice that they will automatically jump to the beginning of the session. This requires even less work than Slip mode because you only have to drag the region just outside the Regions list onto the tracks you want them to appear on in the Edit window.

18. *Hit Command+S* (Mac) or *Ctrl+S* (PC) to save.

Now that you have your drum tracks laid in, you should have a good listen to them. Never assume that because everything looks right that it is right. Only your ears can tell you if something is missing or wrong.

The drums should all be in order now. If they are not, you may want to start over from Exercise 2.5.1 to make sure you have not missed any part of the exercises.

## Exercise 2.6.1 The Music

The piano is the next order of business, so let's get straight to it. According to the producer, the piano part was punched in three sections to get the performance right, and they should just lay in end to end. This would account for the extra Piano takes you have in the Regions list.

1. *Select* Ex 2.6.1 from the **Memory Locations** window.

2. *Use* the *small open quote* key ( ) to get back to Spot mode and start dragging and dropping.

3. *Click/drag* the **Piano_01** region from the **Regions** list out on to the Piano track. The Spot Dialog box once again tells you from the original time stamp that the region lays in at bar 1 beat 1.

4. *Click* on the **up arrow** next to the Original Time Stamp and *hit* **OK**.

5. *Hit* the *F1* key to switch to Shuffle mode. This will allow you to snap the remaining Piano regions directly to the end of the Piano_01 region you just laid in.

6. *Click/drag* the **Piano_02** region from the **Regions** list and *drop* it onto the Piano track anywhere after the Piano_01 region.

7. *Drag* and *drop* the **Piano_03** region after the Piano_02 region. Your Piano track should now look something like Figure 2.19.

8. Have a listen to the placement of the Piano regions to make sure they have been placed properly. You can start by *clicking* on the **Intro** marker in the **Memory Locations** window and *hitting* the **spacebar** to start playback.

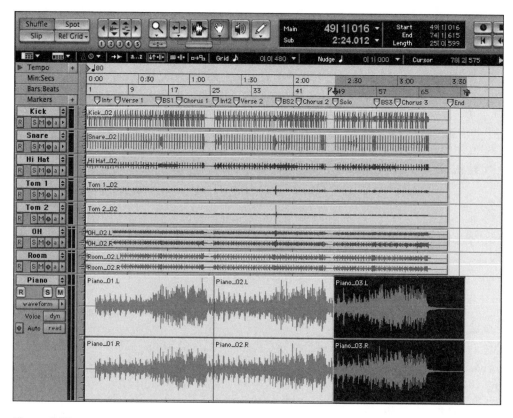

**Figure 2.19**
The Piano regions laid in back to back to back.

9. Do the same for the Intro 2 and Solo markers to verify that the editing and timing are free of glitches.

10. *Hit Command+S* (Mac) or *Ctrl+S* (PC) to save.

I cannot overemphasize the importance of checking your edits as you work. There is nothing more embarrassing for an engineer than saying you've finished an edit, only to have it be wrong when you play it for the client. So LISTEN, LISTEN, LISTEN to your work!!!

## Exercise 2.6.2 The Music: Part 2

Next up are the Acoustic Gtr, Bass, and Guide Vocal tracks.

1. *Select* Ex2.6.2 from the **Memory Locations** window.

2. *Hit* the *F3* button on your keyboard, and you will be back to Spot mode.

3. *Click/drag* each of the three remaining regions, **Acoustic Gtr_01**, **Bass_02**, and **Guide Vocal_01**, from the **Regions** list onto the associated track. In each case, *select* the **up arrow** next to the original time stamp and *hit* OK to place it on the track.

4. *Select* the **Intro** marker from the **Memory Locations** window and have a listen.

## *Exercise 2.6.3 The Music: Part 3*

Didn't I just tell you that you have to listen to your edits? Obviously the Bass and Acoustic Gtr tracks are not lined up properly.

1. *Select* the **Ex2.6.3** marker from the **Memory Locations** window. As you can see, the Acoustic Gtr and Bass tracks start a bar later than the Piano track does. Your screen should look something like Figure 2.20.

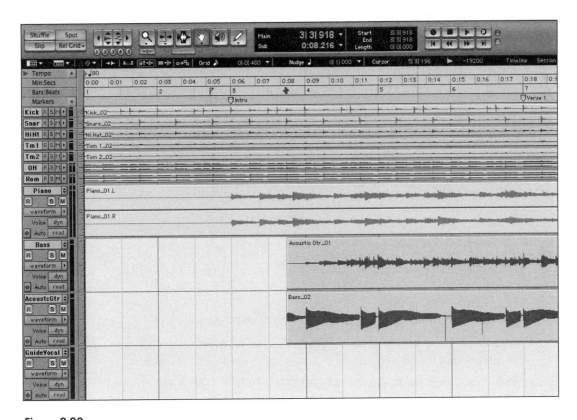

**Figure 2.20**
The Bass and Acoustic Gtr tracks are not in line with the Piano and Drum tracks.

2. *Click* once on the **Acoustic Gtr_01** region and look at the Start Time as indicated in the Event Edit area directly to the right of the Main Counter section in the Edit window (see Figure 2.21). As you can see, the region start time is 34000 (bar 3, beat 4, and tick 000). This makes it a good candidate for Absolute Grid mode.

**Figure 2.21**

This figure shows the Event Edit area. It displays the start, end, and length of any selected region.

3. *Switch* to **Absolute Grid** mode by holding the *Option* key (Mac) or *Alt* key (PC) and *hitting* the alphanumeric *4* key. You might have to do this more than once to get to Absolute Grid mode.

4. *Click/drag* the **region** to your left until the Start Time number in the Event Edit area reads 24000 (bar 2, beat 4, tick 000).

5. *Click* once on the **Bass_02** region and look once again at the Event Edit area. The Start point is 33918 (bar 3, beat 3, tick 918). You cannot use Absolute Grid mode in this case because the region start will be moved to an exact grid increment and offset the Bass track by 42 ticks.

6. Switch to **Relative Grid** mode by *holding* the *Option* key (Mac) or *Alt* key (PC) and *hitting* the alphanumeric *4* key. The Grid mode button should now say Rel Grid.

7. *Click/drag* the **Bass_02** region to the left by one whole bar. The Event Edit area Start Time should now read 23918. *Hit* the **spacebar** and have a listen.

8. *Hit Command+S* (Mac) or *Ctrl+S* (PC) to save.

The Bass and Acoustic Gtr tracks should now be in good order. If this is not the case, revisit this exercise to make sure you have not missed anything.

## Exercise 2.6.4 The Vocals

Your last task for this chapter is to check out the vocal track placement.

1. *Select* Ex 2.6.4 from the **Memory Locations** window, *hit* the **spacebar**, and have a listen. It appears that the Guide Vocal_01 region is also out of sync by one bar.

2. *Select* the *F3* key to change your status to Spot mode.

3. Once there, *click* once on the **Guide Vocal_01** region to open the Spot Dialog box.

4. *Enter* **71000** as the Start Time and *select* OK. *Select* the **spacebar** again to verify the correct entrance of the Guide Vocal.

5. **Hit Shift+Command+M** (Mac) or **Shift+Ctrl+M** (PC) to open the User Time Stamp box, as shown in Figure 2.22.

**Figure 2.22**

The User Time Stamp box.

6. **Click** on the **up arrow** next to Current Selection and **hit OK**.

7. **Click** on the **Guide Vocal** region again, and you will now see the newly created user time stamp available in case of future disaster.

8. **Hit Command+S** (Mac) or **Ctrl+S** (PC) to save.

Hopefully these simple examples have shed a little light on the Edit modes and how they work when moving regions. Because moving regions is the most basic and perhaps the most common task when editing audio, the Grabber tool is the perfect way to exhibit the function and design of the Edit modes. The remaining Edit tools will not change the fundamental design of the Edit modes; in fact, they will only expand the possibilities of what can be done when editing audio.

The next chapter focuses on the Edit tools and breaks down how each one works. Understanding the fundamental logic behind each tool will open up a world of possibilities, and most importantly, show you how to use them for editing audio.

# 3 The Edit Tools

In Chapter 2 you learned how the Edit modes define the working method or approach for any given task. Each mode has a specific set of guidelines that will define the way in which a task will be performed. If a carpenter set out to build a house, he or she would first look at the problems or challenges that are presented by the landscape of the property, drainage issues, how to connect to utilities, and so on, and decide on an approach to the initial task. Once decided upon, the tools most suited to accomplish this task would be selected, and the work would begin. In Pro Tools, the Edit modes are the approach to editing your audio, and the Edit tools are your hammers and saws. Each tool is designed for a specific task and purpose, and how you use it is determined by your approach (the Edit modes). A hammer can be used to drive a nail, knock down a wall, or gently position a pane of glass in a window frame. The ease of use of the Edit tools is what separates Pro Tools from all other audio editing applications. The design is simple, and the application even easier.

Even if you feel you are familiar with the Edit tools, I invite you to take another look. There is always something to be gained with a review, even if it just confirms what you already knew. So grab your tool belt, and let's take a closer look at the Edit tools and their functions in the program.

## Setting Up Chapter 3

If you have not already done so, boot Pro Tools. If you are continuing from Chapter 2 you will want to *select* **Close Session** from the **File** menu and *select* **Show Workspace** from the **Window** menu. From the Workspace, locate the Chapter 3 folder you have copied to your hard drive from the CD-ROM. Once located, open the folder and *double-click* on the **Chapter 3 Start** session template. Mac users *select* **New Session** from the pop-up; PC users *select* **Save As** from the **File** menu. Rename it anything you like and then *select* **Save**.

If you have not copied the files for Chapter 3, place the CD-ROM included with this book into your CD drive. If the CD-ROM does not automatically load, *double-click* on the **disk image** on the Mac Finder or Windows Explorer to view the contents. *Double-click* on the link for your computer type, **Start.osx** (Mac) or **Start.exe** (PC), and preview the License agreement. If acceptable, *select* **I Agree**. *Click* once the **Chapter Files** link at the bottom of the screen, and you will be given a list of chapters. *Select* **Chapter 3**. This will open your default browser, and you can *right-click* to **Save As** or *drag/drop* the **Chapter 3** folder onto your hard drive along with the folders for Chapter 1–2. Try to keep your files all on the same drive and folder if possible, to avoid any confusion. If you have not copied any of the files, you may want to revisit the "Loading Files from the CD-ROM" section in Chapter 1 to review the process of copying files from the CD-ROM to your hard drive.

## Navigating the Edit Tools

When editing audio in Pro Tools, you will find that the majority of your work will be best accomplished using the Smart tool. (More on the Smart tool later in the chapter.) However, when editing audio, you may find the need to change the Edit tools often in order to accomplish certain tasks. As you become more familiar with the way each of the Edit tools acts and interacts, switching between them will become a seamless part of your workflow.

Before you begin learning how the Edit tools work, you must familiarize yourself with the many ways you can select or change them. Let's start with some matter-of-fact information.

The Edit tools are located between the Edit modes in the top-left corner of the Edit window and the Main Counter display at the top-center of the Edit window, as shown in Figure 3.1. There are seven basic Edit tools available: the Zoomer, Trim, Selector, Grabber, Scrubber, Pencil, and Smart tools. The Smart tool is really a set of tools combining the use of the Trim, Selector, and Grabber tools that will change based on the cursor position within a region.

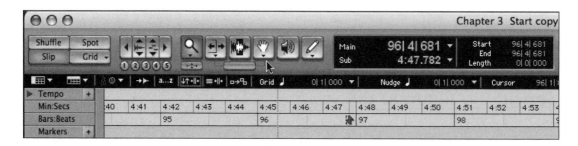

**Figure 3.1**
The Edit Tools are located between the Edit modes and the Main Counter in the Edit window.

You will note that the Zoomer, Trim, Grabber, and Pencil tools all have a small triangle at the bottom of the button. As mentioned in Chapter 2, whenever you see this little triangle on any button, you will find more than one way to use that particular feature. With a simple click and hold on the triangle, you will open up a list of available variations for each tool's function. The Pencil tool's options are shown in Figure 3.2.

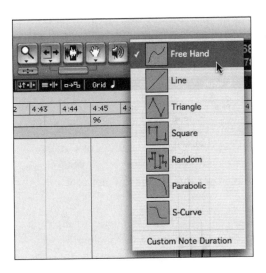

**Figure 3.2**
The different shapes available when using the Pencil tool.

The Edit tools can be changed using any one of four different methods:

- *Position* the **cursor** over the desired **Edit** tool and *click* once or *click/hold* to select the variation of the selected tool.

- *Use* the **Esc** key located in the top-left corner on both Mac and PC keyboards. This allows you to cycle through the Edit tools.

- *Use Function keys F5 through F10* on both Mac and PC keyboards. Note that pressing the F5, F6, F8, or F10 key more than once will toggle the available options for each of the assigned Edit tools—Zoomer, Trim, Grabber, and Pencil tool, respectively. Laptop users may have to hold the Fn key at the bottom-left of their keyboard to access the Function key set.

- *Use* the *Command+1—7* keys (Mac) or *Ctrl+1—7* keys (PC). Note that pressing the Command (Mac) or Ctrl (PC) and the alphanumeric number 1,2, 4, or 6 keys more than once will toggle the available options for each of the assigned Edit tools—Zoomer, Trim, Grabber, and Pencil tool, respectively.

Try using all of the above-mentioned techniques. Remember, it is very important to put your fingers to the computer and dabble a little. This will help you to memorize these valuable shortcuts. I will ask you to use different methods for each of the exercises to help aid this process.

# Using the Edit Tools

Now that you know how to navigate the Edit tools, let's get to the heart of how they work. As I stated previously, there are seven Edit tools, including the Smart tool, and each Edit tool performs a unique and useful function when editing audio. The first seven exercises will detail each Edit tool's design and function when editing audio.

As you go through each Edit tool, I will again direct you to the exercise track located at the top of your Track list in the Edit window. You will use the Memory Locations window to navigate your way around the Edit window from exercise to exercise.

## Working with the Zoomer Tool

The Zoomer tool is really a Navigation tool rather than an Edit tool, but its function cannot be underestimated. Zooming in and out is a large part of making your edits as accurate as possible, and is most often accomplished using shortcuts, rather than using the Zoomer tool. But before you start sending hate letters to the Digidesign Tech Support, a closer look at the Zoomer tool will reveal some valuable options.

The Zoomer tool has two options, Normal Zoom and Single Zoom, as shown in Figure 3.3. In Normal Zoom mode, the Zoomer tool remains selected after zooming. In Single Zoom mode, the previously selected tool is reselected after zooming. The Single Zoom mode is identified by a curved arrow to the right of the Zoom icon on the button.

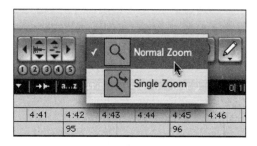

**Figure 3.3**
The options available for the Zoomer tool.

There are three basic ways to use the Zoomer tool: single-click, click/drag, and waveform zoom. Let's break them down one by one.

### Exercise 3.1.1 Method One: Single-Click
The single-click zoom is the easiest of all methods—just position your cursor and click.

1. *Select* Ex 3.1.1 from the **Memory Locations** window and begin your first exercise.

2. *Select* Slip mode by *hitting F2* on your keyboard.

3. *Click/hold* on the **Zoomer** tool button and *select* **Normal Zoom**. Notice that your cursor turns into a magnifying glass with a plus sign in the middle when placed over a region.

4. *Click* once at the beginning of the **first region** in the exercise track, and you will zoom in by one level.

5. *Click* again at the beginning of the **second region** on the display, and you will zoom in another level, and the screen will center itself at the selected area.

6. Now *hold* the **Option** key (Mac) or **Alt** key (PC) and *click* once again on the **second region**. You have now zoomed out one level (see Figure 3.4). Notice that your Zoomer tool now has a minus sign in the center of it, allowing you to zoom out.

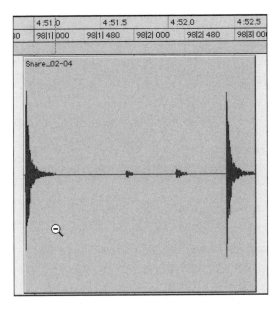

**Figure 3.4**

The Option (Mac) or Alt (PC) key turns the Zoomer tool into a Zoom Out tool.

7. *Option-click* (Mac) or *Alt-click* (PC) once again at the front of the first region, and you will be right back where you started.

## Exercise 3.1.2 Method Two: Click/Drag

The click/drag method for the Zoomer tool requires you to define a zoom selection area.

1. *Select* **Ex 3.1.2** from the **Memory Locations** window to reset the display.

2. *Click/drag* over the first region in the exercise track, as shown in Figure 3.5. Your region will now appear across the Edit window screen zoomed in to the exact zoom area you defined.

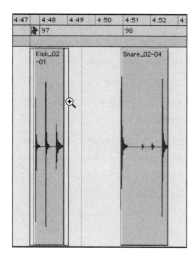

**Figure 3.5**
The first click/drag area for the click/drag method.

3. Now *click/drag* over the **first transient waveform peak** in this region to examine the peak more closely.

## Exercise 3.1.3 Method Three: Waveform Zoom

The third method requires the use of a modifier key. It is the most interactive of the bunch, and definitely the most fun.

1. *Select* **Ex 3.1.3** from the **Memory Locations** window. You will now be zoomed in on your transient peak from the click/drag exercise.

2. *Hold* the **Ctrl** key (Mac) or the **Start** key (PC) and *click/drag* vertically anywhere on the region. The waveform grows larger as you drag upward and becomes smaller as you drag downward. Set the region so the peak is larger than the original size.

3. Now *Ctrl-click/drag* (Mac) or *Start-click/drag* (PC) from the beginning of the peak and *drag* horizontally. You can now zoom in to the peak to sample accuracy, allowing you to make a precise edit!

## Exercise 3.1.4 Zooming Shortcuts

In addition to the Zoomer tool, there are a couple of very commonly used zoom shortcuts that are worth mentioning. The most prominent involves the use of a modifier key with the left (open) and right (closed) brackets on your keyboard. I often find this method quicker than having to mouse around with the Zoomer tool. In this exercise, we will feature this quick and easy method for zooming.

1. From the **Memory Locations** window *select* **Ex 3.1.4**. You will see a selected region on the Edit window display.

2. *Hit Command+]* (Mac) or *Ctrl+]* (PC) twice on your keyboard to zoom in two levels. Notice that the screen centers on the front of the selected region.

3. *Hit* the **right arrow** key on your keyboard, and you will center the screen on the end of your selection.

4. *Hit Command+[* (Mac) or *Ctrl+[* (PC) once on your keyboard to zoom out by one level.

5. *Hit* the **left arrow** key on your keyboard, and you will center the screen, once again, on the front of your selection area.

In Pro Tools, zooming with shortcuts follows a basic set of guidelines that, if understood, will make your zooming experience much more fruitful. When zooming in and out, the assumed zoom-in point will always be the cursor position or the beginning of a selection area. Remember to use your arrow keys to center the selection area on the Edit window. If you find that you are constantly readjusting your cursor position to zoom in where you want to, it may be more advantageous to use the Zoomer tool.

## Working with the Selector Tool

Located in the middle of all the Edit tools is perhaps the most overlooked and yet the most commonly used tool, the Selector tool. As its name suggests, it is used to select regions or parts of regions for editing. It is also commonly used to select start points for playback and zooming. The Selector tool is mostly used to set up an edit or function with another tool or one of the many editing options available in the Edit menu.

To start, let's first take a look at the location of the Selector tool, shown in Figure 3.6. The Selector tool can be used by single-clicking, double-clicking, triple-clicking, and click/dragging. In the following exercises, we look at the features of each method.

**Figure 3.6**
The location of the Selector tool.

### Exercise 3.2.1 The Single- and Double-Click

1. *Select* Ex 3.2.1 from the **Memory Locations** window. You will now see a test dummy set of regions eagerly awaiting the Selector tool.

2. *Hit Command+3* (Mac) or *Ctrl+3* (PC) to enable the Selector tool.

3. *Single-click* anywhere on the **Timeline bar**, as shown in Figure 3.7. You will now see a blue double-arrow in the Timeline bar and a flashing cursor across your tracks. This is your new playback start point.

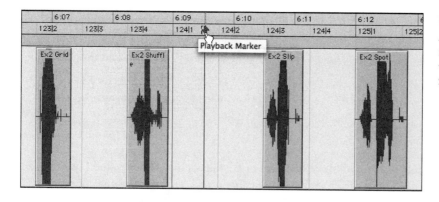

**Figure 3.7**

A Playback Marker point made in the Timeline bar with a single-click of the Selector tool.

4.  *Hit* the **spacebar** once, and you will start playing from this position. Stop after a couple of bars by *hitting* the **spacebar** once again.

    You can also set a start point for playback from a specific place in one of the regions by *placing* the **cursor** anywhere in the **track display** and *single-clicking*. This will allow you to cue your playback for a more precise placement.

5.  *Place* the **Selector** cursor somewhere in the middle of the **Kick** region just before a kick-drum transient and *click* once. *Hit Command+E* (Mac) or *Ctrl+E* (PC). You have now split your region into two!

These are a few of the many possibilities available using the single-click with the Selector tool. The double-click allows you to select a single region for editing. Let's take a look at this feature.

1.  *Place* your **cursor** over the second region in the **Exercise track** and *double-click*. You have now selected that whole region.

2.  Now *press* the **Delete** key (Mac) or **Backspace** key (PC) on your keyboard, and you have deleted the selected region.

3.  *Double-click* in the **Timeline bar** over either the **Bars:Beats** or **Mins:Secs** section and you will now have selected every region in the entire song.

### Exercise 3.2.2 The Triple-Click

Now that you have warmed up your wrist sufficiently, I think you are ready for the triple-click. In the previous exercise, a double-click in the Timeline bar allowed you to select all of the regions in the entire song. But what if you wanted to select all of the regions in a single track?

1.  *Select* **Ex 3.2.2** in the **Memory Locations** window. You will now see an overview of your session.

2.  *Triple-click* anywhere on the **Piano** track, and you will have selected all of the regions in that track. This feature is useful when the entire content of a single track needs to be nudged in time, deleted, or copied and pasted elsewhere (see Figure 3.8).

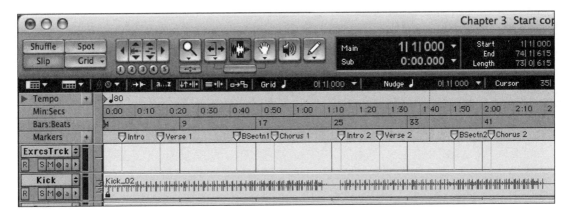

**Figure 3.8**
An overview of the entire session with all regions selected in the Piano track.

If your wrist is not up to the task of a triple-click, or you prefer to lay off the carpal tunnel syndrome–inducing effects that such a feat may produce—you can single-click anywhere in the track and *press Command+A* (Mac) or *Ctrl+A* (PC) to achieve the same effect.

### Exercise 3.2.3 The Click/Drag

Perhaps the most common use of the Selector tool when editing audio is the click/drag. The click/drag allows you to define an area that is not the length of an entire region. You can select a part of a region or a series of regions. This is only limited by the length of time you can hold down the mouse button.

1. *Select* Ex 3.2.3 from the **Memory Locations** window and take a look at some of the possibilities. You are now cued up to the Guide Vocal track from your tracking session. A quick hit of the spacebar will show a stray cough that is distracting the attention of the producer from the rest of the song (see Figure 3.9).

2. *Place* your **cursor** just before this foul ball of phlegm and *click/drag* to just after.

   *Hit* the **Delete** key on your keyboard so you can move on in peace.

   *Hit Command+S* (Mac) or *Ctrl+S* (PC)

As you can see, there are many ways to create location and selection areas for playback, or to just edit or define areas to be copied, pasted, deleted, and so on. As you wind your way through the book, the real power of these selection options will become more apparent. As mentioned at the beginning of this section, the Selector tool is used mostly to set up another tool or edit function. But before we get into these other options, let's take a peek at another location tool, the Scubber tool.

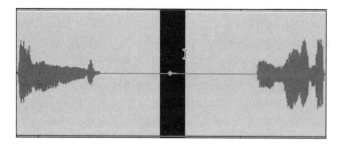

**Figure 3.9**
The selection area shows the
cough that needs to be removed.

## Working with the Scrubber Tool

The Scrubber tool at first look seems to be an innocuous tool that was placed into Pro Tools as a throwback to the analog tape machine days. In the days of analog tape recording, there was no benefit to seeing the waveform on a display to help you perform your edits with accuracy. The only visual aid was the VU meters as you "scrubbed" the tape reels.

Given the capabilities of modern DAWs with waveform displays, editing audio has been greatly simplified by having the ability to *see* the waveform as well as hear it. You may be led to believe that seeing your edit will be enough to get you through all of your editing work, but alas, this is not the case. Although the vast majority of your editing work may be visually based, occasionally you will come across an edit that has no obvious visual transient peak to grab hold of. In such a case, it's time to dust off the Scrubber tool and do a little editing work "old school."

### Exercise 3.3.1 Standard Scrubbing

1. *Select* Ex 3.3.1 from the **Memory Locations** window and take a look at a more pertinent example. In this exercise, you will see a Bass part. There is a little slide just before the cursor position that is bothering the producer, and he wants you to get rid of it.

2. *Hit Command+5* (Mac) or *Ctrl+5* (PC) to enable the Scrubber tool.

3. *Click/drag* the **speaker** icon across the middle note of the Bass part until you hear the transition from the note to the slide. *Scrub back and forth* until you hear the exact transition point and *release* the **click/drag**. Your cursor will now be at the location of the transition.

4. *Press Command+]* (Mac) or *Ctrl+]* (PC) four times to focus in on the exact edit.

5. *Scrub* a little **more** until you can place the cursor on a point between the waveform peaks that touches the "zero" line, as shown in Figure 3.10.

6. From the **Edit** menu *select* **Separate Region**, and you will now have an edit at the transition point. Zoom out by *pressing Command+[* (Mac) or *Ctrl+[* once.

7. **Scrub** the **beginning** of the **next bass note** so that the cursor is placed before the transient peak, as shown in Figure 3.11.

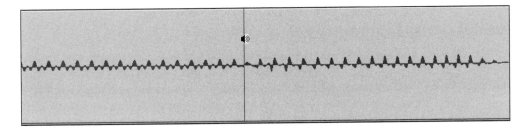

**Figure 3.10**
The Scrub tool is placed at the "zero" line.

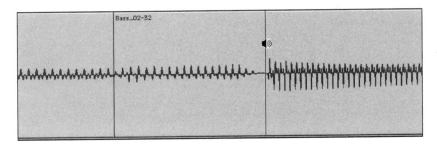

**Figure 3.11**
The cursor here is placed just before the transient peak of the next bass note.

8. *Hit Command+E* (Mac) or *Ctrl+E* (PC) to separate the slide from the rest of the bass part.

9. Now *select Command+3* (Mac) or *Ctrl+3* (PC) to switch to the Selector tool and *double-click* on the **"slide" note** you are attempting to get rid of.

10. *Hit* the **Delete** key on your keyboard. Audition the edit by placing the cursor anywhere before the edited region and *hitting* the **spacebar**. You may want to solo the track to verify that the edit does not have any clicks or pops.

11. *Hit Command+S* (Mac) or *Control+S* (PC)

## Exercise 3.3.2 Shuttle Mode

In addition to scrubbing to find your edit points, it is also a common technique with analog editing to use Shuttle mode to cue up to an edit point. Unlike scrubbing, which will only allow you to audition audio at a speed equal to or less than real time, Shuttle mode allows you to audition at speeds faster than play speed, as well as slower. This can be helpful when you are trying to locate a particular phrase, event, or place in a song in a hurry. Figure 3.12 shows the Shuttle mode icon with the arrow inside the speaker cursor to distinguish it from the Scrub mode. This is a tool for all you obsessive coffee drinkers out there who think the rest of the world is traveling in slow motion. You know who you are!

### Tips on Making Clean Edits

One of the difficulties of editing audio is finding a point where the edit does not create an audible click when played back. Many people will just slap a quick fade-in, fade-out, or crossfade at the edit to solve this problem, which may solve your problem in the short term, but may eventually come back to bite you. Fades of all types eat up additional processing power of the computer, make the hard drive work harder, and can create some difficulties when moving regions.

To avoid these issues, simply zoom in several times and place your edit at the zero crossing or transition point between the positive and negative phase cycles of your waveform. This line of demarcation is displayed as a thin line running horizontally through the middle of your waveform.

Although this does not always guarantee that you will avoid having a click or pop when you play back, it will give you a clean edit more often than not.

The waveform's positive and negative phase cycles are exactly analogous to positive or negative voltage in any analog audio device, the excursion of a speaker outward and then inward, the bunching up (compression) or spreading out (rarefaction) of air particles of a sound wave traveling through air, and finally, your eardrum pushing inward or pulling outward with the incoming acoustic waveform.

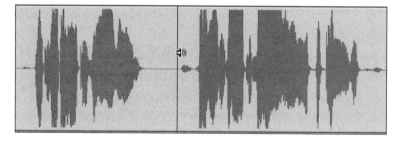

**Figure 3.12**
With Shuttle mode selected, the speaker icon contains an arrow to distinguish it from Scrub mode.

1. *Select* **Ex 3.3.2** from the **Memory Locations** window, and let's have a little bit of fun!

2. Now *select Command+5* (Mac) or *Ctrl+5* (PC) to switch back to the Scrubber tool.

3. *Hold* the **Option** key (Mac) or the **Alt** key (PC), *click/drag* on the **Vocal** track, and see whether you can locate the word "Because."

4. Once you have found it, *release* all **keys** to exit **Shuttle** and enter **Scrub** mode.

5. Now *click/drag* with the **Scrub** tool and *locate* the **cursor** at the beginning of the word "Because."

This is the most basic technique for using Shuttle with the Scrub tool.

# Working with the Grabber Tool

The Grabber tool is designed to select, move, separate, and arrange regions on an audio track. In Chapter 2 you used the Grabber tool to show the function of the Edit modes. Because moving regions is perhaps the most common task when editing audio, this section will need to dig a little deeper into the well to explore some of the valuable resources available when using the Grabber tool.

There are three basic options for using the Grabber tool, which are selectable by click/holding on the Grabber tool button in the Edit window, as shown in Figure 3.13. The three available options are Time, Separation, and Object.

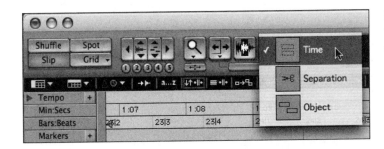

**Figure 3.13**
The location of the Grabber tool and the three options available.

The Time Grabber tool is used for selecting or moving whole regions from one place to another. The word *whole* is important because it defines the fundamental difference between the Time Grabber and the Separation Grabber. The Separation Grabber tool is used to extract *selected* parts of a region to be placed elsewhere. It is almost always used in conjunction with the Selector tool that defines the area to be extracted first. Lastly, the Object tool is used to select or move non-consecutive regions from a single or multiple tracks as a group to another location.

The Grabber tool can be selected by any one of the following shortcuts:

- *Clicking* on the **Selector** button
- *Selecting* the **Esc** key in the upper-left corner of your keyboard until the Grabber tool is highlighted
- *Hitting Function key 8 (F8)*
- *Selecting Command+4* (Mac) or *Ctrl+4* (PC)

The last two options, if selected multiple times, will toggle through the optional ways of using the Grabber tool.

## Exercise 3.4.1 The Time Grabber
The Time Grabber tool is used for dragging whole regions around the Edit window. When the Time Grabber is selected, the Grabber tool button in the Edit window will display a hand and be highlighted in the color blue, as shown in Figure 3.14.

**Figure 3.14**
The Grabber tool button when set to the Time Grabber option.

Because this is the primary tool you used in Chapter 2 for moving regions with the different Edit modes, take a look at a few new options by employing the use of a few modifier keys.

1. *Select* Ex 3.4.1 from the **Memory Locations** window, and you will see two vocal regions. The middle line is on an alternate vocal track that contains a one-line fix and must be placed into the Guide Vocal track.

2. *Select* the **Time Grabber** tool in your **Edit** window by *click/holding* on the **Grabber** tool button and *selecting* the **Time** option.

3. *Hit Option+2* (Mac) or *Alt+2* (PC) to select Slip mode.

4. *Click/drag* the **region** from the **Vocal Fix** track to the Guide Vocal track and drop. If you drag the region straight down, your region will remain locked in time.

5. *Select Command+Z* (Mac) or *Ctrl+Z* (PC) to undo your move.

6. Now *click/drag* the **same region** down to the **Guide Vocal** track and slide it to the left or right to get a feel for how far you must move the region in order to free it from the vertical lock.

7. *Drop* the **region** anywhere and again *press Command+Z* (Mac) or *Ctrl+Z* (PC) to undo your move.

8. Now *hold* the **Ctrl** key (Mac) or the **Start** key (PC) and *click/drag* the **Guide Vocal Fix C1** region to the **Guide Vocal Alt** track. Try to move the region to the left or right. You will notice that the region is locked to vertical movement only, thus preventing any timing issues with your edit.

## Exercise 3.4.2 The Separation Grabber

The Separation Grabber tool is used to extract part of a region from one track to be moved or placed elsewhere. The selection area is defined with the Selector tool. Once the area to be moved is selected, switch to the Separation Grabber to extract and move the region. Using shortcuts to switch between the tools will facilitate this process. You can tell that the Separation Grabber is selected by the pair of scissors displayed on the Grabber tool button in the Edit window, as shown in Figure 3.15.

**Figure 3.15**
The Grabber tool button when set to the Separation Grabber option.

1.  *Select* **Ex 3.4.2** from the **Memory Locations** window, and you will see an exercise similar to the last one, except for the size of the Guide Vocal Fix region.

    The Time Grabber is not useful in this situation because grabbing the region and moving it would cover up the original performance when moved to the Guide Vocal track. It's time to dust off your Separation Grabber tool and put it to work!

2.  *Hit Command+3* (Mac) or *Ctrl+3* (PC) to choose the **Selector** tool and *click/drag* a **selection** area around the waveform on the **Guide Vocal Fix** region.

3.  *Hit Command+4* (Mac) or *Ctrl+4* (PC) twice to choose the Separation Grabber tool.

4.  *Click/drag* and *drop* the **selected area** from the **Guide Vocal Fix** track to the **Guide Vocal** track. Notice that a new region is created, and a hole is left where the selected region was removed.

5.  *Select Command+Z* (Mac) or *Ctrl+Z* (PC) to undo your move.

6.  While *holding* the **Option** key (Mac) or the **Alt** key (PC), *click/drag* and *drop* the **selection** area from the **Guide Vocal Fix** track to the **Guide Vocal** track. You have now copied the selected area to another track without affecting the original region.

To take this one step further, if you wish to both time-constrain and copy the region, you can employ the use of both the Ctrl and Option keys (Mac) or the Start and Alt keys (PC) to copy your region without the worry of losing the region's timing to the track.

### Exercise 3.4.3 The Object Grabber

The Object Grabber tool is used for selecting and moving groups of noncontiguous regions on one or more tracks. Another unusual benefit of this tool is that it ignores Edit groups. Edit groups are discussed in detail in the next chapter. The Object Grabber can best be described as a really neat tool that is great when you need it, but otherwise does not serve the vast majority of your needs when moving regions on a day-to-day basis. The Object Grabber is enabled when the Grabber button displays two boxes superimposed over the hand icon, as shown in Figure 3.16.

**Figure 3.16**
The Grabber tool button when set to the Object Grabber option.

In this exercise, the producer wants to replace two vocal lines in the Guide Vocal with an alternate Guide Vocal take. The second line and the fifth line in the second Guide Vocal track must first be defined as separate regions, and then moved into the Guide Vocal track.

1. **Select** Ex 3.4.3 from the **Memory Locations** window to begin.

2. **Press** the **F7** key on your keyboard to enable the **Selector** tool.

3. **Click/drag** an **area** around the second vocal line in the **Guide Vocal Alt** track and **hit Command+E** (Mac) or **Ctrl+E** (PC) to create a new region. Make sure that the selected area does not contain any of the next or previous vocal lines.

4. Now **click/drag** an area around the fifth vocal line in the **Guide Vocal Alt** track and **press Command+E** (Mac) or **Ctrl+E** (PC) to create another new region. Your edits should look very similar to Figure 3.17.

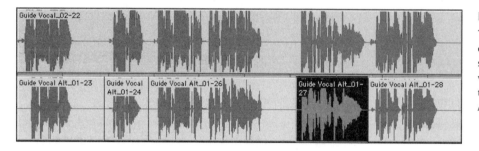

**Figure 3.17**

The regions defined for the second and fifth vocal lines in the Guide Vocal Alt track.

5. **Select** **F8** on your keyboard twice until you enable the **Object Grabber**.

6. **Select** the first of the **two regions** you just created from the **Guide Vocal Alt** track by **clicking** once with the **Object Grabber** tool. It should now have a black box around it.

7. **Hold** the **Shift** key and **select** the second of the **two regions** you just created. Black boxes should now be around both regions.

8. Now **hold** the **Ctrl+Option** keys (Mac) or **Start+Alt** keys (PC) and **click/drag** either one of the two "boxed" regions up to the Guide Vocal track. You have just copied two nonconsecutive regions into the Guide Vocal track while locking the regions in time (see Figure 3.18)

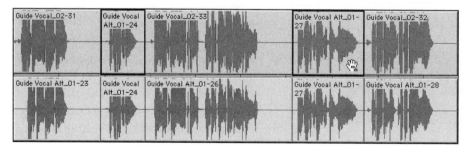

**Figure 3.18**

The final vocal line edits for Exercise 3.4.3.

Given the choice of the three versions of the Grabber tool, I will usually start with the Separation Grabber because it offers the most flexibility for the majority of work done when moving, copying, or extracting regions. The Separation Grabber essentially contains all of the same capabilities of the Time Grabber in that it can still select whole regions, but it also gives you the flexibility of extracting a segment of a region when used in conjunction with the Selector tool. The Object Grabber tool is an odd tool that is limited to a particular task, which is incredibly useful when noncontiguous regions need to be selected and moved.

## Working with the Trim Tool

The Trim tool is designed to trim region boundaries as well as MIDI notes and other data functions, such as automation. For the purposes of this book, we will concentrate on trimming audio regions. Trimming regions allows you to delete unwanted audio from the front or back of a region. Conversely, a region can be extended at the front or back to the full length of the audio file that it represents, but no farther.

In addition to the Standard Trim tool as just described, the Trim tool also has two other functions that can be selected by click/holding on the Trim tool button in the Edit window (see Figure 3.19). They are the TC/E (Time Compression Expansion) tool and the Scrub Trim tool. The TC/E tool is perhaps one of the most innovative and valuable tools when editing loops or regions that need to be adapted to the tempo of the current song or to a defined length, such as a musical cue for a video. The Scrub Trim tool is a combination of the Scrub tool and the Standard Trim tool and is only available on HD systems. It allows the user to hear the audio as if they were scrubbing while simultaneously editing the region boundary.

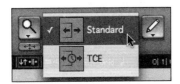

**Figure 3.19**
The available options for the Trim tool on an LE system.

### Exercise 3.5.1 The Trim Tool

1. *Select* Ex 3.5.1 from the **Memory Locations** window and investigate how to use the Standard Trim tool. Once it is selected, you will see two regions that have a waveform in the middle and blank areas to either side.

2. *Select* the **Standard Trim** tool by *clicking* on the **Trim** tool button and *selecting* **Standard Trim** tool. When the Standard Trim tool is selected, the button will display an icon, as shown in Figure 3.20.

**Figure 3.20**
The Standard Trim tool icon.

3. *Move* the Trim tool **cursor** across the first region. Notice that the direction of the Trim tool cursor changes when you pass the halfway point across the region horizontally. This determines the region boundary that will be edited, start or end.

4. To edit the region start boundary, *place* the **cursor** somewhere near the left half of the region and *click/drag* until the region is trimmed just before the audio waveform. *Release* the **mouse button,** and you have just edited the region front.

5. To edit the region end boundary, follow the same procedure, only with the cursor near the right side of the region. *Click/drag* until the **region end** is trimmed just after the waveform. Your edit should look something like Figure 3.21.

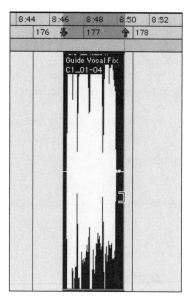

**Figure 3.21**
The region boundary edit for Exercise 3.5.1.

The region start or end can be undone by click/dragging either region end in the opposite direction. The click/drag is only constricted by the limits of the size of the audio file from which the region was derived.

The Trim tool is simple by design and will handle most of your region boundary editing needs. The next tool, however, takes trimming to a whole new level.

## Exercise 3.5.2 The TC/E Tool

The Time Compression Expansion Trim tool (TC/E) encompasses such an incredibly useful part of modern production that it requires its own chapter. That would be Chapter 6, as a matter of fact. This section covers the basic use of the TC/E Trim tool, as well as some general guidelines. You know the TC/E Trim tool is selected when the Trim tool button has a clock superimposed over the Trim icon, as shown in Figure 3.22.

**Figure 3.22**
The TC/E Trim tool icon.

Before you begin this exercise, here are some general guidelines for using the TC/E Trim tool:

- ■ The TC/E tool will create a new audio file and region whenever used. This is necessary because Time Compression/Expansion is a function that cannot be performed in real time.

- ■ Make sure the TC/E tool settings are optimized for the task you are performing. Optimized settings can be made and stored when dealing with different program material. This is covered in more detail in Chapter 6.

- ■ Only select the TC/E Trim tool when you are using it, and then deselect it immediately. This will prevent you from creating accidental regions when trying to perform a standard trim.

1. *Select* Ex 3.5.2 from the **Memory Locations** window and *hit* the **spacebar** to play the region. The region is a shaker loop that is two bars in length.

2. *Hit Option+4* (Mac) or *Alt+4* (PC) to select **Grid** mode. A quick look at the grid lines shows that the tempo of the loop is slower than the tempo of the current session. This is easy to determine by listening to the loop and counting beats. Compare your total with the grid display, and do the math.

3. *Hit Command+2* (Mac) or *Ctrl+2* (PC) on your keyboard until the Clock icon appears. Your Trim cursor will now have the same Clock icon.

4. *Position* your **cursor** over the right region boundary, *click/drag* to the **left** until the length is sized up to two bars, and *release* the **mouse button**. You have just adapted the Shaker Loop region to the tempo of the song. You can use the Length field in the Event Edit area directly to the right of the Main Counter to verify that it is two bars long.

   The TC/E Trim tool is most commonly used with Grid mode when editing loops or audio files that have a beat or tempo. Slip mode is commonly used when non-tempo-related audio files need to be shortened or lengthened.

5. *Reset* the **TC/E** tool back to Standard trim by *click/holding* on the **TC/E Trim** button and selecting Standard.

## Working with the Pencil Tool

The Pencil tool lets you draw automation, MIDI data, tempo changes, and most importantly for the purposes of this book, audio waveforms when zoomed into sample level. The Pencil tool can draw any one of seven different shapes, as shown in Figure 3.23. But before you start redrawing all of your waveforms with all the pretty shapes, Pro Tools only allows the Freehand option for redrawing audio.

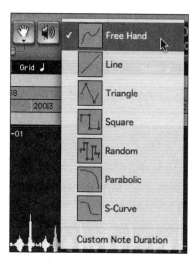

**Figure 3.23**

The seven different shapes available with the Pencil tool.

Drawing audio waveforms to create new sounds, especially with a mouse, would be a fruitless venture. However, it does have one very useful purpose, which is getting rid of clicks and pops. Clicks and pops can be generated by bad cables, bad digital clock sources, or a variety of other reasons, but when they occur during the perfect take, they can be downright annoying. Much effort has gone into designing plug-ins to deal with these annoying little pests. However, with any kind of processing of this nature, there is always some loss of audio quality in the process. If the number of clicks is minimal, it may make more sense to grab your Pencil tool and get to wiping them out one by one.

### *Exercise 3.6.1 Declicking*

1.   *Select* **Ex 3.6.1** from the **Memory Locations** window. Once it is selected, you will see the Bass track in the intro section of your song with two noticeable clicks. Luckily, these are the only two in the track, so let's get to work.

2.   *Select* **Slip** mode by *hitting Option+2* (Mac) or *Alt+2* (PC).

3.   *Hit Command+3* (Mac) or *Ctrl+3* (PC) on your keyboard to enable the Selector tool.

4. *Place* the **Selector** cursor as close to the first click as possible by *single-clicking* on the **waveform** where the first click occurs.

5. Now zoom in by *hitting Command+]* (Mac) or *Ctrl+]* (PC). Keep hitting this combination until the waveform switches from solid to a single line. When the waveform switches from solid to a single line, it is the point where you have officially entered "sample accuracy." You might need to place your cursor closer to the click while zooming so that the click does not disappear off the screen.

6. *Select* the **Pencil** tool by *hitting Command+6* (Mac) or *Ctrl+6* (PC) on your keyboard.

7. Carefully *click/drag* at the **area** where you see the spike to "redraw" the waveform, as shown in Figure 3.24.

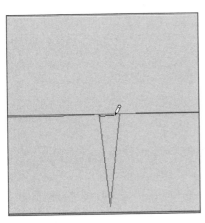

**Figure 3.24**
The Pencil tool redrawing the click on the Bass track.

8. You can quickly zoom out by *selecting* Ex 3.6.1 from the **Memory Locations** window again.

9. Use the same method as earlier to rid yourself of the second click.

10. Zoom out by *hitting Command+[* (Mac) or *Ctrl+[* (PC) until you can see the whole bass notes. If the click is still displayed, don't worry; it is just a waveform redraw issue, which can be corrected. *Click* on the **Selector** tool and *double-click* on the **Bass_02** region.

11. Open up the Regions list by *clicking* on the **double-arrow** in the bottom-right corner of the **Edit** window.

12. *Click* once at the top of the list where it says **Region**, and *select* **Recalculate Waveform Overviews**. It might take a second, but the spike will disappear.

13. *Hit Command+S* (Mac) or *Ctrl+S* (PC) to save.

It is important to keep in mind that this process is destructive in that it actually rewrites the file on the hard drive. You can undo a redraw, however. If you feel uncertain about a redraw, you might want to make a copy of your region by highlighting the region and selecting Duplicate from the Audiosuite menu before editing it. Remember kids, safety first!

## Working with the Smart Tool

The vast majority of all of your editing work in Pro Tools will revolve around the use and application of three tools: the Trim tool, the Selector tool, and the Grabber tool. As you have probably noticed over the whole of this chapter, switching between these tools is clumsy at best, especially when you are trying to perform a series of edits that requires you to change tools frequently. Enter the Smart tool.

The Smart tool, as I mentioned earlier in this chapter, encompasses a set of tools. In addition to the three main tools, you also have a Crossfade tool, a Fade In tool, and a Fade Out tool. The Smart tool is located directly beneath the three tools that it activates, as shown in Figure 3.25. The bar directly below the Trim, Selector, and Grabber tools is used to activate this tool set. Once enabled, all three tools will be highlighted blue, in addition to the bar.

**Figure 3.25**
The Smart tool is selected by clicking on the bar located directly below the Trim, Selector, and Grabber tools.

The Smart tool can be activated by any one of the following means:

- ■ *Clicking* on the **Smart toolbar** below the Trim, Selector, and Grabber tools
- ■ *Selecting* the **Esc** key in the upper left-hand corner of your keyboard until the Smart tool highlights
- ■ *Hitting* **Function keys 6 and** 7 simultaneously (F6/F7)
- ■ *Selecting Command+Alphanumeric* 7 (Mac) or *Ctrl+Alphanumeric* 7 (PC)

### Exercise 3.7.1 Navigating the Smart Tool

When the Smart tool is enabled, regions are divided up into eight areas. Each area of the region will activate a different tool, logically based off of the tool that would most likely be used when in that area of the region (see Figure 3.26).

1. *Select* **Ex 3.7.1** from the **Memory Locations** window. You will see a single region on the Exercise track.

2. *Hit Command+7* (Mac) or *Ctrl+7* (PC) to select the **Smart** tool.

3. *Place* your **cursor** in the top half and in the middle of the region. You will have the Selector tool.

4. *Move* your **cursor** down to the lower half in the center, and you will have the Grabber tool.

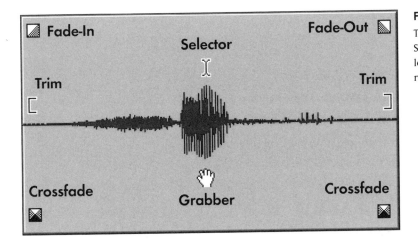

**Figure 3.26**

The tools that appear with the Smart tool when the cursor is located to different areas of a region.

5. Now *move* your **cursor** to the far left or right and near the zero crossing line. This is the Trim tool area.

6. *Move* the **cursor** to the top-left, and you have the Fade In tool.

7. *Move* your **cursor** to the top-right, and you will find the Fade Out tool.

8. Now *move* your **cursor** to the bottom left or right corner, and you will have the Crossfade tool.

9. Finally, *hold* the **Ctrl** key (Mac) or **Start** key (PC) and *place* the **cursor** in the top half of the region, and you will have the Scrubber tool.

Take a little time to navigate the different areas of the region and explore the possibilities with the Smart tool. Given the number of features available, there is really no reason to use any other tool. Because we have covered the use and capabilities of the Trim, Selector, Grabber, and Scrubber tools in detail already, let's take a closer look at the two new tools available with the Smart tool.

### Exercise 3.7.2 The Fade In and Fade Out Tools

The Fade In and Fade Out tools are used to smooth the edges of a tricky edit. I generally try to avoid using them unless it is a necessary part of making an edit work. Every little bit of processing affects the overall quality, as well as drains the CPU of valuable processing power that can be used for other tasks. But when the need does strike, I will dive right in to fix up a rough edit.

The Fade In and Fade Out tools can be accessed by two means. The first is with the Smart tool, as just described in the previous section. The second is by highlighting the area of the fade-in/out and selecting Command+F (Mac) or Ctrl+F (PC). Let's take a look at the Smart tool version.

1.  *Select* Ex 3.7.2 from the **Memory Locations** window, and you will see the Bass track's final note of the song. The producer wants you to put a fade-out on the final note to smooth out the end.

2.  *Select* the **Smart** tool by *hitting Command+7* (Mac) or *Ctrl+7* (PC).

3.  *Select* **Grid** mode by *hitting Option+4* (Mac) or *Alt+4* (PC).

4.  *Move* your **cursor** to the top-right corner of the **Bass** region until you see the Fade Out tool.

5.  *Click/drag* to the left by **two beats**, and you will create a fade-out for the last Bass note, as shown in Figure 3.27.

6.  *Relocate* your **cursor** back before the last bass note with a single click of your Cursor tool, and *hit* the **spacebar** to audition your newly created fade-out.

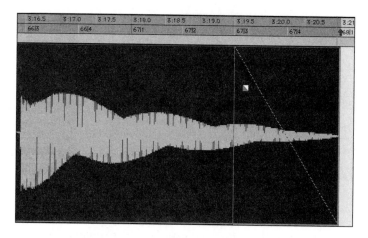

**Figure 3.27**

The fade-out of the last Bass note.

## Exercise 3.7.3 The Crossfade Tool

The Crossfade tool allows regions to overlap one another by a defined amount. The amount is determined by the area you click/drag using the Crossfade tool or by the area you define with the Selector tool. The latter method requires a shortcut command used for creating crossfades, fade-ins, and fade-outs.

1.  *Select* Ex 3.7.3 from the **Memory Locations** window, and you will see two bass notes. A quick listen by hitting the spacebar will reveal that there is a click between the two notes.

2.  *Select* the **Smart** tool by *hitting Command+7* (Mac) or *Ctrl+7* (PC).

3.  *Select* **Slip** mode by *hitting Option+2* (Mac) or *Alt+2* (PC).

4.  *Place* your **cursor** between the **two Bass regions** at the bottom where they meet until you see the Crossfade tool.

5.  *Click/drag* to the **left or right** so that the area of the crossfade extends just beyond the start of the second bass note, as shown in Figure 3.28.

68

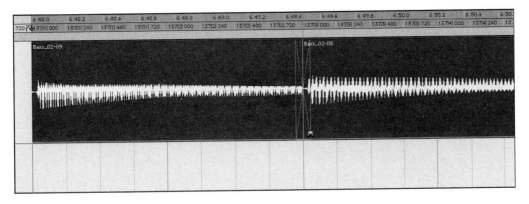

**Figure 3.28**
The Crossfade length between the two bass notes in Exercise 3.7.3.

6. *Place* your **cursor** back before the last bass note, *click* once and *hit* the **spacebar** to audition the crossfade.

7. *Hit* ***Command+S*** (Mac) or ***Ctrl+S*** (PC) to save.

### *Exercise 3.7.4 The Fades Dialog Box*

Now that you have created a fade-out and a crossfade, you might want to edit the shape of your fade to make it a bit more musical. The Fades dialog box allows complete control over fade-in, fade-out, and crossfade shapes to suit just this desire.

1. *Select* **Ex 3.7.4** from the **Memory Locations** window, and you will see the last bass note fade-out you created in Exercise 3.7.2.

2. *Place* your **cursor** on the bottom half of the **fade-out area** until you see the Grabber tool and *double-click*. You will open up the Fades dialog box, as shown in Figure 3.29.

   The Fades dialog box has a number of features to help you get just the right shape for your fade-in/out. The top-left of the box has a Speaker button that allows you to audition the fade shape without leaving the Fades dialog box. A pre-roll and post-roll is automatically induced so you can hear the fade in context.

   Beneath the Speaker button are four different waveform display types you can use to display the waveform in a way to best suit your needs. The up and down arrow buttons allow you to adjust the amplitude of the display if you are creating a fade over low-level material.

   The fade shape can be set to any one of three different options—Standard, S-Curve, and a variety of preset shapes, as shown in Figure 3.30.

   While the preset type of fade shape offers seven options for fade shape, using the Standard and S-Curve shapes allows a much higher degree of resolution.

69

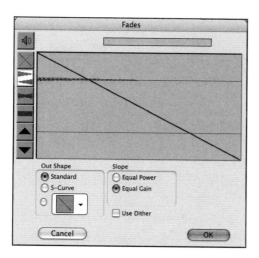

**Figure 3.29**

The Fades dialog box.

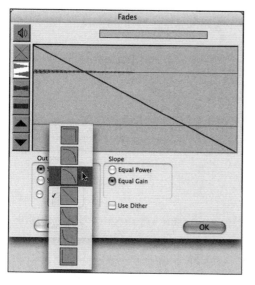

**Figure 3.30**

The preset fade shapes available
in the Fades dialog box.

3. **Select** Standard for the Out Shape and **position** your **cursor** over the blue fade-out shape, as shown in Figure 3.31.

4. **Click/drag** your **cursor**, and you will now have total control over the fade-out shape.

5. Now **select** S-Curve and **click/drag** once again on the **fade shape** to see the realm of possibilities.

6. Audition your fade-out by **selecting** the **Speaker** button. Once you are happy with the fade shape, **select** OK to apply it to the region.

7. **Hit Command+S** (Mac) or **Ctrl+S** (PC) to save.

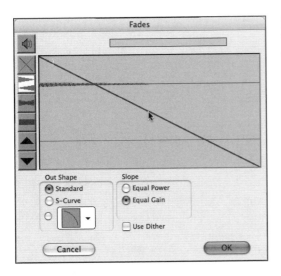

**Figure 3.31**
This is the position of the cursor necessary to change the fade shape at a higher degree of resolution.

The Slope setting has two features, Equal Power and Equal Gain. Equal Power is for non-phase-coherent fades, and Equal Gain is for phase-coherent fades. In simple English, if the crossfade is being performed over the exact same audio, say to get rid of a click or noise, then the material will typically be considered phase-coherent. If the crossfade is being performed over different audio from differing sources, then it would be considered non-phase-coherent. Ninety percent of all the edits I typically create are with the Equal Power slope. As always, let your ears be the best judge.

### Exercise 3.7.5 The Crossfade Dialog Box

The Crossfade dialog box is of very similar design to the Fades dialog box, with a couple of additional features. You have control over two fades (In and Out) and you have the ability to link the fade shape (see Figure 3.32). If the Link option is set to Equal Power or Equal Gain, the fade shape will be duplicated for the fade-out and fade-in shapes. If it is set to None, however, the fade-in and out shapes are independent of each other. Let's investigate.

1. *Select* **Ex 3.7.5** from the **Memory Locations** window. You will now see the Bass note crossfade you worked on in Exercise 3.7.3.

2. *Double-click* on the **crossfade** with the **Grabber** tool to open the Crossfade dialog box.

3. Change the Fade shape by *click/dragging* on either the **Fade-In** or **Fade-Out** shape, as you did in the previous exercise. Notice how both fade shapes adjust when you move just one.

4. *Hold* the **Option** key (Mac) or **Alt** key (PC) and *click* once on the **Fades** display to reset the fade shapes.

5. *Select* **None** from the **Link** section of the **Fades** dialog. You will now see four small black boxes appear in each corner of the Fades display. Click/dragging on any box will alter the start or end of the selected fade shape.

71

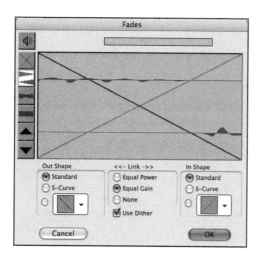

**Figure 3.32**
The Crossfade dialog box.

6. *Hold* the **Option** key (Mac) or the **Alt** key (PC) and *click/drag* anywhere in the **Fades** display. You are now adjusting the fade-in curve only.

7. *Hold* the **Command** key (Mac) or the **Ctrl** key (PC) and *click/drag* anywhere in the **Fades** display again. You are now adjusting the fade-out curve only.

8. Audition your fade-out by *selecting* the **Speaker** button. Once you are happy with the fade shape, *select* **OK** to apply it to the region.

9. *Hit Command+S* (Mac) or *Ctrl+S* (PC) to save.

## Exercise 3.7.6 The Batch Fades Dialog Box

Many of today's recordings employ the use of repeated loops throughout a song. Should the need arise to create crossfades across a series of repeated regions, it is not practical to do them one by one. Enter the Batch Fades dialog box (see Figure 3.33). As you can see, there are a number of new options available to accommodate your batch fade needs.

In the Operation section of the Batch Fades dialog box, there are three options: Create New Fades, Create New Fade Ins & Outs, and Adjust Existing Fades. The fade length can be defined in milliseconds (1/1000 of a second). Selecting Create New Fades will create new crossfades across the selected regions. Selecting Create New Fade Ins & Outs will create new fade-ins and fade-outs across all selected regions. Adjust Existing Fades will change all existing fades within the selection area to the new preset values. Any combination of these three settings is possible. If all three are selected, then crossfades will be created where selected regions abut one another. Fade-ins and fade-outs will be created wherever a region boundary does not touch another region. Any pre-existing fades and crossfades will be rewritten.

The placement of the fades can be made pre-splice, centered, or post-splice. The placement of the fades is based on the region boundary. Let's take a closer look.

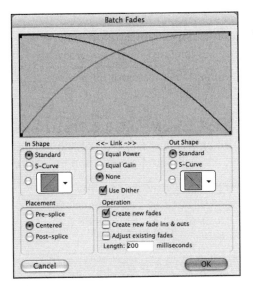

**Figure 3.33**
The Batch Fades dialog box.

1. *Select* **Ex 3.7.6** from the **Memory Locations** window. You will now see a series of Bass notes.

2. Using the **Selector** tool, *click/drag* across all of the **regions**.

3. *Select Command+F* (Mac) or *Ctrl+F* (PC) to open the **Batch Fades** dialog box. You can find this selection in the Edit menu, Fades/Create.

4. *Select* **Create New Fades** and **Create New Fade Ins & Outs** from the **Operation** section, and *select* **Pre-Splice** from the **Placement** section of the Batch Fades dialog box.

5. *Set* the **Length** to **50** milliseconds. Your Batch Fades dialog box should now look like Figure 3.34.

6. *Select* **OK**, and you will see the results of your batch fade.

### Default Fade Settings

As you become more familiar with using fades and crossfades, you will find certain settings that you use most often. These can be stored in the Pro Tools Preferences.

*Select* **Preferences** from the **Setup** menu and then *select* **Editing** (see Figure 3.35). You can set the default fade type for fade-ins, crossfades, and fade-outs. Selecting one of these three buttons will open up a Fades dialog box for you to set your default settings. In addition, the conversion quality of the fade can be set to determine how accurately your fades will be processed. Remember, the better the quality, the longer it will take to process the fade.

As you can see there are quite a lot of possibilities available with the Edit tools. When used in conjunction with the Edit modes, the ability to achieve any desired edit is only limited by your ability to quickly figure out what combination of tools and modes will best accomplish the task.

73

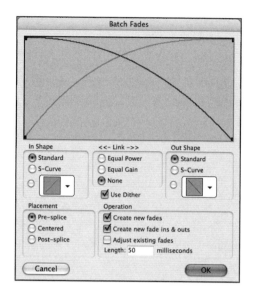

**Figure 3.34**

The Batch Fades dialog box for Exercise 3.7.6.

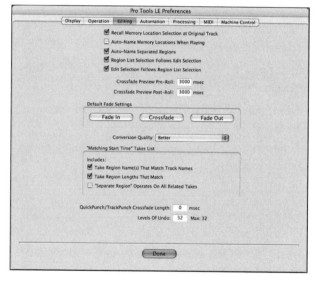

**Figure 3.35**

The Default Fade Settings section in the Preferences menu.

Understanding the design of the Edit tools and modes is critical to making the best decisions for whatever task you have. Experience and practice are the only ways to make this process flow seamlessly. But with every project comes a new challenge, and hopefully a new learning experience that will make the next project go even smoother.

The next chapter starts to tie some of these possibilities together as you explore the interaction of the Edit tools and modes for editing audio in Pro Tools.

# 4 Integrating the Edit Modes and Edit Tools

The remainder of your audio editing experience in Pro Tools will involve the integration of the Edit modes and Edit tools. The last two chapters discussed in detail the conceptual design and basic application of each mode and tool. This chapter starts the process of learning how the two are inextricably intertwined. Though the early part of this chapter might seem like review of Chapters 2 and 3, it is worth clarifying the connection between the tools and modes because this will be the foundation of all your editing work. Every feature you learn for the rest of this book and beyond will be an extension of the basic principles of the Edit tools or will be conceptually based on the Edit modes.

To wrap up this chapter you will delve a little more deeply into the navigation of regions to help facilitate your ability to get where you need to quickly. As you will see, getting to the job site quickly and efficiently is half the battle.

## Setting Up Chapter 4

If you have not already done so, boot Pro Tools. If you are continuing from Chapter 3, you will want to *select* **Close Session** from the **File** menu and *select* **Show Workspace** from the **Window** menu. From the Workspace, locate the Chapter 4 folder you have copied to your hard drive from the CD-ROM. Once located, open the folder and *double-click* on the **Chapter 4 Start** session template. Mac users *select* **New Session** from the pop-up; PC users *select* **Save As** from the **File** menu. Rename it anything you like, and then *select* **Save**.

If you have not copied the files for Chapter 4, place the CD-ROM included with this book into your CD drive. If the CD-ROM does not automatically load, *double-click* on the **disk image** on the Mac Finder or Windows Explorer to view the contents. *Double-click* on the link for your computer type, **Start.osx** (Mac) or **Start.exe** (PC), and preview the license agreement. If acceptable, *select* **I Agree**. *Click* once on the **Chapter Files** link at the bottom of the screen, and you will be given a list of chapters. *Select* **Chapter 4**. This will open your default browser, and you can *right-click* to **Save As** or *drag/drop* the **Chapter 4** folder onto your hard drive along with the folders for Chapters 1–2 and 3. Again, try to keep your files all on the same drive and folder, if possible, to avoid any confusion. If you have not copied any of the files, you may want to revisit the "Loading Files from the CD-ROM" section in Chapter 1 to review the process of copying files from the CD-ROM to your hard drive.

# The Edit Modes and Edit Tools

The following exercises go through all the combinations of the different modes and tools. To simplify things a little bit, you will work primarily with the Smart tool because you will be able to access all of the basic Edit tools without having to switch between them using the cursor or shortcuts. The Smart tool should be the starting point for all your editing work because 95 percent of all your work will require the tools encompassed in this tool set.

Because most of your editing tools are instantly available with the Smart tool, you will cycle through the Edit modes one by one and review each tool's function. The Zoomer and Scrubber tools work independently of the Edit modes because their primary function is to provide proper visual resolution or aid in the process of locating an edit point. The Pencil tool's only function with editing audio is redrawing waveforms and is again independent of the Edit modes. Because of these facts, the following exercises concentrate only on those tools that are affected by a change in the Edit mode.

## Spot Mode and the Edit Tools

I have purposely started with Spot mode because it is mostly an offline editing tool—offline in the sense that it requires manual input of data for placement. In that respect, it differs from the other modes that work in real time. They move, trim, or select as you move, trim, or select. For those of you who think and operate with specific known locations in mind, Spot mode allows you to place regions at a specific time or bar:beat number. It is also quite handy for relocating lost or mistakenly moved regions.

### Exercise 4.1.1 The Selector Tool with Spot Mode

The Selector tool is not affected in any way by Spot mode. It will operate in every respect the same way it does when you are in Slip mode. Let's take a quick look.

1. *Select* **Ex 4.1.1** from the **Memory Locations** window, and you will see a Shaker region on the exercise track. Verify that you are set to Spot mode and the Smart tool is enabled.

2. *Place* your **cursor** in the upper-half center of the **Shaker** region and *click* once. The flashing play cursor will now move to the location of the selector cursor.

3. *Click* twice with the **Selector** tool, and you will have selected the whole region.

4. **Triple-click**, and you will select every region in the track.

5. Finally, **click/drag** an area, and you will have performed all the basic functions of the Selector tool using Spot mode.

### Exercise 4.1.2 The Grabber Tool with Spot Mode

The Grabber tool's function is typically to move regions from point A to point B. When used in conjunction with modifier keys, it can also perform functions such as copying regions (Option key for Mac, Alt key for PC). In Spot mode these functions still exist, but the location data must be entered manually.

The Grabber tool's Separation and Object modes are not available in Spot mode. If you select the Separation Grabber tool in Spot mode, the Grabber cursor will appear and act exactly like the Time Grabber tool. If you attempt to select the Object Grabber, Pro Tools will notify you with a dialog pop-up indicating that the Object Grabber cannot be selected while in Spot or Shuffle modes and will automatically select Slip mode when you hit OK.

1. **Select** Ex **4.1.2** from the **Memory Locations** window.

2. **Click** once with the **Grabber** tool on the displayed **Shaker** region, and the familiar Spot Dialog box will appear, as shown in Figure 4.1.

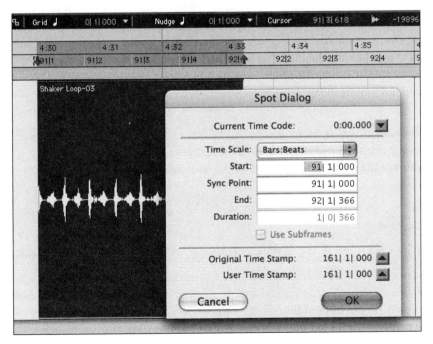

**Figure 4.1**

The Spot Dialog box.

3. **Type** in bar **93**1**000** as the new **Start** time, and the region will move to bar 93**1000**. This is offline movement of a region.

4. Now *hold* the **Option** key (Mac) or **Alt** key (PC) and *click* again with the **Grabber** tool.

5. *Type* in bar **911000** as the new **Start** time, and you will have created a copy of the original region and placed it at bar 911000 (see Figure 4.2).

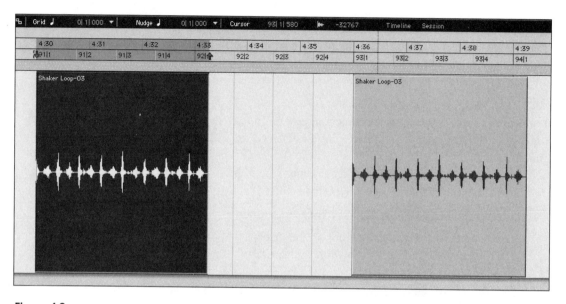

**Figure 4.2**
The newly copied Shaker region created using the Spot Dialog box.

## Exercise 4.1.3 The Trim Tool with Spot Mode

The Trim tool's primary function, of course, is to trim or resize region boundaries. When used with Spot mode, the amount of trimming is determined by the numerical values entered through the Spot Dialog box.

1. *Select* **Ex 4.1.3** from the **Memory Locations** window. You will again be confronted with the now familiar Shaker region.

2. *Place* your **cursor** to the far left of the **region** until you see the Trim tool cursor and *click* once. The Spot Dialog box will appear once again, as shown in Figure 4.3. Notice how only the Start and Duration fields are available for data entry.

3. *Enter* **952000** in the **Start** time field. You can use the right arrow key to tab over to the Beats field to enter the number 2.

4. *Select* **OK** to execute your Spot trim. Your region should now look like Figure 4.4.

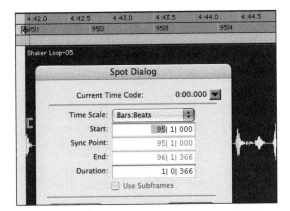

**Figure 4.3**

The Spot Dialog box when used with the Trim tool.

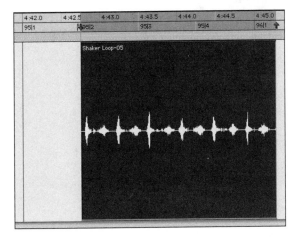

**Figure 4.4**

The left region boundary spot trimmed by one beat.

5. Now *place* your **cursor** to the far right of the **region** until you see the Trim tool cursor and *click* once. The Spot Dialog box will appear once again, but only the End and Duration fields will be available for data entry.

6. *Enter* 96|000 in the **End** time field and *select* OK. You have now trimmed the end of the Shaker region.

## Exercise 4.1.4 The TC/E Tool with Spot Mode

When the Trim tool is set to TC/E (*Time Compression/Expansion*) in Spot mode, the amount of time compression or expansion is determined by the entered value using the Spot Dialog box.

1. *Select* Ex 4.1.4 from the **Memory Locations** window.

2. *Hit Command+2* (Mac) or *Ctrl+2* (PC) until the Trim tool button shows the Trim icon with a clock, as shown in Figure 4.5.

**Figure 4.5**

The Trim tool set to TC/E.

The Shaker region shown is a one-bar loop that is at a slower tempo than the current session. Because the Shaker region start is already placed exactly on the beginning of a bar, you can use the TC/E tool to trim the end value.

3. *Click* once with the **TC/E** tool on the right side of the region to open up the Spot Dialog box. As with the Standard Trim tool in Spot mode, the End and Duration fields once again become available for editing. The difference will be how the file is processed. The Standard Trim tool will just create a new region. The TC/E tool, however, will create a new time compressed/expanded audio file based off of the entered values.

4. *Enter* a **Duration** time of **10000** and *select* **OK.** The file is now at the session tempo (see Figure 4.6).

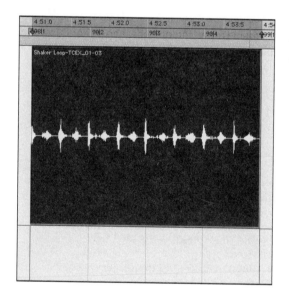

**Figure 4.6**

The one-bar Shaker Loop region now set to the tempo of the session.

5. Finally, *move* your **cursor** over the **Trim** tool button and *select* the **Standard Trim** tool. Reselect the Smart tool by *clicking* on the **small bar** below the Trim, Selector, and Grabber tools. It is important to reset the TC/E tool when you are finished using it; otherwise, you will find yourself accidentally creating all sorts of useless TC/E'd regions that will eat up valuable hard drive space.

## Exercise 4.1.5 The Crossfade and Fade-In/Out Tools with Spot Mode

As with the Grabber and Trim tools, the Crossfade and Fade In/Out tools also require the use of the Spot Dialog box.

1. *Select* Ex 4.1.5 from the **Memory Locations** window. You will see a pair of Shaker regions back to back.

2. *Place* your **cursor** to the top far-left corner of the **first Shaker region** until you see the Fade In tool cursor appear.

3. *Click* once, and you will see the **Spot Dialog** box with only the End and Duration fields available for data entry. If you were to perform a Spot Fade Out, the Start and Duration fields would become available for data entry.

4. *Select* the **Duration** data entry box and *enter* **01000**, as shown in Figure 4.7, and then *hit* OK. You have now created a fade-in of one-quarter note length.

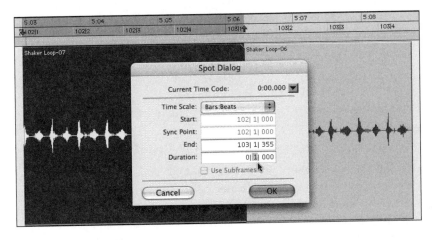

**Figure 4.7**

A Duration entry of one-quarter note for the fade-in length in the Spot Dialog box.

5. Now *place* your **cursor** at the bottom where the **two Shaker regions** meet until you see the Crossfade tool cursor and *click* once. You will see the Spot Dialog box with the Start, End, and Duration fields available for data entry as shown. Entering values for the start and end will define the crossfade's length. If the entries are invalid, the spot crossfade will be ignored.

6. *Enter* **1031000** for a **Start** time and **1032000** for an **End** time, and *select* OK. You now have created a crossfade for the two Shaker regions, as shown in Figure 4.8.

81

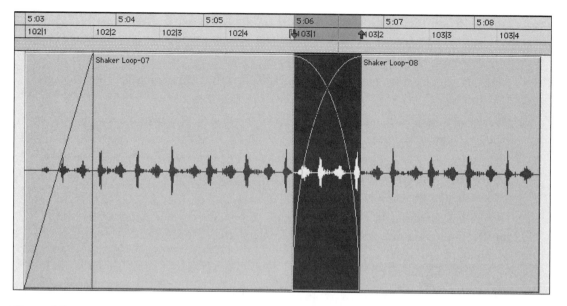

**Figure 4.8**
The spot crossfade created from the Spot Dialog box.

## Slip Mode and the Edit Tools

Using Slip mode with the Edit tools is the easiest of all the modes to understand because there is no math involved. Wherever you place the cursor, move your region, or trim your selection to is exactly where it goes. The accuracy of your edit is only limited by the amount you are zoomed in or out. Zoom in to sample accuracy, and you can edit to sample accuracy. Zoom out to get an overview of your whole session, and you can edit or manipulate whole files or sections of the song to create your arrangement.

The next set of exercises will break down each of the Edit tools using Slip mode.

### Exercise 4.2.1 The Selector Tool with Slip Mode

Using the Selector tool in Slip mode is exactly the same as using the Selector tool in Spot mode. You are completely free to place the cursor or select any area to sample accuracy. Let's investigate.

1. *Select* Ex 4.2.1 from the **Memory Locations** window. You will see a Bass region on the Exercise track.

2. *Hit Option+2* (Mac) or *Alt+2* (PC) to enable **Slip** mode.

3. *Place* your **cursor** in the upper-half center of the **Bass** region and *click* once. The flashing play cursor will now move to the location of the selector cursor.

82

4. *Click* twice with the **Selector** tool, and you will have selected the whole region.

5. *Triple-click*, and you will select every region in the track.

6. Finally, *click/drag* an **area**, and you will have performed all the basic functions of the Selector tool using Slip mode. Note that the placement and movement of your cursor is not restricted.

## Exercises 4.2.2 The Grabber Tool with Slip Mode

As mentioned before in the section on Spot mode, the Grabber tool's function is to move regions from one place to another. When used in conjunction with modifier keys, it can also perform functions such as copying regions (Option key for Mac, Alt key for PC).

The Grabber tool's Standard, Separation, and Object modes are all readily available in Slip mode. Slip mode is the mode of choice when you need to move regions, parts of regions, or groups of regions without restriction. The following exercises will best illustrate this principle.

1. *Select* Ex 4.2.2 from the **Memory Locations** window.

2. *Click* once with the **Grabber** tool at the bottom-center of the displayed **Bass** region, and you will have selected the entire region.

3. *Click/drag* the **Bass** region from the Exercise track to the Bass track directly below it and *release*. Notice how you are free to move the Bass region anywhere in time on the Bass track without restriction.

4. Now, while *holding* the **Control** key (Mac) or **Start** key (PC), *drag* the **Bass** region back to the **Exercise** track. If you attempt to drag the region to the left or right, your horizontal movement will be restricted.

5. *Holding* the *Control+Option* keys (Mac) or *Start+Alt* keys (PC), *drag* the **Bass** region again from the Exercise track to the Bass track. You have now made a copy of the original Bass region onto the Bass track while locking it in time.

## Exercise 4.2.3 The Separation Grabber Tool with Slip Mode

The Separation Grabber tool is most commonly used in conjunction with the Selector tool. The following exercise will show you how.

1. *Select* Ex 4.2.3 from the **Memory Locations** window to start the next exercise.

2. Now *select* the **Separation Grabber** tool by *hitting Command+4* (Mac) or *Ctrl+4* (PC) until you see the Grabber icon with scissors, and then *hit Command+7* (Mac) or *Ctrl+7* (PC) to reselect the Smart tool (see Figure 4.9).

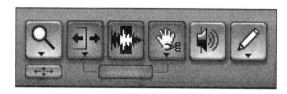

**Figure 4.9**
The Separation Grabber selected with the Smart tool.

3. **Move** your **cursor** over the **Bass** region in the upper half of the second bass note until you see the Selector tool, and *click/drag* your **cursor** to capture a selection area that covers the second bass note (see Figure 4.10).

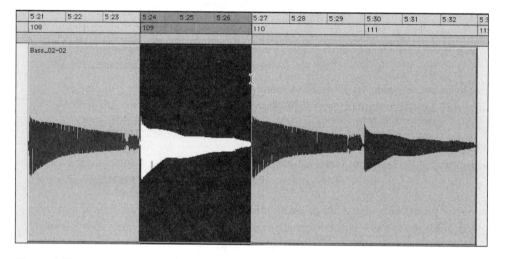

**Figure 4.10**
The second bass note selection area with the Selector tool.

4. **Move** the **cursor** to the lower half of the selection area until you see the Separation Grabber cursor and *click/drag* the selected area down to the **Bass** track. This is a very common method for extracting regions to create compilations of multiple takes. Conversely, with the Time Grabber tool, you would have to separate the region first before being able to extract it.

### *Exercise 4.2.4 The Object Grabber Tool with Slip Mode*
The Object Grabber is used to select nonconsecutive regions. When used with Slip mode, the selected regions may be moved without restriction.

1. **Select** Ex 4.2.4 from the **Memory Locations** window. In this exercise there are two notes missing on the Bass track below.

2. *Select* the **Object Grabber** tool by *hitting Command+4* (Mac) or *Ctrl+4* (PC) until you see the Grabber icon with two small boxes superimposed, as shown in Figure 4.11. Because the Object Grabber does not work with the Smart tool, you will continue the remainder of this exercise with only the Object Grabber selected.

**Figure 4.11**

The Separation Grabber selected with the Smart tool.

3. Select the region above the first missing bass note by *clicking* on it once with the **Object Grabber** tool. *Hold* the **Shift** key (Mac or PC) and select the region above the second missing note until they are both selected. Black boxes will now appear around both regions to indicate that they have been selected.

4. While *holding* the *Control+Option* keys (Mac) or *Start+Alt* keys (PC), *drag* the two bass regions from the **Exercise** track to the **Bass** track. The net result of this action will look very much like Figure 4.12.

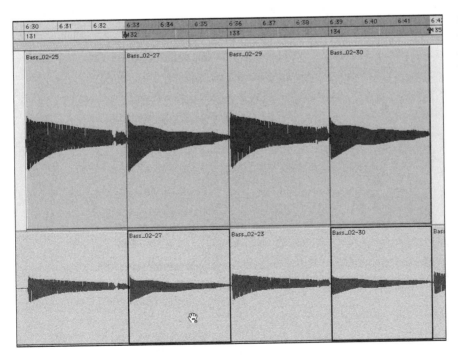

**Figure 4.12**

The two bass regions moved to the bass track using the Object Grabber tool.

This exercise shows another very common method for compiling takes from one performance into another. The use of the Control+Option (Mac) or Start+Alt (PC) key combination, especially with Slip mode, is a great way of copying what you need while preserving the timing and not affecting the original regions from the alternate take. In this scenario, normally you would have to create these regions first using the Selector tool.

### Exercise 4.2.5 The Trim Tool with Slip Mode

The Trim tool's primary function, of course, is to trim or resize region boundaries. When used with Slip mode, trimming regions can be done to sample accuracy. This is a great way to really get in there and fine-tune the region edits that do not fall precisely on a beat or grid value. This, of course, allows you to clean up any unwanted noise.

1. **Select** Ex 4.2.5 from the **Memory Locations** window. At the beginning of the Bass note, there is a glitch that you need to get rid of.

2. **Select Command+4** (Mac) or **Ctrl+4** (PC) to reset the Object Grabber tool back to Time mode.

3. **Hit Command+7** (Mac) or **Ctrl+7** (PC) to reselect the Smart tool.

4. **Place** your **cursor** at the far left of the **region** until you see the Trim tool cursor and **click/drag** to the **right** until the glitches before the first bass note disappear.

5. Now **place** your **cursor** at the far right of the **region** until you see the Trim tool cursor and **click/drag** to the **left** until the last bass note is removed (see Figure 4.13).

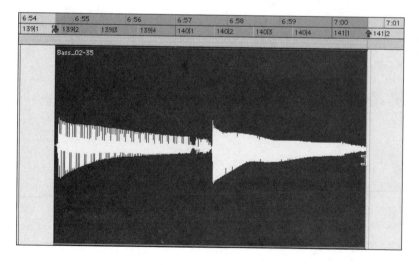

**Figure 4.13**
The last note trimmed from the bass region.

These two simple examples are the most common uses of the Trim tool in Slip mode.

### Exercise 4.2.6 The TC/E Tool with Slip Mode

Usage of the TC/E tool in Slip mode is mostly for extending existing notes of a performance cut short by poor musicianship or poor recording. When confronted with such an edit, it is important to make sure the TC/E tool settings are properly configured to the type of audio you are editing. If the edit is percussive in nature, the TC/E preferences must be set to be most accurate rhythmically. If the edit is a sustained note, the TC/E preferences must be set to provide the best sound quality.

1. *Select* Ex 4.2.6 from the **Memory Locations** window.

2. *Hit Command+2* (Mac) or *Ctrl+2* (PC) until the Trim tool button shows the Trim icon with a clock. In the following exercise, the bass note needs to be extended to match the length of the Piano region. Before you begin, however, you will need to set your TC/E preferences to the Sound setting.

3. *Select* **Preferences** from the **Setup** menu. Then *select* the **Processing** tab. You will find the Default Settings selector for the TC/E tool, as shown in Figure 4.14. *Select* the preset called **Sound** and *click* on **Done**. If you do not see this setting, you will need to revisit the section in Chapter 1 called "Edit Menu Preferences" to set up your TC/E tool for the upcoming exercises.

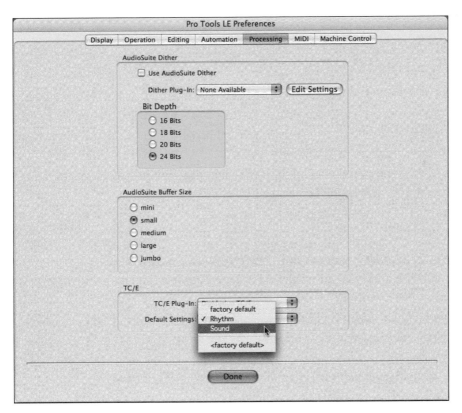

**Figure 4.14**

The Preference settings for the TC/E tool being set to the Sound preset.

4. *Move* your **cursor** to the end of the last **Bass** region until you see the TC/E tool and *click/drag* your **cursor** to the **right** until you have matched the length of the Piano note. *Release* the **mouse button** to time-stretch the last note of the Bass (see Figure 4.15).

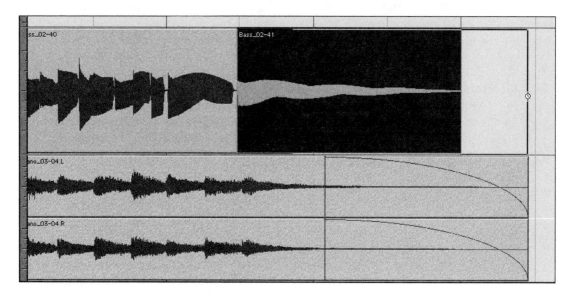

**Figure 4.15**
The Bass note is extended to the length of the Piano note using the TC/E tool.

5. *Hit* the **spacebar** to have a listen to your edit. You will notice a click at the end of the bass note. In the next exercise, you will deal with this click.

6. *Hit Command+2* (Mac) or *Ctrl+2* (PC) until the Trim tool is selected to Standard mode, and reselect the Smart tool by *pressing Command+7* (Mac) or *Ctrl+7* (PC).

7. *Hit Command+S* (Mac) or *Ctrl+S* (PC) to save.

### Exercise 4.2.7 The Crossfade and Fade In/Out Tools with Slip Mode

As with the Grabber and Trim tools, the Crossfade and Fade In/Out tools can be used to perform fades and crossfades to sample accuracy.

1. *Select* Ex 4.2.7 from the **Memory Locations** window. You will see the TC/E edit you have just performed on the Bass track.

2. *Place* your **cursor** at the top-right corner of the region until you see the Fade Out tool and *click/drag* to the **left** about halfway across the region before you *release*.

3. *Hit Command+S* (Mac) or *Ctrl+S* (PC) to save.

Using the Fade In and Crossfade features is identical to the Fade-Out exercise just shown. The moral of the story here is that using any of the tools in Slip mode will allow you total freedom of placement without restricting your movement in time. In the upcoming section, you will see how restricting the movement of your cursor can be very handy.

## Grid Mode and the Edit Tools

Grid mode is next in line and offers the best perks with the Edit tools for editing audio in songs that are tracked to a defined tempo. Editing in this mode, when the Grid standard is set to Bars:Beats, is the easiest way to make musical edits. Grid mode, when using Mins:Secs as your standard, is great if you are working with commercial spots or music for movies where the musical cues must be a defined length.

The following exercises will break down each of the Edit tools in Grid mode. As you may remember, there are two types of Grid mode, Absolute and Relative. Rather than double up the number of exercises, I will only create a distinction between the two types of Grid modes where there is a difference.

### Exercise 4.3.1 The Selector Tool with Grid Mode

Using the Selector tool in Grid mode is unlike any other mode. Restricting the placement of the cursor, as done in Grid mode, has great benefits if the standard and resolution are set to something that is fitting for the type of edit you are trying to perform.

The following exercise will be done in Absolute Grid mode because the Selector tool works in identical fashion with Relative Grid mode selected. Let's take a closer look.

1.  *Select* Ex 4.3.1 from the **Memory Locations** window.

2.  *Select* **Absolute Grid** mode by *hitting Option+4* (Mac) or *Alt+4* (PC).

3.  *Select* the **grid arrow** above the **Timeline Bar** and make sure the grid standard is set to Bars:Beats and the resolution is set to ? note, as shown in Figure 4.16.

4.  *Place* your **cursor** anywhere in the upper-half center of the **Kick** region and *click* once. The play cursor will now move to the nearest grid mark.

5.  The double-click and triple-click functions for Grid mode are identical to all other Edit modes. A double-click will select a region, and a triple-click will select all regions in the track.

6.  Finally, *click/drag* an area across the **Kick** region, and you will have performed all the basic functions of the Selector tool using Grid mode. Notice that the click/drag selection area is confined to the grid standard/resolution lines.

This exercise will work in identical fashion in Relative Grid mode.

**Figure 4.16**
The grid standard set to Bars:Beats and
the grid resolution set to quarter notes.

## Exercises 4.3.2 The Grabber Tool with Grid Mode

The Grabber tool's Standard, Separation, and Object modes are all available in Grid mode. Using any of the Grabber tools with Grid mode is preferable when you want to preserve the timing of a performance that was cut to a specific tempo or click track.

The Time Grabber tool will select and move whole regions. The Separation Grabber tool will extract selected areas, and the Object Grabber will allow you to move nonconsecutive regions all locked to the grid standard and resolution settings. Because you have already moved regions around in Grid mode in the previous chapters, I will concentrate here on some of the not-so-obvious ways to use the Grabber tool in Grid mode.

1. *Select* **Ex 4.3.2** from the **Memory Locations** window.

2. *Click* once with the **Grabber** tool by placing it in the bottom-center of the displayed Kick region, and you will have selected the entire Kick region.

3. *Click/drag* the **Kick** region and move it to the left or right. Notice how you are locked to the grid lines.

4. Now *hold* the **Command** key (Mac) or the **Ctrl** key (PC) and move the selected region. Notice how you are free to move the region as you would in Slip mode.

5. From the **Edit** menu, *select* **Undo** to return the region to its original location. You may need to do this more than once.

6. *Select* the **Kick** region once again and, while *holding* the **Shift** key, *select* the **Snare** region as well.

7. *Release* the *Shift* key, and you can now move the two regions as a pair locked to the grid lines.

8. Now *hold* the **Command** key (Mac) or the **Ctrl** key (PC) and move the selected regions. You are no longer restricted to the grid.

## Exercises 4.3.3 The Separation Grabber Tool with Grid Mode

In the following exercise, the Kick and Snare parts are locked to the grid lines. In this situation, using Grid mode with the Separation Grabber has the added benefit of making it easy to extend existing musical parts.

1. *Select* Ex 4.3.3 from the **Memory Locations** window to start the next exercise.

2. Then select the Separation Grabber tool by *hitting Command+4* (Mac) or *Ctrl+4* (PC) until you see the Grabber icon with scissors.

3. *Hit Command+7* (Mac) or *Ctrl+7* (PC) to reselect the Smart tool.

4. *Click/drag* your **Selector** tool so that you capture an area that covers the second and third bars of the Kick region. Now *hold* the **Shift** key and *click* once with the **Selector** tool in the top half of the Snare region to add it (see Figure 4.17).

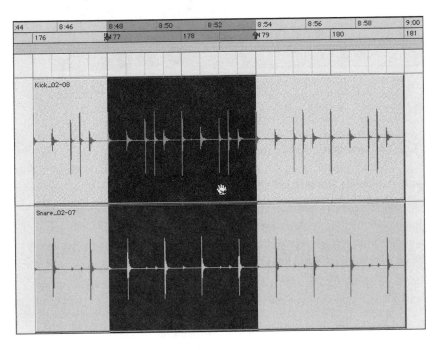

**Figure 4.17**

The selection area on the Kick and Snare tracks for Exercise 4.3.3.

5. *Move* the **cursor** to the lower half of either region in the **selection area** until you see the Separation Grabber cursor appear.

6. *Hold* the **Option** key (Mac) or the **Alt** key (PC) and *click/drag* the **selected** area to the right until the copied selection area is placed directly after the current Kick and Snare regions on the tracks, as shown in Figure 4.18. Notice how the original selection area is unaffected by the copy function.

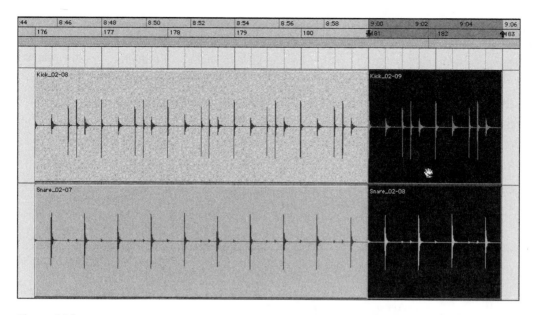

**Figure 4.18**

The copied Kick and Snare selection moved to extend the length of the tracks using the Separation Grabber.

## Exercises 4.3.4 The Object Grabber Tool with Grid Mode

As with all other modes, the Object Grabber does not work with the Smart tool, so you will need to do this exercise with only the Object Grabber selected.

1. *Select* Ex 4.3.4 from the **Memory Locations** window. In this exercise there is a series of Shaker regions copied over two bars. If you hit the spacebar to listen to the track, you will notice that it is panned to the left. Using the Object Grabber, you are going to move every other region to the second exercise track that is panned to the right side.

2. *Hit Command+4* (Mac) or *Ctrl+4* (PC) to select the **Object Grabber** tool until you see the Grabber icon with two small boxes superimposed.

3. *Hold* the **Shift** key and *select* the second **Shaker** region and every other region in the track, as shown in Figure 4.19.

4. *Select* any one of the **Shaker** regions and *drag* it down to the **Exercise 2** track. Because the regions are cut to the grid, the movement will stay locked in time musically when moved. The end result should look exactly like Figure 4.20.

5. *Hit* the **spacebar** to take in this masterpiece of musical production.

Although the Object Grabber is not the most commonly used tool, you can get a sense from this last exercise how, in just the right scenario, it can be a helpful tool.

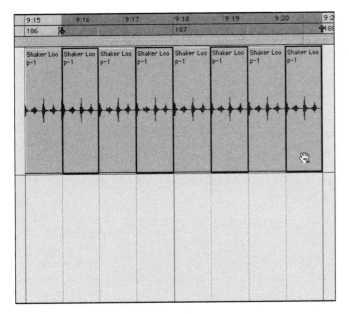

**Figure 4.19**

Every other Shaker region selected on the exercise track using the Object Grabber tool.

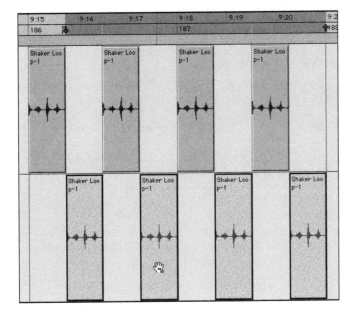

**Figure 4.20**

The Shaker regions moved to the second exercise track using the Object Grabber.

## Exercises 4.3.5 The Time Grabber Tool with Relative Grid Mode

Lost in all this madness is the use of Relative Grid mode with the Grabber tool. Relative Grid mode works equally well with each of the three modes—Time, Separation, or Object Grabber. Let's take a quick peek.

93

1.  *Select* Ex 4.3.5 from the **Memory Locations** window. In this exercise you will see the Bass part starts one bar before the Piano. The lead-in note of the Bass starts just slightly before the quarter-note grid line, necessitating the use of Relative Grid mode to move the region by one bar.

2.  Select Relative Grid mode by *pressing Option+4* (Mac) or *Alt+4* (PC) until the Grid button says **Rel Grid**.

3.  Now *select Command+4* (Mac) or *Ctrl+4* (PC) until you have selected the **Time Grabber** tool.

4.  *Select Command+7* (Mac) or *Ctrl+7* (PC) to reselect the **Smart** tool, and let's begin.

5.  Using the Grabber tool, *click/drag* the **Bass** region to the right by one bar to line it up musically with the Piano part (see Figure 4.21).

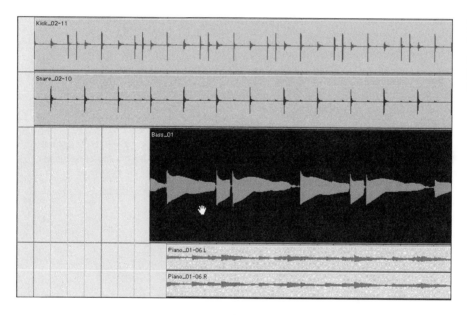

**Figure 4.21**

The Bass region moved in time musically with the Piano part.

6.  *Hit* the **spacebar** to audition the edit.

This is perhaps the most common use of Relative Grid mode when editing audio. Because much of music either anticipates or lays on the backside of the beat, this Grid option allows the editor to work quickly and easily while maintaining the exact performance.

### Exercises 4.3.6 The Separation Grabber Tool with Relative Grid Mode

The Separation Grabber and the Object Grabber work in exactly the same fashion. With the Separation Grabber, any selected area not locked to the grid can be extracted and moved containing its relative timing.

94

1. *Select* Ex 4.3.6 from the **Memory Locations** window. In this exercise the selected Bass note must be copied to replace the same note two bars earlier, which is low in volume and does not sustain long enough.

2. *Press Command+4* (Mac) or *Ctrl+4* (PC) until you have selected the Separation Grabber tool with the scissors superimposed over the Grabber icon.

3. *Press Command+7* (Mac) or *Ctrl+7* (PC) to reselect the Smart tool, and let's begin.

4. *Holding* the **Option** key (Mac) or **Alt** key (PC), carefully move the **Separation Grabber** tool over the selected area and *click/drag* the **area** two bars to the left, as shown in Figure 4.22. Should you accidentally lose the selection area, simply reselect Ex 4.3.6 from the Memory Locations window. In real life, of course, you would have to reselect the area manually!

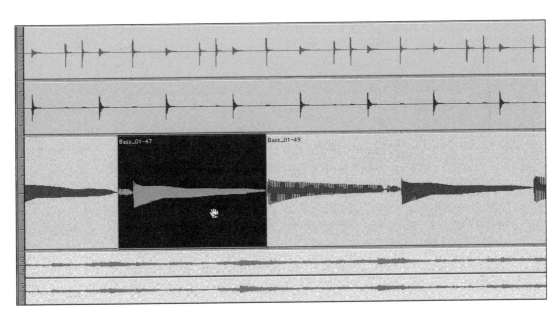

**Figure 4.22**
The selected Bass note moved to replace the bad note.

This again is a very easy and common way of correcting poor performances, bad notes, inadequate timing, and a plethora of other engineering abnormalities. Learning these techniques will go a long way toward improving your production and engineering skills when editing audio in Pro Tools.

### Exercises 4.3.7 The Object Grabber Tool with Relative Grid Mode

When used with Relative Grid mode, the Object Grabber is a handy way of moving nonconsecutive regions relatively by grid increments. The techniques and methods involved are identical to the two previous exercises, with the exception of the method used to select the regions.

1. **Select** Ex 4.3.7 from the **Memory Locations** window. The following exercise shows a series of Shaker regions. You will need to select every other region and move them to the end of the existing pattern so the part only happens every other beat.

2. **Select Command+4** (Mac) or **Ctrl+4** (PC) until you have selected the Object Grabber tool with the two small boxes superimposed over the Grabber icon.

3. Using the Object Grabber, **select** the second **Shaker** region and, while **holding** the **Shift** key, **select** every other **region** afterward so that the selection area looks like Figure 4.23.

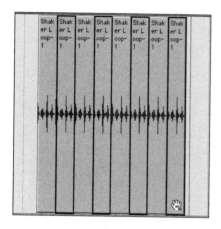

**Figure 4.23**

The correct selection for the Object Grabber tool exercise.

4. **Click/drag** on the first of the selected **regions** and move them to the right so that the regions are equally spaced to complete the prescribed pattern, as shown in Figure 4.24. Notice how the regions move relative to the grid markings, maintaining their relative timing to the beat.

Now that you have explored the uses of the Grabber tool in both Relative and Absolute Grid modes, it is time to forge forward into the realm of possibilities with the Trim tool.

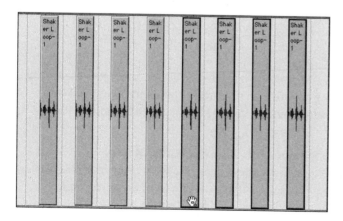

**Figure 4.24**

The final edit for Exercise 4.3.7

### Exercise 4.3.8 The Trim Tool with Grid Mode

When used with Grid mode, the Trim tool allows region trimming to be locked to a set grid standard and resolution. This combination is invaluable when region trimming must be performed to an exact Bar:Beat or Min:Sec value.

1. *Select* Ex 4.3.8 from the **Memory Locations** window. The following exercise shows Kick, Snare, and Piano tracks. The Kick and Snare tracks start two bars before the entrance of the Piano. Using the Trim tool, you will need to make the drum tracks start at the same time as the Piano track.

2. Select the Time Grabber tool by *hitting Command+4* (Mac) or *Ctrl+4* (PC) until you see the **Time Grabber** icon.

3. Select the Smart tool by *hitting Command+7* (Mac) or *Ctrl+7* (PC).

4. Select Absolute Grid mode by *pressing Option+4* (Mac) or *Alt+4* (PC) until the Grid button says Grid.

5. Using the Smart tool, *place* your **cursor** to the far left and center of the **Kick** region until you see the Trim tool cursor appear. *Click* once.

6. Now *select* the **Snare** region by holding the **Shift** key and *clicking* once at the far left of the **Snare** region.

7. *Hold* the **Shift** key and *click/drag* to the **right** until the region start is moved to the same start as the Piano track (see Figure 4.25).

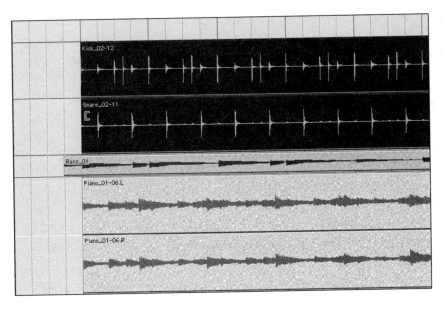

**Figure 4.25**

The Kick and Snare regions start trimmed to the beginning of the Piano region.

This last exercise is a classic example of how the Trim tool is most commonly used with Grid mode. The beauty of this combination lies mostly with tracks that are programmed or cut to a click. The ability to make edits to define grid settings helps to simplify the work. Even in tracks where a performance may be slightly ahead or behind the grid marking, this mode will get you very close to the exact edit. From there, a simple zoom in to the edit will allow you to refine your edit by holding the Command key (Mac) or Ctrl key (PC). Remember, this will temporarily suspend Grid mode to allow sample-accurate editing, as in Slip mode.

### Exercise 4.3.9 The TC/E Tool with Grid Mode

Using the TC/E tool in Grid mode is perhaps the most common combination for your loop-crunching needs. Assuming that your loop has already been properly trimmed (we will discuss this in more detail in Chapter 6), adjusting the tempo of your loop to the tempo of the song you are currently working on should be a piece of cake. In this example, your grid standard will be set to Bars:Beats. When working with music cues for video or commercial spots, Grid mode used with the Min:Secs can be helpful to readjust the overall length of the cue to match the required time should your music cue prove to be a little short or long.

1. *Select* Ex 4.3.9 from the **Memory Locations** window. In the following exercise, there is a one-bar drum loop that is slightly faster in tempo than the song. Your mission is to resize this drum loop to the tempo of the song. But before you begin, you must first check your TC/E preference settings.

2. *Hit Command+2* (Mac) or *Ctrl+2* (PC) until the Trim tool button shows the Trim icon with a clock.

3. From the Setup menu, *select* Preferences. Then *select* the **Processing** tab, and you will find the Default Settings selector for the TC/E tool, as shown in Figure 4.26. *Select* the preset called **Rhythm** and *click* Done. If you do not see this setting, you will need to revisit Chapter 1, "Getting Started," under the subsection "Edit Menu Preferences" to set up your TC/E tool for the upcoming exercises.

4. *Move* your **cursor** to end of the last **Drum Loop** 1 region until you see the TC/E tool. This will allow you to expand the length of the region. Because the region start is already placed at the beginning of the bar, you will not have to reset the start time of the region.

5. *Click/drag* your **cursor** over the **Drum Loop** 1 region to the right until the length is 1 bar long, as shown in Figure 4.27. *Release* the **mouse button** to time-stretch the loop to the tempo of the song.

6. Now *select* Loop Playback from the **Options** menu and *hit* the **spacebar** to listen to the loop and verify the edit.

7. *Hit Command+2* (Mac) or *Ctrl+2* (PC) until the Trim tool button is set to Standard mode.

8. *Deselect* Loop Playback by *hitting Shift+Command+L* (Mac) or *Shift+Ctrl+L* (PC).

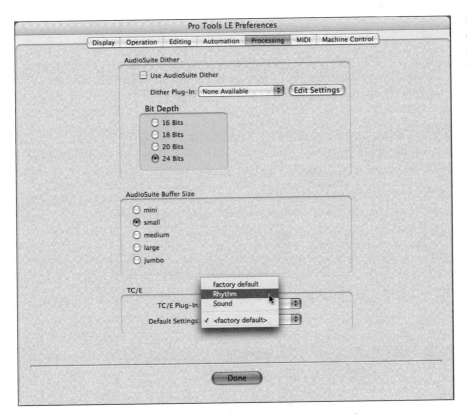

**Figure 4.26**
The Preferences
settings for the
TC/E tool being
set to the Rhythm
preset.

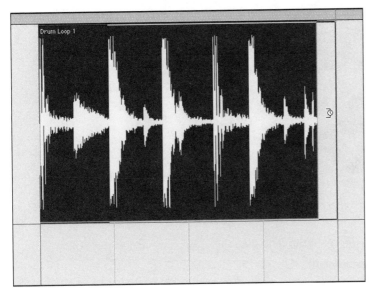

**Figure 4.27**
The Drum loop is time-stretched
to the tempo of the song using the
TC/E tool.

Honestly, that's about as simple as it gets! Chapter 6 goes more in depth into the editing proce-dures that lead up to the use of the TC/E tool. The TC/E tool operates the same in Relative Grid mode as it does in Absolute Grid mode. This is unfortunate because many loops sound better when they push or pull the beat and do not edit exactly on the grid line. The ability to time-stretch by grid values relative to the grid line would be a great feature.

### Exercise 4.3.10 The Crossfade and Fade In/Out Tools with Grid Mode

As with the Grabber and Trim tools, the Crossfade and Fade In/Out tools can be used to perform fades and crossfades to any defined grid standard and resolution.

1. **Select** Ex 4.3.10 from the **Memory Locations** window. You will see an acoustic guitar part with a sustained note that has some noise at the end you need to fade out.

2. Select the Smart tool by *hitting Command+7* (Mac) or *Ctrl+7* (PC).

3. *Place* your **cursor** at the top-right corner of the **region** until you see the **Fade Out** tool cursor appear.

4. *Click/drag* to the **left** to extend the fade-out three-quarter notes in length, as shown in Figure 4.28.

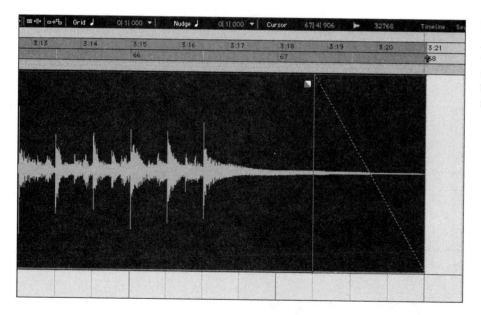

**Figure 4.28**

A fade-out of three-quarter-note length being performed in Grid mode.

5. *Release* the **mouse button** to create the fade-out.

6. *Hit* the **spacebar** to audition the edit.

Using the Fade In and Crossfade features in Grid mode operates identically to the fade-out exercise just shown. The length of the fade-in/out or crossfade will be restricted as it is with all the other tools by the Grid Standard and Grid Resolution settings. The use of Relative Grid mode has no bearing whatsoever on the use of the use of the fade-in/out and crossfade features. In other words, Relative Grid mode will operate exactly as Absolute Grid mode when dealing with fade-ins/outs and crossfades.

Grid mode is perhaps the most commonly used mode for editing work when dealing with programmed music or music cut to a click track. It allows the most flexibility by allowing you to edit synchronously with the music. This is particularly true when editing MIDI information. (That's a whole other book!) Any glitches that may result from the edit can easily be fixed with a quick switch to Slip mode to adjust for anticipated or laidback performances.

Next up on the menu is the often misunderstood and yet very powerful Shuffle mode. When using the Edit tools in conjunction with Shuffle mode, an interesting world of possibilities opens up. Let's take a look!

## Shuffle Mode and the Edit Tools

Using Slip and Grid modes with the Edit tools will encompass the vast majority of your music editing work in Pro Tools. Using Shuffle mode with the Edit tools, although it is not the most often-used mode, still offers very useful features when editing musical material. I find this mode most useful for editing dialogue or voiceover content, to the point where I use it almost exclusively. Shuffle mode is primarily used when regions need to be placed or moved together end to end, or when regions need to be reordered or "shuffled" into a different order.

The following exercises break down each of the Edit tools using Shuffle mode. As with the previous sections of this chapter, I will attempt to avoid repeating redundant information already covered in the previous chapters and dig a little deeper into the finer aspects of each tool's use in Shuffle mode. So follow along with me on this little journey called Shuffle mode.

### Exercise 4.4.1 The Selector Tool with Shuffle Mode

Using the Selector tool in Shuffle mode at first glance works identically to using the Selector tool in Slip mode. And for the most part, this is exactly true. You are completely free to place the cursor or select any area to sample accuracy. The use of single-, double-, and triple-clicks with your cursor will also work, as in Slip mode. The differences come into play when you start to use many of the optional editing features (Cut, Copy, Paste, and so on) in conjunction with the Selector tool. Then, things get interesting. Let's take a peek.

1. *Select* Ex 4.4.1 from the **Memory Locations** window. You will see two drum loop regions on the display.

2. Select Shuffle mode by *hitting* the **small open quote** key located directly above the Tab key until **Shuffle** mode button is highlighted.

3. *Hit* the **spacebar** to listen to the two drum loops. You will notice that the second loop is a "Fill" loop. The combination of the two loops totals two bars, and you need to make the total length four bars long so that the Fill loop only occurs in the final bar.

4. *Place* your **cursor** in the upper-half center of the **first drum loop** region and *double-click*. The region should now be highlighted.

5. Now *select Command+D* (Mac) or *Ctrl+D* (PC). The "D" stands for Duplicate Selected Regions. You can find this feature in the Edit menu. Notice that the Fill loop has moved to the right by one bar.

6. Now *select Command+D* (Mac) or *Ctrl+D* (PC) once again. You should now have three Shuffle loops and one Shuffle Fill loop, as shown in Figure 4.29.

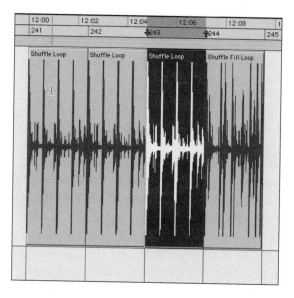

**Figure 4.29**

The newly created drum pattern using the Duplicate feature in Shuffle mode.

7. Finally, *double-click* on the first of the four **regions** with the **Selector** tool and, while *holding* the **Shift** key, *double-click* on the last of the four **regions**. All four regions should now be highlighted.

8. *Hit Command+Shift+L* (Mac) or the *Ctrl+Shift+L* (PC) to enter **Loop Playback** mode.

9. *Hit* the **spacebar** to listen to the newly configured loop pattern.

This is one of the many possible ways of using Shuffle mode to help edit regions in Pro Tools. There are many others hailing from the Edit menu that can be used with Shuffle mode, and I cover them in more detail in Chapter 6.

## Exercises 4.4.2 The Grabber Tool with Shuffle Mode

When using the Grabber tool with Shuffle mode, regions may be reordered, thus allowing you to create new arrangements from pre-existing regions. Remember, the Grabber tool's primary function is to move regions from point A to point B. Hopefully point B sounds better than point A!

The Grabber tool has three modes: Time, Separation, and Object. The Time and Separation modes are the only two available with the Grabber tool in Shuffle mode. Object mode is not available, perhaps due to the complexity of possibilities available when moving nonconsecutive regions. If you select the Object Grabber tool in Shuffle mode, a warning box will appear, informing you that you are not allowed to use it in Shuffle or Spot modes. Your Edit mode will then be unceremoniously switched to Slip.

1. **Select** Ex 4.4.2 from the **Memory Locations** window. The series of loops you have just edited in the previous exercise will reemerge. In this exercise, you will now rearrange some of the work from your last attempt.

2. **Click** once with the **Grabber** tool on the **last** of the four **Shuffle Fill Loop** regions and **click/drag** this region to the **left** until a line appears between the first two regions, as shown in Figure 4.30. **Release** the **mouse button**. The highlighted line indicates the destination point of your region when the mouse button is released.

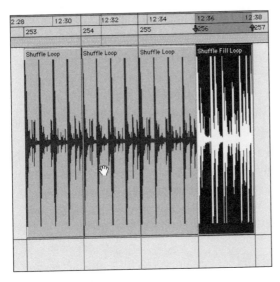

**Figure 4.30**

The Shuffle Fill Loop region being moved between the first two regions. Notice the highlighted line that appears between the first two regions.

3. **Click** once on the first of the **Shuffle Loop** regions with the **Grabber** tool and, while *holding* the **Shift** key, **click** once on the **last** of the four regions. *Hit* the **spacebar** to audition your newly created drum pattern.

Although this exercise is hardly going to get you closer to a Grammy award, it does display yet another way to use Shuffle mode with the Grabber tool.

103

### Moving Regions in Shuffle Mode

When moving, deleting, or copying regions within a track in Shuffle mode, it is very important that you are aware of the regions on the track that follow the area you are editing. Remember that all of the regions that follow will be shifted to the left or right by the exact amount you are adding or removing. If the regions that follow need to remain where they are musically, you will need to lock them into place using the Lock function in the Regions menu. Simply highlight the first of the regions that must remain where they are placed musically and select Command+L (Mac) or Ctrl+L (PC). A small padlock will appear in the bottom-left corner of the region. All regions that follow this locked region will be protected from the effects of editing in Shuffle mode.

## Exercise 4.4.3 The Separation Grabber Tool with Shuffle Mode

Using the Separation tool with Shuffle mode also has some distinct advantages when editing the arrangement of a track. In the following exercise, you need to add an extra bar with a fill extracted from the existing Shuffle Loop region. Because you will be extending the entire arrangement by one bar, Shuffle mode is perfect for exactly this task.

1. *Select* Ex 4.4.3 from the **Memory Locations** window. Two loops will now appear with a highlighted section area.

2. Select the Separation Grabber by *click/holding* on the **Grabber** tool icon and *selecting* **Separation** mode. The Grabber icon will now have a pair of scissors displayed inside the hand.

3. Reselect the Smart tool by *clicking* once on the **small bar** directly below the Trim, Selector, and Grabber tools.

4. *Move* the **Grabber** tool over the selected area and, while *holding* the **Option** key (Mac) or **Alt** key (PC), *click/drag* the **region** to the right and *release* it between the two **Shuffle Loop 2** regions. Should you misplay your cursor movement and lose the selection area, reselect Ex 4.4.3 from the Memory Locations list to start anew. If you have mistakenly moved your region to the wrong place, select Undo from the Edit menu until the original selection area reappears.

5. Once moved, *select Command+D* (Mac) or *Ctrl+D* (PC) three times to fill a one-bar section with the new fill. See Figure 4.31 to verify that you have duplicated the designated edit.

6. *Place* the **Selector** tool any place before the new edits, *click* once, and *hit* the **spacebar** to audition the edits.

7. If the edit is correct, reset the Loop Playback feature to normal playback mode by *selecting* *Shift+Command+L* (Mac) or *Shift+Ctrl+L* (PC).

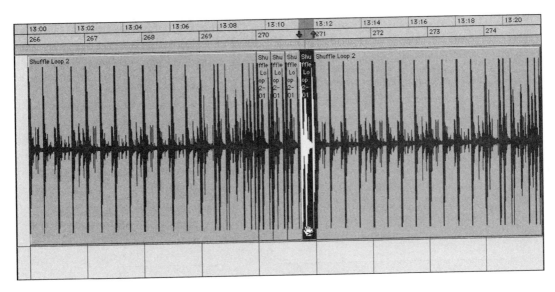

**Figure 4.31**
The new arrangement edit using the Separation Grabber tool in Shuffle mode.

The original selection was created in Grid mode to ensure that it was locked in time musically. The final edit, performed by you, was then created in Shuffle mode so the new arrangement pattern could be formed. As you perform these types of edits over and over, you will get to know the advantages of each mode and switch between them with frequency. I will cover this in more detail later in this chapter.

### Exercise 4.4.4 The Trim Tool with Shuffle Mode

The Trim tool's primary function, as stated earlier, is to trim or resize region boundaries. When used with Shuffle mode, this trimming function can help you quickly remove unwanted region sections while simultaneously moving material you do want closer to where you need it. As always, with Shuffle mode, you must be very conscious of the regions that follow on the track you are editing, lest you unwittingly move them out of their carefully placed locations.

1.  *Select* **Ex 4.4.4** from the **Memory Locations** window. You will see a series of three voiceover regions that must be edited to form a single line.

2.  When the exercise is complete, the line should read: "When using the Trim tool in Shuffle mode, be aware of the regions that follow, and remember to lock the ones you want to remain unaffected by your editing work." Sure, it's not exactly the Gettysburg Address, but you get the point!

3.  Using the Smart tool, *place* your **cursor** to the far left and center of the first region until you see the **Trim** tool cursor appear, and *click/drag* with the **Trim** tool to the right until just before the first voiceover line, as shown in Figure 4.32.

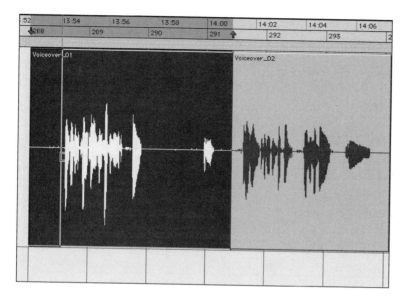

**Figure 4.32**
The beginning part of the voiceover region being trimmed.

4. *Release* the **mouse button** and you will have cleaned up the front end of the first voiceover take.

5. Now *place* your **cursor** to the far right and center of the first region until you see the **Trim** tool cursor appear again and *click/drag* to the **left** until the word "be" and its breath are also removed, as shown in Figure 4.33. Make sure you get as close as possible without clipping the end of the word "mode."

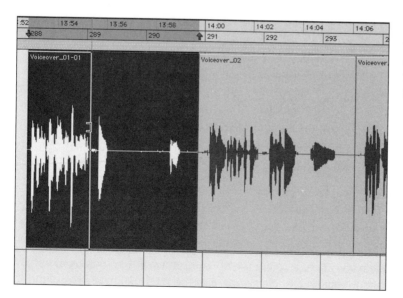

**Figure 4.33**
This figure shows the trim edit on the end of the first voiceover take to remove the unwanted portion.

6. *Release* the **mouse button**, and you will have cleaned up the back end of the first voiceover take.

7. Verify your edit by *clicking* once with the **cursor** anywhere before the first voiceover region and *hit* the **spacebar**. Adjust the edit if necessary by trimming the region until the transition sounds correct.

8. *Place* your **cursor** to the far right and center of the second region until you see the **Trim** tool cursor appear again, and *click/drag* to the **left** until the word just after the word "follow," as shown in Figure 4.34. Again, make sure you get as close as possible to the end of the word without clipping.

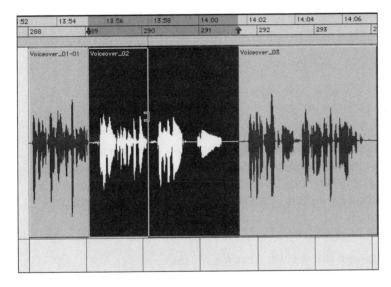

**Figure 4.34**

The trim edit to remove the unwanted portion of the second voiceover take.

9. *Release* the **mouse button**, and you will have cleaned up the back end of the second voiceover take.

10. You can verify the second edit by *clicking* once again with the **cursor** anywhere before the second edit and *hitting* the **spacebar**. Adjust the edit if necessary by trimming the region until the transition between the second and third voiceover regions sounds correct.

11. Finally, if you haven't already noticed, the third voiceover region has a click on the end.

12. *Place* your **cursor** to the far right and center of the third region until you see the **Trim** tool cursor appear, and *click/drag* to the **left** until the click is removed. The final edit should look something like Figure 4.35.

This is a classic example of how to use the Trim tool with Shuffle mode. Even if you are not editing voiceovers and working on music, this can be a convenient method to edit a spoken part in a verse that has multiple takes, or a series of interstitial material that must be edited together and placed at the beginning or end of your track.

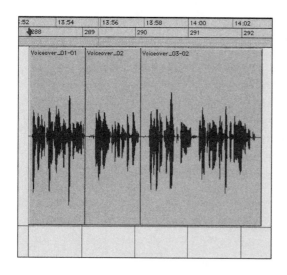

**Figure 4.35**
The final result of your voiceover edit exercise.

### The TC/E Tool with Shuffle Mode

Using the TC/E tool in Shuffle mode is essentially no different than using it in Slip mode because you can time-compress or expand to sample accuracy. The difference is a simple matter of how much you compress or expand the region. This difference is the amount by which all succeeding unlocked regions will move. I do not believe there is any obvious advantage to the TC/E tool with Shuffle mode other than that it might allow you to keep succeeding regions always at the same distance from the end of your current edit.

### The Crossfade and Fade In/Out Tools with Shuffle Mode

The Crossfade and Fade In/Out tools can also be used to perform fades and crossfades to sample accuracy with Shuffle mode. Remember that Shuffle mode will reorder, displace, or move regions that are moved, deleted, or trimmed in length. Because the creation of fades and crossfades does not actually change the length or move or delete the regions, this combination will work identically to using the Crossfade and Fade In/Out tools when working in Slip mode. If you feel that you want to review the Crossfade and Fade In/Out tools with Slip mode, you can refer back to Exercise 4.2.7.

Whew! That is a lot of information to take in. The reason for meticulously documenting the combinations of all of the Edit modes and Edit tools is that it should at least give you a taste of the many ways that Pro Tools can be used when editing audio (if it doesn't make you suicidal). The chapter to this point has highlighted the essence of what makes Pro Tools tick. Understanding all of these options will give you a solid foundation for all of your editing work. If you feel that you do not understand any of the combinations of the Edit modes and Edit tools, it is worth a review of them now. The following exercises in this and all remaining chapters will assume that this information is completely understood. What follows next is an avalanche of additional features and ways of working that will expand greatly on all of the information you have just been bombarded with.

# Navigating Regions and Edits

The ability of an engineer to edit audio quickly, efficiently, and accurately is the sign of an engineer who works often and is in demand. Much of this, of course, is due to an intimate knowledge of the program's design and features, as this book is attempting to cover. However, if you've ever watched such a person operate, you might notice that much of his or her quickness and agility with the system is in the ability to get to where he or she needs to be quickly and efficiently. In summation, half the battle is just getting there in the first place. The faster you get there, the sooner you will be editing the audio, and the sooner you will finish the job.

Some of the available navigation features have been dealt with in earlier sections of the book and will be reviewed or commented on as a reminder. Rather than engaging in repetition, this section of the book expands upon all of the previously learned navigation techniques and adds a few new tricks to greatly enhance your navigation skills.

## Selecting Regions

Chapters 2 and 3 discussed some of the basic ways to select regions with the Selector and Grabber tools. These tools on their own allow you to select a region, all the regions in a track, or all the regions in a song. Although this will suit many of your region selection needs, what if you wanted to select a range of regions? What if the regions you want to select are not currently displayed in the Edit window? Profuse amounts of zooming may take care of this problem, but it will also eat up valuable time that can be better spent making your edits.

Enter the Shift, Tab, and Return keys (Mac) or Shift, Tab, and Enter keys (PC). The Shift, Tab, and Return/Enter keys, when used on their own or in conjunction with the Selector and Grabber tools, allow you to quickly and easily select ranges of regions for editing work. The ability to select series or ranges of regions together quickly will make much of your arranging work a breeze. Mix and match the combinations here or there, and you will have opened up a plethora of possibilities. This section looks at some of these alternative means to selecting regions for editing.

### Exercise 4.5.1 Selecting Regions with the Shift Key

Many of the editing features in Pro Tools, as with most other audio applications, employ the use of functions that are taken from standard word processing programs. Features such as Cut, Copy, and Paste are classic examples of this. The only difference is that you are cutting, copying, and pasting regions instead of text.

One other convention of the word processing world that is commonly used in audio editing programs is the Shift key. In a standard word processing program, the Shift key is commonly used to select a range of text. In Pro Tools, it can be used to select a range of regions.

1. *Select* Ex 4.5.1 from the **Memory Locations** window to have a look at this simple feature. In this exercise you will see an overview of the song.

2. *Hit* the **small open quote** key at the top-left of your keyboard until Slip mode is selected.

3. Select the first Piano region by *clicking* once with the **Grabber** tool.

4. While *holding* the **Shift** key, *select* the last **Piano** region with the **Grabber** tool. You have now selected all three Piano regions, as shown in Figure 4.36.

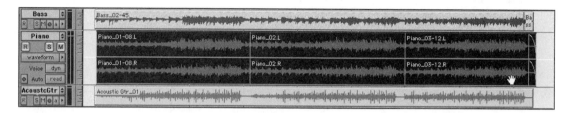

**Figure 4.36**
All of the Piano regions selected using the Shift key with the Grabber tool.

5. Now *move* the **Grabber** tool over the **Kick_02** region and *click* once. The Kick_02 region should now be selected.

6. While *holding* the **Shift** key, *click* once on the **Snare_02** region. Both regions will now be selected.

7. Finally, *move* the **Grabber** tool over the **OH_02** region, and *click* once while *holding* the **Shift** key. Your selection should now look like Figure 4.37. Notice the regions in between are not selected.

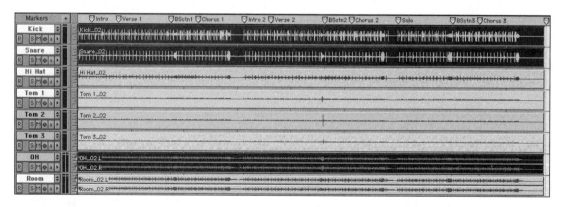

**Figure 4.37**
The Shift key will allow you to add region selections that are not on adjacent tracks.

8. To select a whole range of regions across several tracks, *place* the **Selector** tool somewhere in the middle of the **Room_02** region and *click/drag* toward the uppermost left corner of the **Edit** window. You now have selected a range that covers all of the drum tracks (see Figure 4.38).

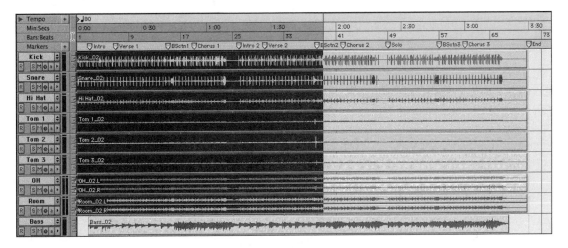

**Figure 4.38**
A selection area that covers all of the Drum tracks.

9. To extend the region selection to cover the all of the Drum regions for the whole song, *hold* the **Shift** key and *click* once to the **right** of any drum region. The selection area will now cover all of the drum regions, as shown in Figure 4.39.

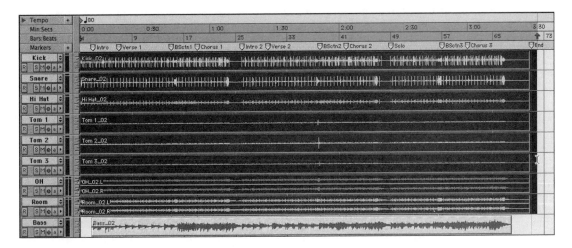

**Figure 4.39**
All the Drum regions selected by using the Shift key and Selector tool to extend the selection area.

III

These three simple exercises show you how to select all the regions in a track or series of tracks in three unique ways. In addition, remember that you can select all of the regions in all of the tracks by double-clicking on the Timeline bar. Depending on your needs, any one of these options may help you select what you need to without having to reorder or hide tracks. Once selected, the necessary editing task may be performed. For example, the selected regions may be shifted later in time by a few bars to accommodate an extended intro section. The next chapter discusses track and region grouping, which can make many of these common tasks even simpler.

### Exercise 4.5.2 Selecting Regions with the Tab and Shift Keys

The Tab key's normal function in word processing is to locate to predefined areas across the document from left to right. This will allow you to line up your text vertically for the purpose of listing items neatly or allow you to create a consistent indentation for the start of each paragraph. In region editing, the Tab key is used to locate your cursor to the next region boundary or transient peak. The latter feature is enabled by selecting the Tab to Transients function, as shown in Figure 4.40.

**Figure 4.40**

The location of the Tab to Transients feature.

The Tab key, when used in combination with the Shift key, offers you the ability to create selection areas that can be tied to region boundaries or even to transient peaks within those regions. It is also useful for selecting regions that extend beyond the viewable area of the Edit window.

1. *Select* Ex 4.5.2 from the **Memory Locations** window, and let's have a closer look. In the following exercise, there is a drum loop with a series of edited fills that are outside of the screen display, for a total of five regions encompassing four bars. You will first need to select this series of regions, and then copy and paste them directly after the current edit to create an eight-bar section of this loop. Knowing that the four Fill regions follow the one viewable region, there is no need to zoom out and display them all.

2. *Press* the *Tab+Control* keys (Mac) or *Tab+Start* keys (PC) once to bring the cursor to the front of the **Shuffle Loop** region boundary and select it simultaneously. Notice that the screen conveniently moves over to end of your selection.

3. Now *hold* the **Shift** key and *select* the **Tab** key four more times. You have now selected a four-bar section, as shown in Figure 4.41. Notice the Length field in the Event Edit area to the right of the Main Counter display. This will verify that you have indeed selected a four-bar section.

**Figure 4.41**
The new four-bar selection area. Note that the Length field in the Event Edit area verifies the selection's length.

4. To complete the assigned task, *press Command+D* (Mac) or *Ctrl+D* (PC) to duplicate the selection area. You have now created the required eight-bar section without zooming.

5. Now *press Command+[* (Mac) or *Ctrl+[* (PC) twice to view your work. It should look like Figure 4.42.

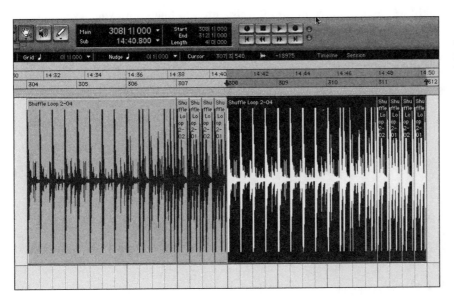

**Figure 4.42**
An overview of the newly created eight-bar loop section.

When you get absorbed in editing work on a song, you will be well aware of where you are, what follows, and what task you are attempting to perform. This awareness has the added benefit of negating the need to constantly zoom in and out to verify your work. Obviously, if you are not sure of the situation, it is better to be safe than sorry, so zoom away.

### Exercise 4.5.3 Making Selections with Tab to Transients and the Shift Key

A more recent and very valuable addition to the Pro Tools palette of editing features is the Tab to Transients feature. The Tab key on its own allows the benefit of locating or selecting regions based on region boundaries, but what if the region boundaries are not edited to the start of the waveform or to an exact beat or sub-beat? A more musical solution to this problem is the Tab to Transients feature. Tab to Transients can be very useful for defining or extracting regions when the region boundaries have no relationship to the content. As always, an example is worth a thousand words.

1. *Select* Ex 4.5.3 from the **Memory Locations** window, and let's take a look at a classic example of this feature. In the following exercise, a tambourine loop region has not been edited properly to the first hit and therefore must be edited so that a loop may be extracted and used in your song.

2. Select Tab to Transients by *clicking* once on the **Tab to Transients** icon in the black bar just below the Waveform Zoom buttons at the top-left of the Edit window. The icon will appear as an arrow pointing to a waveform.

3. *Hit* the **Tab** button once, and the cursor will now tab to the first hit in the region.

4. Now *hold* the **Shift** key and continue to *hit* the **Tab** button 16 times until you have selected a region area that is one bar in length, as shown in Figure 4.43.

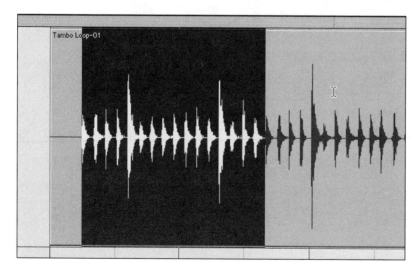

**Figure 4.43**
The one-bar selection area for your tambourine loop.

5. To verify your loop selection, *select* **Loop Playback** from the **Options** menu and *hit* the **spacebar** to confirm you have indeed selected one musical bar of tambourine.

6. Once you are satisfied with the selection, *hit Command+E* (Mac) or *Ctrl+E* (PC) to define a new one-bar loop as a separate region.

7. *Double-click* on the newly created **region** with the **Grabber** tool, and you can now *rename* the region **Tambo Loop 1 bar** so that it is not confused with other unrelated Tambo Loop regions.

The benefit of this feature should now be apparent, as it can allow you to quickly define and extract loops or other audio samples from otherwise unneeded material. The renaming of the region is important because it will allow the loop to be easily identified and used at a later time. The few seconds it takes to organize your work as you go can save you hours of headaches later. It will also make your work more accessible to other engineers working on the same project who do not have the intimate knowledge of the song that you do.

### Exercise 4.5.4 The Shift and Return/Enter Keys

The Return (Mac) or Enter (PC) keys perform many functions in Pro Tools. The most obvious is to finalize the entry of data as it relates to the various dialog boxes that require a response to perform the called upon function. When the Return key (Mac) or Enter key (PC) is used on its own, it will perform a return to zero function. This will allow you to start playback from the beginning of your song.

When used in conjunction with the Shift key, the Return/Enter key can select a range of regions that extend to the beginning of the song. If you throw in the Option (Mac) and Alt (PC) key along with the Return (Mac) or Enter (PC) key, it can be used to select all regions through the end of your song. Let's take a look with an exercise.

1. *Select* **Ex 4.5.4** from the **Memory Locations** window, and you will once again see an overview of your session. The Piano track is displayed larger than the other tracks.

2. *Select* the middle of the three **regions** on the **Piano** track by *clicking* once on it with the **Grabber** tool.

3. Now, while *holding* the **Shift** key, *hit* the **Return** key (Mac) or **Enter** key (PC). You should now have extended your selection area from your currently selected region all the way to the beginning of the song (see Figure 4.44).

4. Now, *select* the *Shift+Option+Return* keys (Mac) or *Shift+Ctrl+Enter* keys (PC), and you will have extended your selection area all the way to the end of the song.

The selection area will always extend to the end of the latest existing region on *any* track, not just the one on which you are currently working. This will explain the selection area extending beyond the Edit window display. These two simple features are incredibly helpful and used often in day-to-day editing work. Once again, although not shown in this exercise, it is an easy way to select regions beyond your Edit window display without the need to zoom.

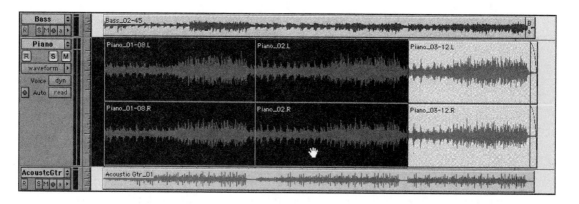

**Figure 4.44**
The Shift-Return keys (Mac) or Shift-Enter keys (PC) can be used to quickly extend the selection area to the beginning of the song.

These few extra locating tips, along with the many of the others scattered throughout the book, can be incredibly helpful for increasing your workflow. It is worth a little extra time to Tab around and familiarize yourself with them before moving on. As I have stated before, repetition can go a long way in aiding the memorization process. What may seem awkward at first will soon become a fluid part of your work.

## Locating Regions

Locating regions may at first seem to be an easy matter of zooming out and then zeroing in on your desired location. But as sessions become more complicated with mazes of edits and arrangement changes, finding these little buggers starts to become a little more like finding Waldo. Pro Tools offers some features that can make this process a little less like finding the proverbial needle in a haystack. Once you have cornered the little sucker, the arrow keys make navigating the Edit window display around your region an easy task.

To start, take a quick look at the Regions list and investigate how this section can help you locate regions in the Edit window. Once there, you will investigate how some simple keystrokes can facilitate the navigation of these regions.

### Exercise 4.6.1 The Regions List

The Regions list can be very helpful for locating and maintaining regions that have been created by the recording, importing, and editing work done in your session. Located on the right side of the Edit window display, it can be accessed by selecting the double arrow at the bottom-right corner of the Edit window.

Whenever a region is edited in any way, new regions are created to reflect the work that has been done, good or bad. There are three basic types of regions: Whole-File Audio regions (represented in bold type), User-Defined regions (represented in normal text), and Auto-Created regions (also represented in normal text). Auto-Created regions are created whenever an edit is performed on any type of region. Once an Auto-Created region is renamed, it becomes a User-Defined region.

1. *Select* Ex 4.6.1 from the **Memory Locations** window.

2. Open the Regions list by *clicking* once on the **double-arrow** at the bottom-right corner of the **Edit** window.

3. Select the Piano_01 region by *clicking* once on the name in the **Regions** list. The region will now be highlighted in the Edit window.

Although this example is perhaps an obvious one due to the size of the region, it is a clear example of the connection between the two areas. When we get into file maintenance work, it will be an easy way to verify whether a region is being used before it is removed or deleted. Although there are other mechanisms to protect against deleting a region that is in use, verifying them may keep you out of such a situation in the first place.

### Exercise 4.6.2 The Tab and Arrow Keys

The Tab and arrow keys can further assist the process of locating to region boundaries. As you have seen in the previous exercises, the Tab key can be used with the Shift key to select regions or extend region selections. When used on its own, it will simply locate to the next region boundary or next transient peak. If the next region boundary or transient is beyond the Edit window display area, the Edit window display will re-center around the new cursor position.

For the purpose of editing audio, I believe the left and right arrow keys are the most useful. When stopped, the left or right arrow key will center the cursor position in the Edit window. Should you ever find your cursor outside the current display area, a press stroke of the left or right arrow key will bring you back home. However, if a region selection area is created, by highlighting a region or click/dragging with the Selector tool, the left and right arrow keys will center the selection area's start or end point, respectively, in the Edit window. The following example will best display the usefulness of this feature.

In the following exercise, the Heavy Gtr track needs to be cleaned up with crossfades and edits.

1. *Select* Ex 4.6.2 from the **Memory Locations** window, and let's take a look at the ways you can use the Tab and arrow keys to locate to your edits.

2. With the Tab to Transients feature selected, *hit* the **Tab** key once to cue to the beginning of your Heavy Gtr part and *press Command+E* (Mac) or *Ctrl+E* (PC) to separate the region.

3. Now *select* the **blank region** with the **Grabber** tool and *hit* the **Delete** key (Mac) or the **Backspace** key (PC) to remove the unneeded region (see Figure 4.45).

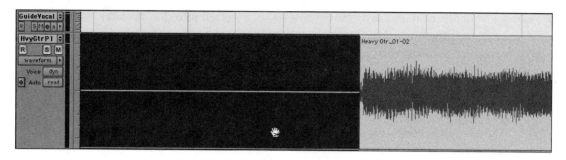

**Figure 4.45**
The blank Heavy Gtr region being selected for deletion by the Grabber tool.

4. Use the Fade In tool by *moving* your **cursor** to the uppermost left corner of the **Heavy Gtr** region and *click/drag* to the **right** to create a small fade-in.

5. *Click* once with the **Grabber** tool on the Heavy Gtr region and *hit* the **right arrow** at the bottom-right of your keyboard to move the selection area to the end of the first Heavy Gtr region.

6. Create a small crossfade by *click/dragging* with the **Crossfade** tool between the two Heavy Gtr regions.

7. *Click* once on the second **Heavy Gtr** region using the **Grabber** tool and *hit* the **right arrow** key once again to move the selection area to the end of the second Heavy Gtr region.

8. Now, using the Crossfade tool again, create a small crossfade by *click/dragging* between the next two **Heavy Gtr** regions.

9. Finally, *select* the last **Heavy Gtr** region with the **Grabber** tool and then *hit* the **right arrow** key on your keyboard.

10. *Create* a **fade-out** at the end by using the Fade-Out tool, as shown in Figure 4.46.

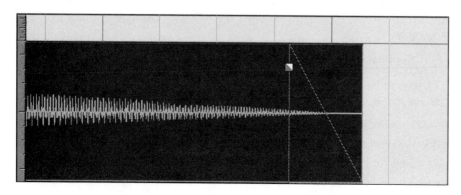

**Figure 4.46**
A fade-out being performed on the last Heavy Gtr region.

In this example, the use of the Tab and arrow keys allows a stream of similar edits to be performed in rapid succession without the need to zoom in or out. In context, each of these edits would require an audition to verify that it indeed works. As you know, the one time you don't listen to your edit is always the one time it doesn't work!

### Auto Scrolling's Benefits and Issues

Auto scrolling is great for a good portion of the work you do that involves recording and mixing, but it is not always your best friend when editing audio. This will soon become apparent when you try to audition a very detailed edit you are performing at sample accuracy, only to find that your page has scrolled and you have now lost your visual. If you are not careful, you might lose an edit point that you must now relocate.

When the work you are doing is general arrangement editing or involves far less visual detail, auto scrolling will help prevent the carpal tunnel–inducing effects of having to manually move the Edit display positioning. Unfortunately, there is no shortcut to turn on and off this great feature.

### Shortcut Tips for Fast Locating

Many of the features just covered in the "Navigating Regions and Edits" section might be a bit confusing or difficult to understand at first. To help guide you through this maze of options, here are some basic tips you might wish to consider that will keep you pointed in the right direction:

- **Don't zoom unless you need to.** Zooming can senselessly slow down your editing time and workflow.

- **Use the Shift, Tab, and Return keys.** These simple features allow you to locate and select many regions with a few simple keystrokes; they facilitate the editing process greatly.

- **Don't forget the Memory Locations window.** The Memory Locations window offers quick-access store points for common location points, such as verses and choruses. In addition, selection areas and zoom settings can also be stored. The exercises in this book would not be possible without the Memory Locations window.

- **Take the time to properly name and organize your regions.** An ounce of prevention is worth a pound of cure. Need I say anything more?

- **Deactivate the Scrolling feature when editing.** The Scrolling feature will quite often change your display window just as you are about to zoom in for the kill. Save yourself the aggravation and turn it off, especially when you are doing detailed editing.

Now that we have built a solid foundation in the basic editing principles of Pro Tools, it is time to dig into all the features that will greatly expand your ability to use the system to its full potential. If the Edit modes and tools are your meat and potatoes, the remaining chapters are the gravy, cranberry sauce, and pumpkin pie. One without another is just not quite as satisfying.

We will start by investigating one of the most powerful features in Pro Tools—grouping. Edit one, and many will follow. Then, perhaps the most often-used, most misunderstood editing principle—looping. Because loops are the foundation of most modern productions, they are well deserving of a chapter's worth of exercises and explanations. Pull up a chair; it's time to take this production in a whole new direction!

# 5 Grouping

Now that you have put a little sweat equity into learning the foundation of the Pro Tools editing system, it is time to start having a little more fun. Without getting into a maze of really bad metaphors to explain the importance of understanding the fundamentals of editing audio, I think it will be clear as you complete this book that without this foundation, all of the remaining features would leave you hopelessly misguided. If you feel that you are still not confident with the Edit modes and tools, it may be worth a review of Chapters 2 through 4 before you embark on the next part of your journey.

*Grouping* is a concept that allows many objects to be controlled by a single object. Rather than having to duplicate the same function across many tracks or regions one at a time, the chosen function or edit will happen to all members of the group. In Pro Tools, tracks and regions can be connected in many ways to facilitate your editing and mixing needs. This chapter takes a look at these two very powerful forms of grouping.

## Setting Up Chapter 5

If you have not already done so, boot Pro Tools. If you are continuing from Chapter 4, you will want to *select* **Close Session** from the **File** menu and *select* **Show Workspace** from the **Window** menu. From the Workspace, locate the Chapter 5 folder you have copied to your hard drive from the CD-ROM. Once located, open the folder and *double-click* on the **Chapter 5 Start** session template. Mac users *select* **New Session** from the pop-up; PC users *select* **Save As** from the **File** menu. Rename it anything you like, and then *select* **Save**.

If you have not copied the files for Chapter 5, place the CD-ROM included with this book into your CD drive. If the CD-ROM does not automatically load, *double-click* on the **disk image** on the Mac Finder or Windows Explorer to view the contents. *Double-click* on the **link** for your computer type, **Start.osx** (Mac) or **Start.exe** (PC), and preview the license agreement. If acceptable, *select* I **Agree.** *Click* once on the **Chapter Files** link at the bottom of the screen, and you will be given a list of chapters. *Select* **Chapter 5**. This will open your default browser, and you can *right-click* to **Save As** or *drag/drop* the **Chapter 5** folder onto your hard drive along with the folders for Chapters 1 through 4. Again, try to keep your files all on the same drive and in the same folder, if possible, to avoid any confusion. If you have not copied any of the files, you may want to revisit the "Loading Files from the CD-ROM" section in Chapter 1 to review the process of copying files from the CD-ROM to your hard drive.

The entire content of this chapter will be working on the song that you are required to edit. Therefore, each edit must be performed accurately to enable the following edits to work. Pay close attention to the details of each exercise and follow the figures to verify that your edits and selections are accurate. Should you find that your edits do not line up with the figures and exercises, remember that there is a session template for each set of exercises. For example, booting up the Chapter 5 Ex 5.3 template will start you at the beginning of the Using Region Groups exercises (Ex 5.3.1). Try your best to finish the exercises using only the Chapter 5 Start template. In the real world of editing audio, you will need to get the edits right before you can move on to the next task. Good luck!

# Track Grouping

*Track grouping* is a concept that hails from the mixing and automation systems of analog consoles. As increased track counts became the norm in recording studios, mixing down the final product also became more difficult. You only have 10 digits, after all! It soon became readily apparent that there needed to be a means of controlling many tracks from a single place. For example, once you have achieved proper mix balances between all the elements of a drum kit, it is much easier to move a single fader to raise or lower the level of all the drum tracks than it is to move all the individual faders by equal amounts; thus the creation of track grouping occurred.

On most large-format analog consoles, there is usually a set of dedicated group faders designed for just this purpose. Eventually, the control of many faders could happen with any fader, not just dedicated group faders. This would allow more localized control of a set of faders because the controlling fader could now be one of the elements of the tracks being grouped. Given that Pro Tools is more than just a mixer, the ability to edit audio as a group is easily as valuable a function as grouping levels or mute states. Although Mix groups offer us convenient grouping options for mixing, the following section concentrates on the Edit groups feature, because this after all, is the theme of the book.

# Edit Groups and Mix Groups

The words "track" and "channel" have been thrown around with great frequency, especially in the world of nondestructive editing, often to the confusion of the many people trying to learn or understand the art of audio. In the reel-to-reel era of recording, a track was very easily defined as a discrete input/output of a multitrack recorder. Once your kick drum was recorded on track 1, it would remain there forever, or at least until the next take. The analog console would maintain the channels through which the audio could be monitored and processed. In the modern era of digital audio workstations, a track in many ways encompasses both of these designs—track and channel— into a single virtual device. Because modern recording is mostly software-driven, the whole idea of tracks and channels of audio is blurred by the fact that audio can be played back, moved, bounced, mixed, and processed anywhere you want it to be. Although the flexibility is incredible, it can often leave one pondering what the difference is between a channel and a track. In DAW terms, the difference is essentially nothing.

The concept of grouping tracks for mixing is a simple matter of allowing the software tracks to behave in the same way as they would in the analog console world. This form of grouping is called *Mix groups*. Mix groups allow the levels, mute states, solos, and many other features to be controlled simultaneously on *all* members of the group by *any* member of the group. Mute the snare track, and all the drum tracks will be muted. Un-mute the kick track, and all the drum channels will be un-muted.

The concept of grouping audio, however, is not covered by the analog world. In the realm of regions and nondestructive editing, grouping audio is an open concept. The closest analog equivalent would be editing analog tape, which requires that all the tracks be edited together using a razor blade, a chopping block, and some splicing tape to create the new arrangement. But what if you could just grab the drum performance from the second chorus and copy it to the third chorus without having to drag all the other instruments along with it? This is the concept of Edit groups. With the "tracks" as your canvas, an Edit group will allow any number of audio and MIDI tracks to be moved, cut, copied, pasted, and otherwise processed together. To this point, the majority of your work in this book has been focused on editing regions within a single track. Now it's time to expand these features two-, three-, ten-, or twenty-fold.

## Exercise 5.1.1 Creating Groups

Before getting into the features and capabilities of Edit groups, you must first learn how to create one. The process of creating groups, Edit or Mix, is inextricably connected to the tracks. The following exercise looks a little deeper into creating Track groups.

1.  *Select* Ex 5.1.1 from the **Memory Locations** window. You will now see an overview of the session. To create a group, you must start by selecting the track names of the desired group members. Let's start by creating a group for the drum tracks.

2.  *Single-click* on the track name of the **Kick** track, as shown in Figure 5.1. When selected, the track name box will be highlighted with a white background.

123

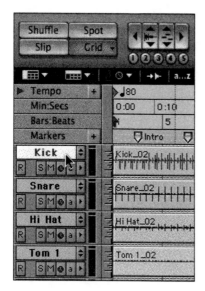

**Figure 5.1**
The track name is selected with a single click.

3. *Hold* the **Shift** key and *click* once on the **Tom 3** track. You have now selected all the tracks between the previously selected Kick track and the Tom 3 track.

4. *Hold* the **Command** key (Mac) or *Ctrl* key (PC) and *click* once on the **Room** track. You have now added the Room track while skipping over the OH track.

5. *Hold* the **Command** key (Mac) or *Ctrl* key (PC) again and *click* once on the **Tom 2** track. You have now deselected the Tom 2 track.

6. *Hold* the **Shift** key (Mac or PC) one last time and *click* once on the **Room** track. You have now selected all of the Drum tracks.

7. To create a group, *select* **Group** from the **Track** menu. You will be presented with the New Group dialog box, as shown in Figure 5.2.

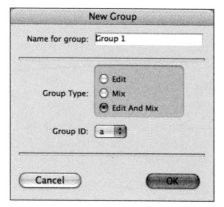

**Figure 5.2**
The New Group dialog box.

In this dialog box you are given options for the name of the group, the group type, and the group ID. The name is important for reference purposes, just as it is for track names and region names. It will be easier to remember that the group called Drums is for the drum tracks than it will be to remember that Group 6 is for the drum tracks.

The group type will be relevant to the purpose of the group. If the purpose of the group is to edit audio only, then Edit would be your selection. If you want to use the group entirely for mix purposes, then Mix would be your best option. The default setting is always Edit and Mix, and this is the best option when you want both group types enabled. Keep in mind that this option is not permanent and can be changed at any time.

Finally, the group ID is a unique letter—a to z—that will be assigned for each created group. You can create up to 26 total groups, comprising any combination of the group types. This feature is important for adding or subtracting group members, as you will investigate more fully later in this section.

8. *Type* **Drums** into the **Name for Group** box and *select* **OK**.

9. *Select Command+=* (Mac) or *Ctrl+=* (PC) to switch to the Mix window.

10. Now *select* a **Mute** button on any of the drum tracks, and all drum tracks will mute. Changing the level of any group member's fader will change all the other group members' levels by the same relative amount. This is critical because the balance of the individual elements of the drum kit will remain intact.

11. Now, *hold* the **Control** key (Mac) or **Start** key (PC) and *select* the **OH Mute** button. This modifier key allows you to temporarily suspend Mix group functions to change a single group member's settings. This modifier function will work identically with fader levels.

12. Finally, *click* once on the **Mute** button of any of the drum channels to un-mute all drum tracks so that you can continue with the exercises.

13. *Select Command+=* (Mac) or *Ctrl+=* (PC) to switch back to the Edit window.

14. *Select Command+S* (Mac) or *Ctrl+S* (PC) to save.

In summation, when a Track group is created, a decision must be made as to the purpose of the group—Edit, Mix, or Edit and Mix. Remember, a Mix group is specifically designed for linking levels, mutes, solos, and a variety of other mix functions. An Edit group is specifically geared toward editing audio regions en masse. The next exercise looks at the Group list and the ways you can edit and modify group functions.

## Exercise 5.1.2 The Group List

The Group list contains a list of created groups and controls all group-related activity. From this list area, the creation, deletion, enabling, disabling, editing, and display of all Track group functions can be modified. Within a session, up to 26 groups can be created.

The Group list can be accessed from either the Edit or Mix window by selecting the double-arrow at the bottom-left (see Figure 5.3.). It is located below the Track list and to the left of the Edit window display.

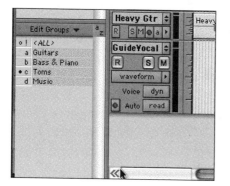

**Figure 5.3**

The Group list in the Edit window.

I. *Select* Ex 5.1.2 from the **Memory Locations** window to start this exercise. At the head of the Group list display, the heading reads Edit Groups, indicating that only Edit groups or Edit and Mix groups will be displayed. To change this function, click/hold the down arrow next to the Edit Groups heading and move your cursor over the Display option, as shown in Figure 5.4. From here you can set the display for Edit or Mix groups.

**Figure 5.4**

The Display option from the Group list in the Edit window.

In addition to the display preferences, the ability to create a new group, delete groups, or suspend all groups also appears. The Delete Groups function is helpful for deleting multiple groups. Simply select the group names in the list you want to delete and select Delete Groups from the Group list menu. If you want to delete a single group, you can click/hold on the group name you want to delete.

2. *Click/hold* on the **Piano & Bass** group in the Group list and *select* **Delete Group** from the pop-up menu, as shown in Figure 5.5.

3. You will then be confronted by a pop-up window telling you that "Deleting groups is not undoable." *Select* **Delete**, and the Bass & Piano group will soon be a thing of the past.

4. *Select Command+S* (Mac) or *Ctrl+S* (PC) to save.

**Figure 5.5**
The Delete Group function selected from the Group pop-up menu.

## Exercise 5.1.3 Activating/Deactivating Groups

When an individual member of an Edit group needs to be edited independently of the other group members, it would be inconvenient to have to delete the group and then recreate it once the individual edit is performed. Thus with all the wisdom and foresight of a great sage, the developers of Pro Tools gave us the ability to temporarily suspend a group and subsequently re-enable it with the single click of our mouse. The following exercise takes a look at a couple different ways to select or deselect groups.

1. *Select* Ex 5.1.3 from the **Memory Locations** window.

   The process for selecting or deselecting a group name also activates or deactivates the group, respectively. Using the Option key (Mac) or Alt key (PC) and clicking on any group name allows you to activate or deactivate all of the groups with a single click. When a group is deactivated, the individual track members are now free to be edited or mixed independently of the group. Once the group is reactivated, any further changes will be once again reflected in all of the group members. This is the first method for activating or deactivating your groups.

   Another way of deactivating groups is the Suspend All Groups function. The Suspend All Groups function can be selected by opening up the Group list pop-up menu (the down arrow) at the top of the Group list and selecting Suspend All Groups.

2. *Select* **Suspend All Groups** from the **Group list** pop-up menu. You will notice that the entire Group list is now dimmed. The individual "activated" tracks are now suspended from group activity. Selecting or deselecting them at this point will not change their suspended status.

3. Now use the shortcut *Shift+Command+G* (Mac) or *Shift+Ctrl+G* (PC) to remove group suspension. This shortcut will toggle back and forth between suspended and active group function.

This shortcut is a quicker way to stop group activity temporarily to perform a quick edit, especially if the Group list window is closed. Rather than sifting through the Group list to find the correct group to deactivate, this shortcut is a quick "turn it off, edit, turn it on, and continue working" function. The first two methods discussed in this exercise are more helpful for long-term deactivation, where other group activity is helpful or necessary.

### Exercise 5.1.4 The (ALL) Group

Included automatically with the creation of any session in Pro Tools is the (ALL) group. The parentheses indicate the fact that this group is a permanent fixture in every session. Although you can enable or disable its activity, it cannot be deleted. Whenever all the tracks in a session must be edited together as a single large group, the (ALL) group enables this to happen without having to create or re-create such a group every time you add a new track. It is important to note that the (ALL) group will only function on tracks that are shown in the Edit window display. If tracks are hidden in the Track Show/Hide list, the edits will not be performed on those hidden tracks. Let's take a closer look at how this feature is useful when editing the arrangement of your song.

1. *Select* Ex 5.1.4 from the **Memory Locations** window. The producer wants to move the whole arrangement forward by six bars so there is an eight-bar introduction to the song.

2. *Click* once on the **(ALL)** group in the **Group** list. When the (ALL) group is activated, it acts as an Edit and Mix group, and all shown tracks will now be affected by the edit or mix function performed.

3. *Move* the **cursor** over any drum region until the **Grabber** tool icon is displayed, and *click* once. You have now selected all the regions in the song.

4. Now *click/drag* the **regions** to the right with the **Grabber** tool while looking at the Start Time in the Event Edit area located to the right of the Main Counter.

5. *Drag* the regions to the right until the **Start Time** reads **71000**, and *release* the **mouse button**. Although this may be a simple example of how to use the (ALL) group, when the edits start to become more complicated, you will love this simple but powerful feature.

6. *Deselect* the **(ALL)** group by *clicking* once on it in the **Group** list to set up the next exercise.

7. *Select* **Command+S** (Mac) or **Ctrl+S** (PC) to save.

### Exercise 5.1.5 Adding/Subtracting Group Members

As sessions start to grow in track count, you might find yourself in a situation in which you need to add or subtract an individual track or two from a created group. Pro Tools allows you to do this by giving each group a unique group ID. When creating a new group, you have the ability to select the group ID letter that will be assigned to the new group. As you will see, this is the key to editing your group members and settings. This group ID also conveniently shows up in the Group list for quick access.

Whenever you need to add or subtract a track from a group, you will need to select the names of the tracks you want to include in the group first. With this in mind, let's take look at a few easy ways to streamline this process.

1. *Select* **Ex 5.1.5** from the **Memory Locations** window.

2. Make sure that the Group list is open. If it is not, *click* once on the **double-arrow** at the bottom-left of the **Edit** window. Directly to the left of the group names in the Group list are two rows of characters; the letters that you see, a to z, are the group IDs. A single click on a group ID will highlight or select the names of the tracks that are members of that group.

3. *Select* the **group ID** for the group called **Music** in the Group list, as shown in Figure 5.6. You will now see all the music track names highlighted.

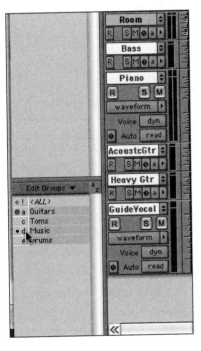

**Figure 5.6**

The track names of the members of the Music group are highlighted when the Group ID is selected.

4. If you want to remove the Guide Vocal track from the Music group, you must first deselect the Guide Vocal track. *Hold* the **Command** key (Mac) or the **Ctrl** key (PC) and then *click* once on the **track name** for the Guide Vocal track.

5. *Select* ***Command+G*** (Mac) or ***Ctrl+G*** (PC) to open the New Group dialog box.

6. *Click/hold* on the **Group ID** arrow and *select* the **Music** group, as shown in Figure 5.7. Once selected, the group name will appear in the Name for Group box.

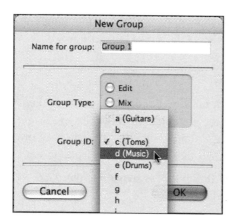

**Figure 5.7**
The Music group is selected from the New Group dialog box.

7. *Select* **OK**, and the Music group will no longer include the Guide Vocal track.

8. *Select* **Command+S** (Mac) or **Ctrl+S** (PC) to save.

To edit the group name or change its function (Edit, Mix, or Edit and Mix) **double-click** on the **group ID** in the **Group** list to open up the New Group dialog box. Once opened, any of these parameters including the group ID can be changed.

Now that you have uncovered the function, setup, and management of your Track groups, it's time to sink your teeth into the song and put your tools to the task of arranging the song form.

## Arranging Your Basic Tracks Using Edit Groups

Edit groups are very useful and powerful tools when you are arranging or rearranging a song. The ability to edit many tracks at once has the obvious advantage of simplifying your workload. In this section, you will look at some of the ways you can edit and clean up your song using Track groups.

### Exercise 5.2.1 Editing Your Drum Tracks

To start, you will take a look at some edits that will help clean up your drum tracks. You will need to edit the intro and ending of the drum performance so that it will start cleanly on the downbeat of the song and the ending will not linger on too long with the ambient noise of the room. The drum tracks have a two-bar lead-in programmed in that you need to get rid of.

1. *Select* Ex 5.2.1 from the **Memory Locations** window.

2. Verify that the Drums group is active and that the (ALL) group is not active. If Grid mode and the Smart tool are not selected, then select them now.

3. *Move* your **cursor** over the **Drum** tracks to the far left of the regions that now start at bar 71000 until you see the Trim tool.

4. *Click/drag* on the **Drum** regions to the right until the **Start Time** is moved to bar **91000**, as shown in Figure 5.8.

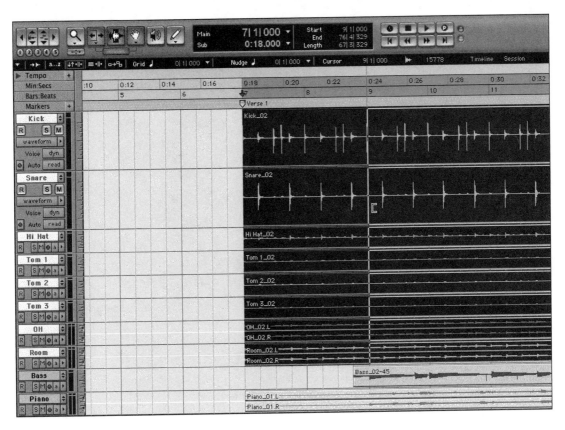

**Figure 5.8**

The two-bar lead-in of the Drum performance being trimmed to start at bar 91000.

5. *Click* once **anywhere** on the **tracks display** before the drums start and *hit* the **spacebar** to verify that the edit is glitch free.

6. Reselect the Drum regions by *clicking* on any Drum region with the **Grabber** tool and *hit* the **right arrow** on your keyboard to view the end edit of the Drum regions.

7. *Move* your **cursor** to the right end of the **Drum** regions until you see the Trim tool. *Click/drag* to the left until the Drum region's **end time** reads bar **753000** in the Event Edit area (see Figure 5.9).

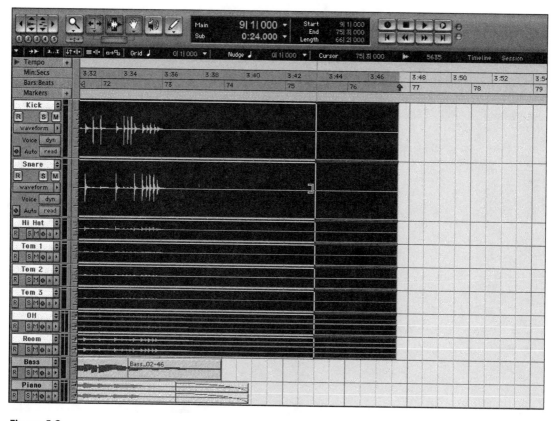

**Figure 5.9**

The lead-out of the drum performance being trimmed to end at bar 753000.

8. *Place* the **cursor** at the top-right of any of the **Drum regions** until you see the Fade Out tool. *Click/drag* to the **left** to create a fade-out of one and a half bars. You can verify the length in the Event Edit Area to the right of the Main Counter.

9. *Click* once **anywhere** on the **Timeline** bar before the Drum region fade-out and *hit* the **spacebar** to verify that the fade-out length and shape sounds natural.

10. *Select Command+S* (Mac) or *Ctrl+S* (PC) to save.

Now that the drums are tidied up, it is time to take a closer look the overall arrangement of your song. Using track grouping is an easy way to change the arrangement of your song.

## Exercise 5.2.2 Changing a Song's Arrangement: Part 1

One of the most common uses of track grouping when editing audio is to facilitate the arranging or rearranging of a song. Perhaps the greatest benefit of nondestructive editing is the ability to arrange and rearrange with reckless abandon a song's format. It allows you to take pre-existing recorded material and piece it together in any way, shape, or form that best suits the meaning of the song. The ability to do this quickly and efficiently will greatly aid in the flow of the creative process whether you are a songwriter, arranger, producer, or engineer.

When editing a whole arrangement, there are a few things to consider before you break out your toolbox and start hacking away. The edits must always take place across all the tracks in your arrangement. The use of the (ALL) Edit group will aid greatly in this process. However, it is important to note that this is only possible if all the tracks are showing in the Track list on the far left of the Edit window. For the purposes of this book, all the necessary tracks you need to work on will be displayed when you select the memory location of the exercise you are working on. Once you have changed your arrangement, you will need to change the Memory Location markers to reflect the changes in the arrangement. We will deal with this in a later exercise.

1. *Select* Ex 5.2.2 from the **Memory Locations** window. The producer would like to extend the intro once again by another eight bars. Loops and other assorted samples will be coming soon to fill this empty area.

2. *Click* once on the **(ALL)** group in the Group list.

3. *Double-click* on the **Timeline bar** at the top of the **Edit** window display to select all the regions in the song.

4. From the **Edit** menu, *select* **Shift** to move the selected regions over by a fixed amount. The Shift dialog box should now be displayed, asking you enter a direction, earlier or later, and an amount (see Figure 5.10).

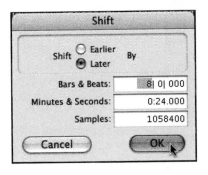

**Figure 5.10**
The Shift feature can be used to move selected regions by set amounts earlier or later in the arrangement.

5. *Set* the **Shift** selection to **Later** and the amount to **80000**. *Hit* OK to apply the shift amount to the selected regions.

6. *Select Command+S* (Mac) or *Ctrl+S* (PC) to save.

### Exercise 5.2.3 Changing a Song's Arrangement: Part 2

The next part of your arrangement journey will involve expanding the length of the solo section to 16 bars. To do this, you can employ the use of the Edit modes to assist in the edit.

1. *Select* Ex 5.2.3 from the **Memory Locations** window. You will see that the cursor is placed exactly at the beginning of the Solo section of the song. Because you have changed the arrangement of the song a few times already, your markers are now out of line with the arrangement, so you will have to take my word for it! In the next exercise, you will learn how to quickly correct the markers to reflect the changes in the arrangement.

2. *Hold* the **Shift** key and *click/drag* to the **right** until you have selected the first four bars of the **Solo** section. You can check the selection size in the Length field in the Event Edit area located to the right of the Main Counter display (see Figure 5.11).

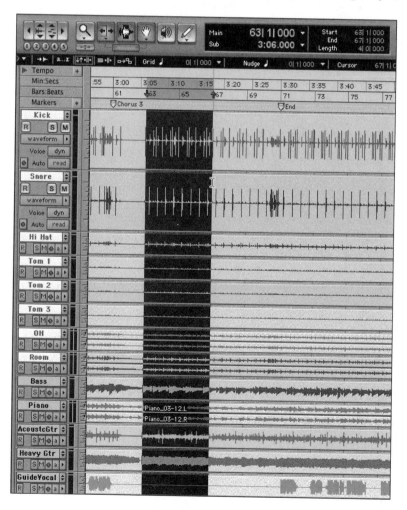

**Figure 5.11**

The first four bars of the Solo section selected using the *(ALL)* group and the Shift key.

3. Once selected, change the Edit mode to **Shuffle** by *selecting Option+1* (Mac) or *Alt+1* (PC).

4. *Hit Command+D* (Mac) or *Ctrl+D* (PC) twice on your keyboard. Because you are in Shuffle mode, the Duplicate function you just performed will slide the rest of the regions to the right and preserve the rest of your arrangement. The result of your edit should look like Figure 5.12.

**Figure 5.12**
The first four bars of the Solo section duplicated twice using Shuffle mode.

5. *Click* once on the **track** display with the **Selector** tool, anywhere before the first duplicated region selection, and *hit* the **spacebar** to verify that you have edited the arrangement correctly.

6. *Select* **Grid** mode once again to prevent any accidental editing catastrophes and to set you up for the next exercise, Moving Markers.

7. *Click* once on the **(ALL)** group in the **Group** list to deselect it.

8. *Select Command+S* (Mac) or *Ctrl+S* (PC) to save.

## Exercise 5.2.4 Moving Markers

Of course, now that you have changed the arrangement, your markers no longer line up to the music. Moving your markers to reflect arrangement changes is quite simple and can save you hours of headaches after a long session, when you are too tired to remember that the Chorus 2 marker is really the start of Verse 2. In this exercise, you will review some quick tips on moving your markers so that they are accurate to the arrangement changes.

The important thing to remember when moving markers is that there are only two methods for doing it. Markers can be individually click/dragged to a new location along the Timeline bar, or they can be cut and pasted as a group to a new location. When moving them using either of the two methods, it is important to note that the markers will follow the selected Edit mode's design. Moving a marker in Grid mode will lock the movement to the grid lines. Moving a marker in Slip mode will allow it to be moved to sample accuracy. Spot mode will allow you to enter the new start point just as you would any region.

1. **Select** Ex 5.2.4 from the **Memory Locat** window. The first step will be to move all of your markers over to reflect the exp the Intro section. To start you must first select the markers at the Marker b

2. Carefully **place** your **cursor** to th he marker called **End** and **click** once. It is important not to click on the M itself or the Timeline bar above. This will place the cursor across the regions d you will end up selecting and moving the regions you have so carefully rearran

3. **Hold** the **Shift** key and **clicl** the **Intro** marker. In this case, since the cursor is now in the Marker bar and the tracks, only the markers will be selected. Notice the selection Start Time in the lit area. The Start Time should read 3|1000 (see Figure 5.13).

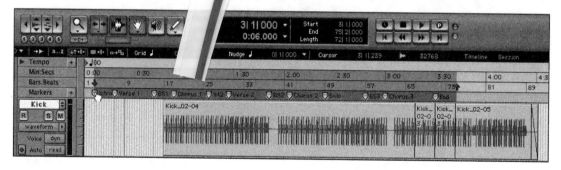

**Figure 5.13**
All the markers selected and ready to be moved.

4. **Select Command+X** (Mac) or **Ctrl+X** (PC) to cut the markers and place them in the paste buffer.

5. Now *place* the **cursor** on bar **171000** in the Marker bar and *click* once. Verify your cursor placement in the Event Edit Area.

6. *Press Command+V* (Mac) or *Ctrl+V* (PC) to paste the markers to the new location.

7. Now *click/drag* the **Intro** marker to the left and move it all the way to beginning of the arrangement.

8. *Click* again on the **Marker** bar just to the right of the **End** marker, and then *click* once on the **B Section 3** marker. Because of the zoom level, the marker will be displayed as "BS3" in the marker bar.

9. *Press Command+X* (Mac) or *Ctrl+X* (PC) to cut the three markers.

10. *Click* once on the **Marker** bar at bar **791000** and verify your cursor placement in the Event Edit area. You might need to click a few times to find the right bar number. Alternatively, you can zoom in on the display to aid your placement.

11. *Press Command+V* (Mac) or *Ctrl+V* (PC) to paste the markers to the new location.

12. Finally, switch to Spot mode by *hitting Option+3* (Mac) or *Alt+3* (PC) on your keyboard.

13. *Click* once on the **End** marker and *enter* in a value of **913000**. The End marker is now just after the drum fade-out you created earlier.

14. Switch back to Grid mode by *hitting Option+4* (Mac) or *Alt+4* (PC) on your keyboard.

15. *Press Command+S* (Mac) or *Ctrl+S* (PC) to save.

Okay, not exactly "easy as pie," but these are the only ways to do it! The couple of minutes spent fixing these markers will be a great help later on, when the edits and the song format start to get a little more complex. A small investment now equals fewer headaches later!

Track grouping is one way to rearrange and edit your tracks in bunches, or to clean up bad edits and performances. Another way to deal with these types of tasks is the use of region grouping. The second half of this chapter looks in detail at how region grouping can offer you a whole new level of ease with region handling when editing audio.

# Region Grouping

*Region grouping* is a revolutionary development in the world of nondestructive editing, and is one of the many reasons that Pro Tools is at the head of the class in the audio editing world. Imagine an audio track with many edits that need to be moved. Track groups are of no help because they will only duplicate edits across multiple tracks. Selecting all of the regions in a track is easy enough, but moving them all together without messing up can be a slippery matter. One false move can leave you wondering whether you accidentally changed an edit or two.

Region groups allow these valuable edits to be moved together as a group, without the worry of accidentally changing an edit. Region groups can be created across a single track or many tracks.

In addition, once grouped, these newly created groups can be exported to other sessions. The associated audio files can be copied when imported into the new session without the worry of importing the wrong parent files from which the regions and edits were created. The beauty of this is that the underlying edits contained in the Region group will then be available for further editing in the new session.

## Using Region Groups

Region groups encompass capabilities that are far beyond simple Track groups. Whereas a Track group connects specifically defined track parameters, a Region group encompasses a series of regions across one or many tracks and places them in a container that looks and behaves exactly like a standard region. Because the Region group acts like a region unto itself, it can be moved, trimmed, copied, cut, pasted, and crossfaded in exactly the same way a standard region can. If you need to get back to the original edits that lie underneath the Region group, you can do so at any time to fix the problem, and then simply regroup the region.

The following exercises explore the wide world of possibilities when using Region groups. You will start by learning how to create one in the first place, and follow through the process of ungrouping, regrouping, and editing Region groups.

### Exercise 5.3.1 Creating a Region Group

All Region grouping features can be found in the Region menu, as shown in Figure 5.14. Before a Region group can be created, you must first make a selection area. The selection area can encompass regions as well as blank space. This is important, as you will see in the upcoming exercise.

**Figure 5.14**

The Region grouping features in the Region menu.

138

1. *Select* Ex 5.3.1 from the **Memory Locations** window.

2. *Un-mute* the **Tambo Loop** track in the **Track Name** section.

3. *Triple-click* on any of the **Tambo Loop** regions with the **Selector** tool. Because there are no other regions on the track, this will select all of the regions on the display.

4. Once selected, create a Region group by *selecting* **Group** from the **Region** menu.

   Once you have grouped the region, it will look ominously like a standard region except for the Region Group icon in the lower-left of the Region group. The icon is a waveform enclosed in a box.

   Now open the Regions list by *clicking* once on the **double-arrow** at the bottom-right of the Edit window display. At the bottom of the list, you will see the same Region Group icon with the group name "Tambo Loop.grp-12." Since there are already other region groups in the list with the same name, it will add a dash with a number on the end to distinguish it from the other region groups with the same base name. The producer says that these extra region groups are not needed and can be removed from the session.

5. *Select* the **Tambo Loop.grp-01** region group by *clicking* on it once. It will now be highlighted.

6. *Holding* the **Shift** key, *click once* on the **All B Section 3-01** Region group to select all the unneeded region groups. The selected Region groups are displayed in Figure 5.15.

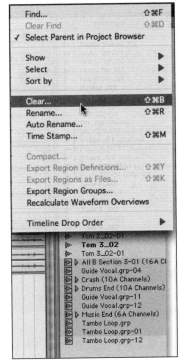

**Figure 5.15**
The selected Region Groups can be removed from the session using the Clear feature in the Regions list menu.

7. Now *click/hold* on the **down arrow** at the top of the **Regions** list and *select* **Clear** from the pop-up menu, as shown in Figure 5.15. You will be presented with a Clear Regions dialog box. The Clear Regions dialog box allows you to remove or delete regions. Only whole audio and MIDI files can be deleted. Whole audio or MIDI files are distinguished by bold text in the Regions list. Selecting Remove will not delete whole audio or MIDI files from the hard drive, it will just remove them from the Regions list. Since a Region group is not a whole audio file or MIDI file, it can only be removed, not deleted.

8. *Hold* the **Option** key (Mac) or **Alt** key (PC) and *click* on the **Remove** button. Holding the Option (Mac) or Alt key (PC) will instantly remove all selected regions. If you are sure that all the selected regions are not needed, then this method will save you the pain of having to manually select the removal of each region one at a time. If any of the select regions are active on a track, they will also be removed from the track, so use this feature with caution.

9. You can now rename the newly created Region group by *double-clicking* on the **Tambo Loop.grp-12** Region group in the Regions list. Edit the name so that it reads **Tambo Loop.grp** without the "-12." *Select* **OK.**

10. *Press* **Command+S** (Mac) or *Ctrl+S* (PC) to save.

The fact that the Region group appears in the Regions list is valuable because it may now be dragged onto a track the same as any other standard region. The Region Group icon and the .grp extension distinguish it as a Region group as opposed to a standard region.

Should you decide, in the course of your work, that you want to edit the contents contained within a Region group, you will need to employ the use of the Ungroup feature. In the following exercise, you will explore benefits of this useful feature.

### Exercise 5.3.2 Ungrouping Regions

The Ungroup feature in the Region menu allows a selected Region group to be stripped back down to the original edits contained within the Region group. In the event that you need to edit the underlying contents of a Region group, the Ungroup feature is the key to your lockbox of regions.

Your mission in this exercise, should you decide to accept it, is to open the Tambo Loop Region group and delete the second from the last Tambo hit.

1. *Select* **Ex 5.3.2** from the **Memory Locations** window. You will see the Region group you just created in the previous exercise.

2. *Click* once on the **Tambo Loop** Region group with the **Grabber** tool. The Region group should now be selected.

3. *Open* the **Region** menu and *select* **Ungroup**. The contents of your group will now be revealed.

4. There are three short Tambo hits at the end of the now ungrouped regions. To select the second from the last short Tambo hit, *click* once with the **Selector** tool anywhere close to it.

5. *Press Command+]* (Mac) or *Ctrl+]* (PC) three times to zoom in. The screen should look very much like Figure 5.16. You will notice three short Tambo hits on the display.

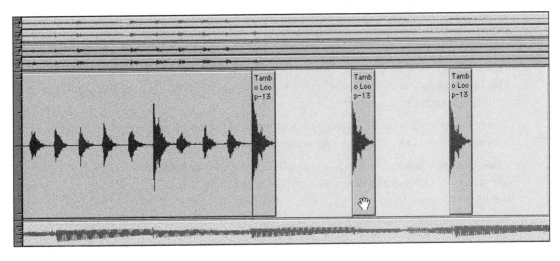

**Figure 5.16**
The zoom selection area displaying the three short Tambo hits.

6. *Select* the **middle** of the three short **Tambo** regions by *clicking* once with the **Grabber** tool and *hit* the **Delete** key (Mac) or the **Backspace** key (PC).

7. *Press Command+S* (Mac) or *Ctrl+S* (PC) to save.

Now that you have completed the first part of your mission, you will need to recreate the Region group you have just ungrouped. Fortunately, Pro Tools has a feature that allows you to do just this.

### Exercise 5.3.3 Regrouping Regions

Once you have finished editing the underlying edits, the Region group can be easily recreated by selecting Regroup from the Region menu. The Regroup feature will only work once and will only regroup the last Region group that was ungrouped.

This feature is important because you might need to ungroup a Region group to fix an underlying edit, as shown in the previous exercise. Once finished, your Region group is easily recreated with the Regroup feature. Without this feature, you would have to recreate your selection area and create a new Region group to return everything to its "grouped" state.

1. **Select** Ex 5.3.3 from the **Memory Locations** window. You should now see the area where you just deleted a Tambo hit.

2. **Select** Regroup from the **Region** menu. The group will now be reformed! Notice that the waveform for the Tambo hit you just deleted is no longer there.

3. **Hit Command+[** (Mac) or **Ctrl+[** (PC) four times to view the overall edit.

   If you now look at the Regions list, you will see that a new Region group has been created with a "-12" added to the end. The "-12," rather than "-01," is a byproduct of the Region groups we deleted earlier.

   This logic allows you to now have multiple versions of the Region group that can be used in different sections of your song.

4. **Select** B Section 2 from the **Memory Locations** window and then **hit** the **left arrow** key on your keyboard to center the Edit window display at the new play cursor position.

5. **Click/drag** the **Tambo Loop.grp** Region group out from the **Regions** list onto the display and **place** it exactly at the **downbeat** of B Section 2. Notice that this Region group contains the hit you so carefully removed in the Ungrouping exercise (see Figure 5.17).

6. **Press Command+S** (Mac) or **Ctrl+S** (PC) to save.

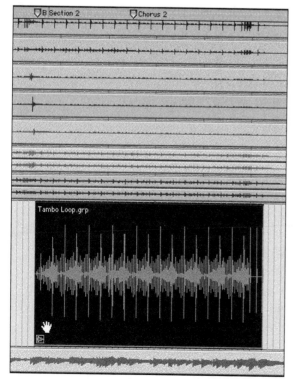

**Figure 5.17**

The original Tambo Loop.grp Region group placed at the start of the second B section.

Now that you have seen a few of the features that region grouping provides on a single track, you might be wondering whether these grouping techniques can be used to edit instruments that encompass several tracks, such as a drum kit. Pro Tools thought of this, too. It's called Multitrack Region groups.

### Exercise 5.3.4 Multitrack Region Groups 1

Unlike normal audio regions that must be contained within a track, Region groups are not constricted by tracks and may be selected across many tracks, both MIDI and audio. Once the Multitrack Region group is created, it can only be moved, copied, and pasted to a set of tracks with a comparable track layout.

To create a Multitrack Region group, you must first select regions across several tracks. Because your Track groups are still active, this will aid in the selection process.

1. **Select** Ex 5.3.4 from the **Memory Locations** window. You will see the Drum tracks most prominently displayed from the Solo section to the end of the song.

2. Select the last big set of Drum regions by **clicking** once on any of the **Drum** tracks with the **Grabber** tool.

3. Now **hold** the **Shift** key and **select** the previous set of Drum regions by **clicking** once on any of the **Drum tracks** with the **Grabber** tool. Your selection area should look like Figure 5.18.

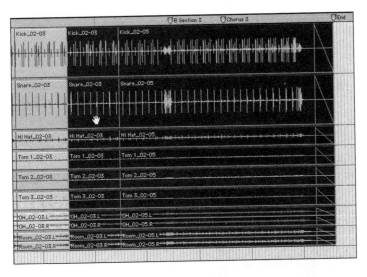

**Figure 5.18**

The selection area for the drums in Exercise 5.3.4.

4. Once you have verified your selection, **hit Option+Command+G** (Mac) or **Alt+Ctrl+G** (PC) to create a new Multitrack Region group. You will notice that the name displayed in this region is generically called Group-01. In a single-track Region group, the name is derived from the track name. In a Multitrack Region group, however, the group name must be generic because there are many tracks involved.

5. To change the Multitrack Region group's name, *double-click* on the newly created **Region** group with the **Grabber** tool and *enter* **Drums End** in the **Name** pop-up box. *Select* OK to make the name change.

6. *Press Command+S* (Mac) or *Ctrl+S* (PC) to save.

The new Multitrack Region group name will now be displayed in the region as well as the Regions list. In addition, the Regions list display will also show the content of the newly created region. The "(10A Channels)" stands for ten audio channels.

## Exercise 5.3.5 Multitrack Region Groups 2

To expand on this concept a little, let's create a Multitrack Region group for the music as well.

1. *Select* **Ex 5.3.5** from the **Memory Locations** window. You will now see the Music and Vocal tracks most prominently displayed from the Solo section to the end of the song.

2. *Select* the **Music** track group from the **Groups list** in the lower-left corner of the Edit window so that it is active. This will aid in the selection process.

3. Once selected, *click* once with the **Grabber** tool on the second-to-last **Piano** region from the end of the song.

4. Now *hold* the **Shift** key and *place* the **cursor** on the yellow marker line for the **End** marker and *click* once.

5. Finally, *move* the **Grabber** tool over the **last vocal region** and *click* once. Your selection area should look like Figure 5.19.

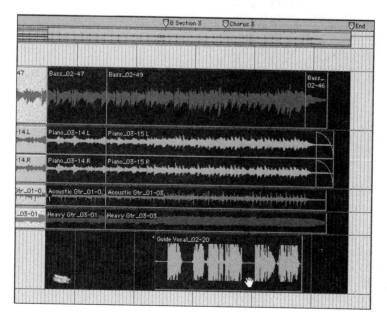

**Figure 5.19**

The correct selection area for Exercise 5.3.5.

6. Once you have verified your selection area, *hit Option+Command+G* (Mac) or *Alt+Ctrl+G* (PC) to create a new Multitrack Region group.

7. Change the new Multitrack Region group's name by *double-clicking* on the new **Region** group with the **Grabber** tool. *Enter* **Music End** in the **Name** pop-up box and *select* **OK**.

8. *Press* **Command+S** (Mac) or **Ctrl+S** (PC) to save.

These two new Multitrack Region groups will be used in the next section, when you shape your new arrangement even further. Now that you have created a series of Region groups, how could you make them all go away with a single click of the mouse? Ungroup All is up next.

## Exercise 5.3.6 Ungroup All

The Ungroup All feature allows you to ungroup all active Region groups at once, and also ungroup nested Region groups. You might find in your editing work the need to layer your groups in order to move groups of groups. All I can say here is, never say never!

Let's start by creating a new Multitrack Region group that contains existing Region groups.

1. *Select* **Ex 5.3.6** from the **Memory Locations** window. As always, no group can be created until a selection area is created.

2. *Select* the **Drums End** Multitrack Region group by *clicking* on it once with the **Grabber** tool.

3. *Hold* the **Shift** key and *select* the **Music End** Multitrack Region group by *clicking* on it once with the **Grabber** tool.

4. Continue to *hold* the **Shift** key, and then *click* once with the **Selector** tool on the **Tambo Loop** track. You have now selected all the audio tracks for the end of the song (see Figure 5.20).

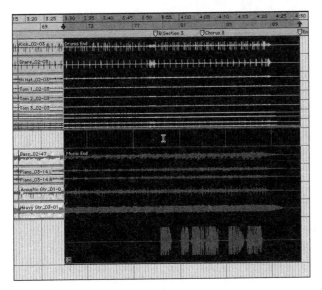

**Figure 5.20**

The correct selection area for Exercise 5.3.6.

5. *Hit Option+Command+G* (Mac) or *Alt+Ctrl+G* (PC) to create a new Multitrack Region group for the whole end section.

6. *Double-click* on the new **Region** group with the **Grabber** tool and *enter* **All End** in the **Name** pop-up box. *Select* **OK**.

7. From the **Region** menu, *select* **Ungroup**. You will now see the Drums End and Music End Multitrack Region groups you created in the previous exercise.

8. *Hit Command+Z* (Mac) or *Ctrl+Z* (PC) on your keyboard to undo the Ungroup. The master All End group should now reappear.

9. Now *select* **Ungroup All** from the **Region** menu. As you can see, all layers of grouping have now been stripped away from the selection area.

10. Finally, *hit Option+Command+R* (Mac) or *Alt+Ctrl+R* (PC) to Regroup all the Multitrack Region groups, including their nested layers.

11. *Press Command+S* (Mac) or *Ctrl+S* (PC) to save.

Okay, now that you have had your primer for Region groups and Multitrack Region groups, it's time to get back to work on the arrangement. This next section covers some of the ways you can edit and manipulate these newly created Region groups to make the process a little more practical.

## Arranging and Editing with Region Groups

In the first part of this chapter, you experienced the usefulness of editing the basic tracks using Track groups; now it is time to experience some of the possibilities when you are using Region groups. Multitrack Region groups are particularly useful for adapting and changing the format of your song, as well as just piling up your edits into a nifty container.

In addition, you will also look at how to use many of the editing features you have used with your standard regions. The sooner you start to look at Region groups, whether multitrack or single track, as just ordinary regions, the sooner you will be able to bust out your editing and arranging tasks with ease.

### Exercise 5.4.1 Arranging with Region Groups

The producer has changed his mind about the extended Solo section you edited earlier in this chapter and has instead opted for a Breakdown section. But before you have a nervous breakdown, remember that you have Region Groups.

1. *Select* **Ex 5.4.1** from the **Memory Locations** window. In this exercise, you will be able to use some of the Multitrack Region groups you created in the last section. Isn't that convenient! First you will need to create an eight-bar hole for your Breakdown section.

2. *Click* once on the **All End** Region group with the **Grabber** tool to select it and *hit Option+H* (Mac) or *Alt+H* (PC) to open the Shift dialog box.

3. *Select* **Later** and *type* in **80000** in the **Shift** dialog box. *Click* **OK** to open the new area for your Breakdown section.

4. Select **Spot** mode by *hitting Option+3* (Mac) or *Alt+3* (PC) to correct the markers that have once again fallen out of line. You will need to add eight bars to each marker.

5. *Click* once on the **End** marker in the **Marker** bar and *type* in **993000**. *Hit* **OK** to move the End marker.

6. *Click* once on the **Chorus 3** marker in the **Marker** bar and *type* in **911000**. *Hit* **OK** to move the Chorus 3 marker.

7. Finally, *click* once on the **B Section 3** marker in the **Marker** bar and *type* in **871000**. *Hit* **OK** to move the B Section 3 marker. Your markers are now back in line with the arrangement.

8. Switch back to **Grid** mode by *hitting Option+4* (Mac) or *Alt+4* (PC).

9. *Click* once on the **B Section 3** marker in the **Marker** bar. The play cursor should now be flashing across the All End Region group.

10. Now *hold Shift+Option* (Mac) or *Shift+Alt* (PC) and *hit* the **Tab** key once. You should now have the selected the contents of the original Solo section, as shown in Figure 5.21.

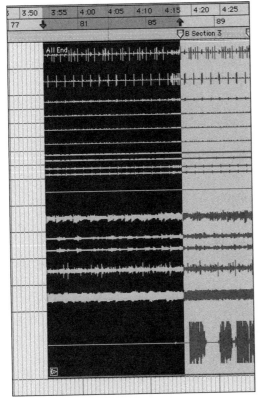

**Figure 5.21**
The selection area of the original Solo section.

11. *Press Command+C* (Mac) or *Ctrl+C* (PC) to copy the selection area into the paste buffer.

12. *Click* once on the **Solo** marker in the **Marker** bar and *press Command+V* (Mac) or *Ctrl+V* (PC) to paste the copied selection area into the Solo section of the song. The end result should look very much like Figure 5.22.

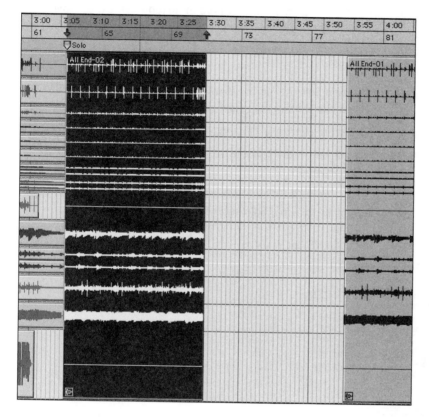

**Figure 5.22**

The newly pasted Solo section Region group.

13. Rename this newly pasted Region group with a *double-click* of the **Grabber** tool on the pasted Region group and *enter* **All Solo Section** into the **Name** dialog box.

14. Finally, you will need to paste a cymbal crash from the Drum tracks onto the downbeat of the new Breakdown section. *Hit Command+]* (Mac) or *Ctrl+]* (PC) once to zoom in on the cymbal crash just before the Solo section.

15. *Click* once on the **cymbal crash** just before the Solo marker with the **Selector** tool. Your cursor position should be at bar 633000. Check the Event edit area to the right of the Main Counter display to verify your cursor placement.

16. *Hold* the **Shift** key and *hit* the **Tab** key once. You should now have selected an area, as shown in Figure 5.23.

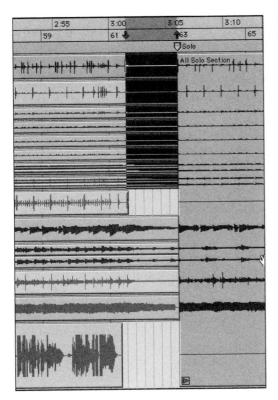

**Figure 5.23**
The selection area for the cymbal crash.

17. *Hit Option+Command+G* (Mac) or *Alt+Ctrl+G* (PC) to create yet another Region group.

18. *Double-click* on the **new Region** group with the **Grabber** tool and *enter* **Crash** into the **Name** dialog box.

19. With the Crash Region group selected, *press Command+C* (Mac) or *Ctrl+C* (PC).

20. *Hit* the **Tab** key twice to move the **cursor** to the end of the new **Solo** section.

21. *Hit* the **right arrow** key to center the display around the new play cursor position.

22. *Select Command+V* (Mac) or *Ctrl+V* (PC) to paste the Crash Region group after the Solo section. Your final edit should now look like Figure 5.24.

23. *Click* once on the **Timeline bar** anywhere before the Solo section and *hit* **Play** to audition your editing work.

24. *Press Command+S* (Mac) or *Ctrl+S* (PC) to save.

If the result of your work does not match Figure 5.24, you might want to close your session, open the session template for Exercise 5.4, and start this section over. As you become more familiar with the features presented, this process, though seemingly complex, will move swiftly and smoothly.

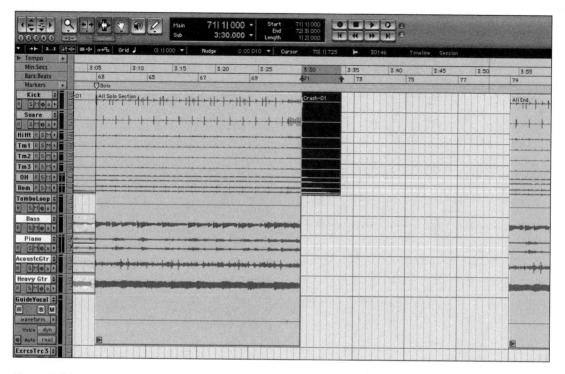

**Figure 5.24**
The final result of your editing work with Region groups.

Under normal circumstances, you would need to solo and go through every edit transition point on each track to verify that your edits are clean. As with any performance, parts will push and pull the beat and not always land exactly on your grid lines. Working with Grid mode is great for editing the overall performance and preserving the relative timing and tempo of the song. Once the gross arrangement is in place, you will need to compensate for the "pushing and pulling" of the individual performances on a track-by-track basis to eliminate clipped or cut-off notes.

The next exercise explores some of the ways you can edit Region groups and clean up your edits.

### Exercise 5.4.2 Editing Region Groups

Region groups are in effect regions unto themselves, and as such, they may be edited in the same way as any audio region. In addition to being separated, trimmed, and moved, Region groups can also be faded in and/or out and crossfaded. This opens up a whole new realm of possibilities as you get deeper into the world of editing and arranging your tracks.

In this exercise, you will take a look at how the Edit tools function the same as they do with standard regions.

1. *Select* Ex 5.4.2 from the **Memory Locations** window. You should now see your final All End Region group centered on the Edit window display.

2. *Place* your **cursor** at the top of the **All End** Region group and slowly move it down the center of the region. The cursor tool will change back and forth between the Selector tool and the Grabber tool. If you look carefully, it changes as it normally would if the underlying regions of the Region group were exposed.

3. Now *place* your **cursor** at the top-left corner of the **All End** Region group, and slowly move it down the left region boundary. The cursor will now change between the Fade In tool, the Trim tool, and the Crossfade tool as it normally would on any region within any track.

4. *Select* an area in the **All End** Region group from the **B Section 3** marker to the **Chorus 3** marker by finding your Selector tool within the Region group and *click/dragging* until your selection looks like Figure 5.25.

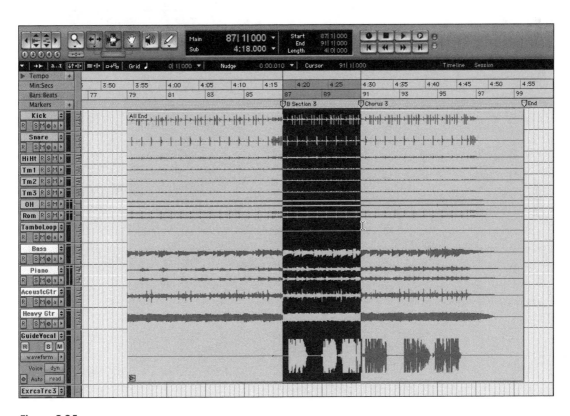

**Figure 5.25**

The selection area from B Section 3 to Chorus 3 in the All End Region group.

5. Once you have verified your selection area, *hit Command+E* (Mac) or *Ctrl+E* (PC) to create a new Region group.

6. *Double-click* with the **Grabber** tool to open up the Name dialog box.

7. *Type* in **All B Section 3** and *click* **OK** to rename.

8. Now move the cursor to the end of the last **All End** Region group, *find* the **Trim** tool, and *click/drag* to the left by two beats so that the end of the track is now moved to bar **99I000** (see Figure 5.26). You have now trimmed all underlying regions and Region groups and shortened the decay of the end of the song.

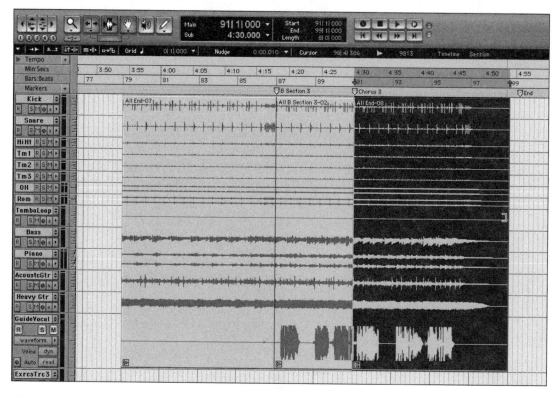

**Figure 5.26**

The end of the All End Region group being trimmed by two beats.

9. Finally, using the **Grabber** tool, *click/drag* the last **All End** Region group to the right by a couple of bars and *release* the **mouse button**.

10. *Select Command+Z* (Mac) or *Ctrl+Z* (PC) to undo this last move.

11. *Press Command+S* (Mac) or *Ctrl+S* (PC) to save.

These are all your basic Edit tool functions and, as you can see, they operate very much the same as they do with standard regions. If you were to change the Edit mode, all of the rules of operation regarding Slip, Shuffle, and Spot would apply equally.

Remember that all edits performed on the topmost layer of your Region groups will be duplicated on all nested Region groups and the underlying individual regions. This is very important to note, as you may lose edits on the underlying layers that you want to keep. Now it is time to investigate fades and crossfades with Region groups.

### Exercise 5.4.3 Fades and Crossfades with Region Groups

The ability to edit Region groups with the Edit tools as you would standard regions creates a nice consistency and greatly simplifies the learning curve when using Region groups. Another feature that follows this same path of consistency is the ability to perform fades and crossfades with Region groups.

Like the previous Edit tools, the Fade In, Fade Out, and Crossfade tools can be accessed using the Smart tool. The same track logic applies to fades and crossfades, so be careful where you place your cursor before you start click/dragging your song into oblivion.

1. *Select* Ex 5.4.3 from the **Memory Locations** window. Once selected, you should see the Crash Region group that you so carefully placed in the new Breakdown section of the song.

2. *Move* your **cursor** to the top-right of the **Crash** Region group until you see the Fade Out tool, and *click/drag* to the **left** for two beats to create a fade-out. This will help the crash decay before clipping.

3. *Click* once on the previous **Region group** with the **Selector** tool to place the play cursor before the Crash Region group, and *hit* the **spacebar** to audition.

4. Now *click* once on the **Crash** Region group with the **Grabber** tool and zoom in by *hitting Command+]* (Mac) or *Ctrl+]* (PC) four times.

5. *Hit Option+2* (Mac) or *Alt+2* (PC) to select Slip mode.

6. *Find* the **Crossfade** tool between the two Region groups and *click/drag* a small **crossfade** area, as shown in Figure 5.27. Notice that a fade-out is created wherever the regions do not meet.

7. *Select* Ex 5.4.3 from the **Memory Locations** window once again and *hit* the **spacebar** to audition the crossfade.

8. *Select Command+S* (Mac) or *Ctrl+S* (PC) to save.

The process here is no different than with standard regions. The only thing to consider when you are creating fades or crossfades on Region groups is that they are not duplicated on the nested Regions groups or underlying regions. Remember that edits performed with the Grabber, Selector, and Trim tools *will* be reflected in the nested Region groups and underlying regions.

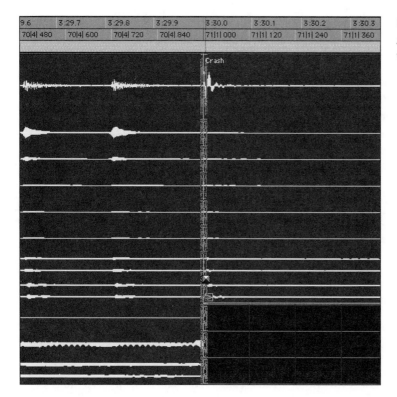

**Figure 5.27**
A crossfade between
two Region groups.

As you can see, the grouping of both tracks and regions is a great way to simplify your editing workload. As you start to group them more frequently in your editing work, you will start to uncover many more of the amazing benefits that are not possible to cover entirely within the design of this book. The ability of these two features to move and manipulate large groups of edits with ease makes for an incredibly powerful arranging and production tool.

Next up, you embark on a journey through the most prominent technique in modern music production—looping. In the next chapter, you will truly transform the vibe of this track by mixing and matching a variety of looping techniques, and you will venture into the all-encompassing loop editing tool—Beat Detective. Once you understand it, Beat Detective will enable you to manipulate and reconstruct loops and live performances to suit your needs with ease.

# 6 Looping, Tempo, and Timing (Beat Detective)

Up to this point in the book, we have discussed all of the foundational principles of the Edit modes and Edit tools. You have taken those principles through the concept of grouping to enable the same editing processes to happen across many tracks. To expand on these processes further, you will need to take a look at the concept of looping. Looping, to some, might just be a simple matter of ordering in a good loop library and building arrangements from preprocessed files. In this chapter, I will take you deeper into the processes of creating and managing loops. This process alone will involve a whole new palette of tools and features to facilitate the process. In addition, you will adapt many of the tools and features you have already learned into a process of organizing these loops within your arrangement. Once understood, these new tools and features will swing open a door into the realm of micromanaging regions. This realm involves dealing with tempo and timing issues.

Whereas grouping is mainly focused on larger issues, such as the form or arrangement of a song or where certain parts play within a song, the world of dealing with tempo and timing issues is one that can quickly become confusing and frustrating. Computer music editing software programs have always been very well adapted to the pure mathematical beauty of clearly defined bars and beats, where everything is just perfectly mathematically in place. Once you step outside these neat little boundaries where inconsistencies in tempo and timing are everywhere, all hell can break loose. Anyone who has ever tried to program, sequence, and edit new parts to a live performance with tempo variations can tell you how the process can seem like you are wearing oven mitts while doing the editing work.

# Setting Up Chapter 6

If you have not already done so, boot Pro Tools. If you are continuing from Chapter 5, you will want to *select* **Close Session** from the **File** menu and *select* **Show Workspace** from the **Window** menu. From the Workspace, locate the Chapter 6 folder you have copied to your hard drive from the CD-ROM. Once located, open the folder and *double-click* on the **Chapter 6 Start** session template. Mac users *select* **New Session** from the pop-up; PC users *select* **Save As** from the **File** menu. Rename it anything you like, and then *select* **Save**.

If you have not copied the files for Chapter 6, place the CD-ROM included with this book into your CD drive. If the CD-ROM does not automatically load, *double-click* on the **disk image** on the Mac Finder or Windows Explorer to view the contents. *Double-click* on the link for your computer type, **Start.osx** (Mac) or **Start.exe** (PC), and preview the license agreement. If acceptable, *select* **I Agree**. *Click* once on the **Chapter Files** link at the bottom of the screen, and you will be given a list of chapters. *Select* **Chapter 6**. This will open your default browser, and you can *right-click* to **Save As** or *drag/drop* the **Chapter 6** folder onto your hard drive along with the folders for Chapters 1 through 5. Try to keep your files all on the same drive and in the same folder, if possible, to avoid any confusion. If you have not copied any of the files, you may want to revisit the "Loading Files from the CD-ROM" section in Chapter 1 to review the process of copying files from the CD-ROM to your hard drive.

# Looping Regions

No single production concept has changed the music industry more in the last 20 years than sampling. The whole concept of taking previously recorded material, extracting selected pieces, and using them to create a new work has become an art form. Although the debate over the legitimacy of this art form ranges from outright thievery to pure genius, one thing is certain—you will be dealing with samples in almost everything that you do. Once you've got the little buggers in hand, how you extract them, process them, and most importantly distribute them in your work will determine whether they will work.

The following exercises deal with some tools and techniques that will help make the process of extracting, processing, and looping these samples the least of your editing concerns.

## Good Loop Editing Habits

The process of gathering and processing loops should follow some simple basic guidelines. Find the part of the loop that contains the groove or sound you are going for. Carefully extract the area you want to use. Adapt the tempo, if necessary, to the session tempo. Adjust its relative timing to the track (sometimes called "finding the pocket"). Finally, copy and paste it wherever you can get away with it!

All of these parts of the process have editing features attached to them that can simplify this process. The upcoming exercises take on these matters one by one. You will learn the editing features of Pro Tools that make this process happen with ease. Each exercise will involve new tools or techniques, as well as adapting some of the tools you have already learned.

### Exercise 6.1.1 Trimming Tops and Tails

The process of finding the loop that best suits your song is one that is inherently personal and relies more on your own musical taste. If you are an engineer and just following orders, however, the choice might not be left up to you. Such is the case today, as you will need to work with a new shaker loop. The Shaker 1 region is longer in length than what you need and is also at a different tempo. The first hit of the loop is cut off, however, so you will first need to extract a good one-bar loop section:

1. *Select* Ex 6.1.1 from the **Memory Locations** window. The cursor will be flashing at the start point for the new loop.

2. *Hold* the **Shift** key and *click/drag* the **Selector** tool to the right of the flashing cursor across the region to create the same selection area, as shown in Figure 6.1. The selection does not need to be exactly edited to the hits right now because you will need to zoom in to correct it anyway.

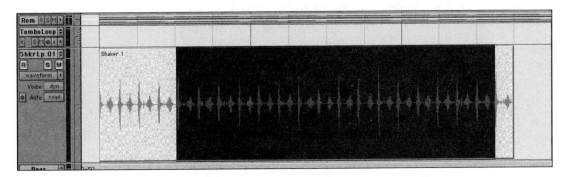

**Figure 6.1**
The selection area for the Shaker 1 loop edit.

3. *Hit Command+E* (Mac) or *Ctrl+E* (PC) on your keyboard to separate the new region.

4. *Hit Command+]* (Mac) or *Ctrl+]* (PC) five times to zoom in to the first hit, and trim the region start using the **Trim** tool, as shown in Figure 6.2.

5. *Hit* the **right arrow** on your keyboard and trim the tail end of the region with the **Trim** tool, as shown in Figure 6.3. Notice that the head and tail cuts are identical in their location to the waveform.

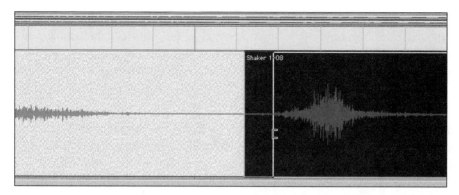

**Figure 6.2**

The exact trim selection for the head of the shaker loop.

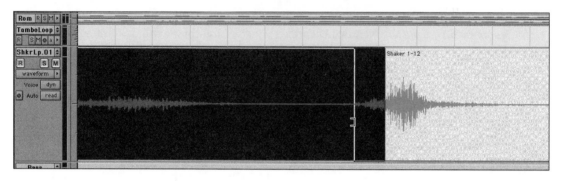

**Figure 6.3**

The exact trim selection for the tail of the shaker loop.

6. *Select* Ex 6.1.1 from the **Memory Locations** window once again to zoom out on the display.

7. Switch to **Grid** mode by *hitting Option+4* (Mac) or *Alt+4* (PC).

8. Now, *click/drag* with the **Grabber** tool to move the newly trimmed region to the left so that the region start time is bar 171000.

9. Select **Loop Playback** by *hitting Shift+Command+L* (Mac) or *Shift+Ctrl+L* (PC).

10. *Hit* the **Solo** button on the **Shaker Loop** track and *hit* the **spacebar** to verify that you have correctly edited the loop. If edited correctly, the rhythm will stay constant when the play cursor cycles back to the beginning of the loop. If you have not properly edited your loop, you might need to reload the session template for this exercise to start over.

11. *Hit* the **spacebar** again to stop the playback and *click* on the **Solo** button of the **Shaker Loop** track once again to enable the playback of all the tracks.

12. *Press Command+S* (Mac) or *Ctrl+S* (PC) to save.

The process for any kind of loop extraction is essentially the same. Always verify that the loop is correctly edited so that it will make sense musically. It is very important to remember not to clip the head and tail of the loop area; although it might be quicker and more convenient at the time, it may come back to bite you later. Once the loop has been successfully extracted, it might be necessary to adapt it to the current session's tempo. The next exercise deals with this exact issue.

### Exercise 6.1.2 TC/E Guidelines

Now that you have defined and extracted the Shaker loop, you will need to adapt it to the tempo of the song. A little trip down memory lane back to Chapter 4 should tweak a few brain cells as you work with Grid mode and our old friend, the Time Compression/Expansion tool.

1. *Select* Ex 6.1.2 from the **Memory Locations** window.

2. *Hit Command+2* (Mac) or *Ctrl+2* (PC) twice so that the **TC/E Trim** tool is selected.

3. *Click/drag* on the **end region boundary** of your extracted **Shaker** loop until the total length becomes **2 bars**. You can verify this in the Length field of the Event Edit area. Once verified, *release* the **drag**, and you have now adapted the loop to the session tempo.

4. *Hit* the spacebar once to verify the timing of the Shaker loop with the track.

5. *Click/hold* on the **Trim** tool button and select **Standard** from the pop-up menu. While you are in the neighborhood, select the **Smart** tool by *clicking* once on the **bar** below the Trim, Selector, and Grabber tools.

6. *Press Command+S* (Mac) or *Ctrl+S* (PC) to save.

The loop has now been extracted and adapted to the session tempo, but your work is hardly done. Next up, you will learn a little about adapting the timing of the loop relative to the song. This relative timing will affect how the Shaker region will push or pull the track. The next exercise introduces two new features that will help streamline this process.

### Exercise 6.1.3 Checking Your Loop for Timing

Just because you have "mathematically" chopped up your loop into a nice little even bar-sized box doesn't mean that it will sit in the track and make your song groove. To do this, you will need to play around a little with its relative position to the existing music. In this exercise, you will uncover a couple of features that should make this process calculated and efficient.

If you remember, when you extracted the Shaker region, you selected start and end points that would not clip the audio at the head or tail of the loop even though this might not be the best start point musically when the region start is set to the grid. To compensate for this issue, Pro Tools offers a great feature that will enable you to adjust the timing of your loop relative to the grid lines and the previously recorded music. That feature is called *nudging*.

Nudging is a great way of moving regions by preset values. The beauty of using preset values to move regions is that you now know exactly how far you are moving a region each time you move it. The selected regions will be moved later or earlier in time with the + and – keys from the numeric keypad. (Note, these are *not* the alphanumeric + and – keys.) Laptop users will need to hold the Fn key on their keyboard and find the superimposed + and – keys. With each hit of the + or – key, the selected regions will be moved by a predetermined value set in the Nudge Value indicator, as shown in Figure 6.4.

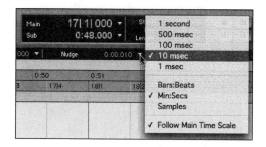

**Figure 6.4**

The location and settings for the nudge standard and resolution.

To start this process, you must first select a nudge standard and resolution. The value entered here will be determined by the task at hand. Regions can be moved by Bars:Beats, Min:Secs, Samples, Timecode (HD systems only), or Feet+Frames (HD systems only) standards. The resolution value will be based on subdivisions of the selected standard. For the purposes of this exercise, you will use the Min:Secs standard and a resolution of 10 msec.

1. *Select* Ex 6.1.3 from the **Memory Locations** window. The Shaker loop should be selected by the Ex 6.1.3 Memory Location. If not, then select it now using the **Grabber** tool, by *clicking* once on the **Shaker** region.

2. *Select* the **down arrow** directly to the right of the **Nudge** value below the **Main Counter** display and *select* the **Min:Secs** standard and a resolution of **10 msec**, as shown in Figure 6.4.

3. *Hit* the **spacebar** once to start playback of the Shaker loop. Notice the feel of the shaker against the rest of the music.

4. Now, while the loop is cycling, *select* the – key on the numeric keypad once to move the region start earlier by 10 msec. It might take a second to buffer, but you should hear a subtle difference in the feel of the shaker.

5. *Select* the – key once again on the numeric keypad to move the region earlier by another 10 msec. Notice how the shaker pushes the track a little more, almost speeding up the tempo.

6. Finally, *select* the + key once on the numeric keypad to move the region later by 10 msec. When this action is multiplied over many tracks, you will find that the feel of the track can be significantly improved. If you feel the best place for the loop lies somewhere in between two selections, you can change the nudge resolution to 1 msec and find the best place in between.

7. **Select Command+S** (Mac) or **Ctrl+S** (PC) to save.

Of course, now that your region has been shifted off of the grid lines, you must be careful when working in Grid mode. When zoomed out, it might not be so obvious that the region is a mere 10 msec off the grid. This problem may be solved with the second feature for this exercise, Sync Points.

Sync Points allow you to make any selected point within a region a locking reference point to your grid lines when working in Grid mode. These Sync Points are used very often in post-production work, where an obvious reference point in the middle of an audio region, such as dog bark, can be matched up to the exact video frame of the dog barking. Sync Points can also be helpful in audio when using loops or other audio segments whose region start does not match up exactly with the grid lines. When working in Grid mode, all movement of the region will now lock the Sync Point, not the region start, to the grid.

8. **Hit Command+]** (Mac) or **Ctrl+]** (PC) five times to zoom in to the head of the **Shaker** region.

9. If it is not already selected, switch to **Grid** mode by **hitting Option+4** (Mac) or **Alt+4** (PC).

10. **Click** once with the **Selector** tool on the **Shaker** region at bar **171000**, as shown in Figure 6.5.

11. From the **Region** menu, **select Identify Sync Point**. You will now see a small green arrow pointing downward at the bottom of the region (see Figure 6.5).

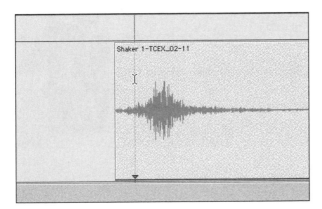

Shaker 1-TCEX_02-11

**Figure 6.5**
The cursor position and the newly created Sync Point at the bottom of the region.

12. **Select Command+S** (Mac) or **Ctrl+S** (PC) to save.

With a Sync Point identified, you will no longer need to worry about the regions being accidentally offset from their carefully placed timing within the track. Because your region start now contains an unclipped version of the shaker part, you will not have to deal with unnecessary fade-ins or fade-outs to clean up bad edits. Now it is time to copy this new loop throughout the track. To do this, you need to employ two editing features that will allow you to quickly copy and paste your way throughout the song. Those two editing features are Duplicate and Repeat.

### Exercise 6.1.4 Other Looping Options

Before region looping came into the consciousness of Pro Tools users with the release of version 7.0 software, there were only two basic practical methods for copying and pasting regions onto a track: Duplicate and Repeat. Using the Copy and Paste commands from the Edit menu serves many valuable purposes when moving regions to other places on the Edit window, but is not practical for copying regions throughout a whole song. Although region looping adds a whole new level of functionality to loop editing, the Duplicate and Repeat commands are still very powerful ways to quickly deal with many of your region looping needs.

1. *Select* **Ex 6.1.4** from the **Memory Locations** window. In the following exercise, you now have the task of copying the Shaker loop in the verses and intro sections of the song.

2. *Select* the **Shaker** region with the **Grabber** tool by *clicking* on it once and *press* **Command+C** (Mac) or **Ctrl+C** (PC).

3. *Press* **Command+D** (Mac) or **Ctrl+D** (PC) once. The Duplicate feature will place a copy of the selected area directly after the selected area.

4. *Press* **Command+D** (Mac) or **Ctrl+D** (PC) four more times so that the loop ends just before the downbeat of B Section 1 (see Figure 6.6).

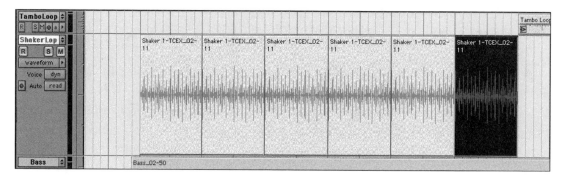

**Figure 6.6**

The newly duplicated Shaker regions up to the beginning of B Section 1.

5. *Press* **Command+D** (Mac) or **Ctrl+D** (PC) one last time and zoom in by *hitting Command+]* (Mac) or **Ctrl+]** (PC) five times.

6. *Hold* the **Command** key (Mac) or the **Ctrl** key (PC) and *click* once with the **Selector** tool between the first two shaker hits, as shown in Figure 6.7. Remember, the Command key (Mac) or Ctrl key (PC) temporarily overrides Grid mode for the Selector tool, allowing you to edit off the grid.

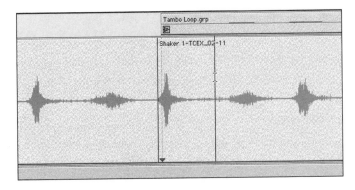

**Figure 6.7**

The placement of the Selector tool
after the first shaker hit in B Section 1.

7. *Hit Command+E* (Mac) or *Ctrl+E* (PC) to separate the region. This extra shaker hit on the downbeat is a common editing technique because it can make the part sound more natural.

8. Remove the remainder of the Shaker region by *clicking* once on it with the **Grabber** tool and *hitting* the **Delete** key (Mac) or **Backspace** key (PC).

9. *Select* **Ex 6.1.4** from the **Memory Locations** window once again, to zoom out to the overall section.

10. *Hit Command+A* (Mac) or *Ctrl+A* (PC) to select all the regions you have just pasted.

11. *Select* **Spot** mode by *hitting* the small **open quote** key above the Tab key until the Spot button is highlighted.

12. *Hold* the **Option** key (Mac) or **Alt** key (PC) and *click* once on the first of the **Shaker** regions.

13. You will be presented with the Spot Dialog box, as shown in Figure 6.8. *Enter* **401000** in the **Sync Point** box and *hit* the **OK** button.

14. Zoom out by *hitting Command+[* (Mac) or *Ctrl+[* (PC) twice to view the copy spot.

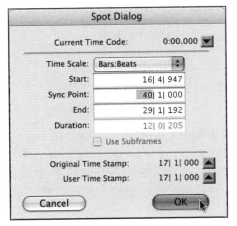

**Figure 6.8**

The Spot Dialog box for the Copy Spot function.

15. From the **Options** menu *select* **Link Timeline and Edit Selection**. This will link our playback position with our editing work.

16. Now *click* once on the **Bridge** marker from the Memory Locations window.

17. *Hit **Command+V** (Mac) or **Ctrl+V** (PC) to paste the **Shaker** region to the beginning of the Bridge section of the song.

18. *Hit* the **right arrow** key to center the screen.

19. Because the region is pasted exactly on the bar, you will need to reset the Sync Point in the region to match the downbeat of the bar. *Click* once on the **region** with the **Grabber** tool to open the Spot Dialog box again. *Enter* bar **791000** in the **Sync Point** box to realign the Sync Point with the bar at the beginning of the Bridge section.

20. From the **Edit** menu *select* **Repeat**. You will be presented with the Repeat dialog box (see Figure 6.9).

**Figure 6.9**

The Repeat dialog box.

21. *Enter* **8** repeats as a value and *select* **OK**. You have now pasted eight copies of your Shaker region to the end of the song.

22. *Click* once with the **Selector** tool anywhere before the first **Shaker** region and *hit* the **spacebar** to audition all the Paste, Duplicate, and Repeat functions you have just performed.

23. *Press **Command+S** (Mac) or **Ctrl+S** (PC) to save.

In cases such as this, it is almost easier to just use the Repeat function to paste a region throughout the whole song. The sections you do not need can easily be discarded by selecting them and hitting the Delete or Backspace key. The nice part is that you have learned some new techniques for copying and pasting your loops throughout a song. The more you do it, the more possible combinations you will find!

Another benefit of this type of looping is that each individual region can be edited independently of all the others. There are times, of course, when you might want to change all of your looped regions at once. This feature is called *region looping*. The next section of this book covers this in vivid detail.

## Region Looping

Pro Tools software revision 7.0 brought many new features, but perhaps none as welcome as region looping. Although manual looping has been used in Pro Tools for quite some time, these features were really nothing more than modified versions of Copy and Paste. The Duplicate and Repeat features are limited in their capabilities to manage regions on a global scale because they just make copies of regions that are separate entities unto themselves. Where region looping differs is in the use of a concept known as *iteration*. An iteration differs from a copy or duplicate in that it is connected to the original region. If the original region is moved, all iterations will follow. If the original is trimmed down in size, all iterations will be trimmed down to the same size. They are inextricably connected until, of course, you un-loop them!

Region looping can be performed on audio regions, MIDI regions, and Region groups. Looping a Region group may be employed to consolidate a series of regions into a single region first, so that they can be looped together. You can also loop regions across multiple tracks. This is helpful for looping multitracked live drums. In the following series of exercises, you will take a peek into region looping and the options for creating and editing iterations.

### Exercise 6.2.1 Looping a Region (Iterations)

The creation of region loops is a simple matter of selecting the region to be looped and selecting Loop from the Region menu. Once you have started the process of creating a region loop, you will need to make a few decisions that will help you achieve the desired result.

Once a selection is made and Loop is selected from the Region menu, the number of copies or length to fill is entered, and the copies are created. Each subsequent copy of the original region is known as an *iteration*. Each iteration is essentially a slave of the original. As such, the iterations will act as a singular entity.

1. *Select* Ex 6.2.1 from the **Memory Locations** window. In this exercise, the producer wants to replace the live drums with drum loop samples. The new Sampled Drums track should now be prominently displayed. To start, you will need to select, deactivate, and hide all of the live drum tracks before laying in your new drum loops.

2. Select **Grid** mode by *hitting Option+4* (Mac) or *Alt+4* (PC) on your keyboard.

3. Open the **Groups list** display by *clicking* on the **double-arrow** at the bottom-left of the Edit window display.

4. Once open, *click* once on the **group ID** letter for the drums, as shown in Figure 6.10. This will select all the track names for the Drums group.

**Figure 6.10**

The track names for the drums are selected with a single click on their group ID letter.

5. From the **Track** menu, *select* **Make Inactive**. The tracks should now be grayed out. The nice part about deactivating tracks versus deleting them is that if you deactivate them, they are accessible later if the producer changes his mind.

6. To hide the drum tracks, *click/hold* on the **Drums** group name in the **Groups** list and *select* **Hide Tracks in Group** (see Figure 6.11). The tracks will now be removed from the Edit window display. Now that you have your old drums neatly tucked away, you can work on region looping the new drum samples.

**Figure 6.11**

The Hide Tracks In Group feature from the Groups list.

7. *Click* once with the **Grabber** tool on the first **Sampled Drums** region on the Sampled Drums track to select it.

8. Now *select* **Loop** from the **Region** menu. You will be presented with the Region Looping dialog box, as shown in Figure 6.12.

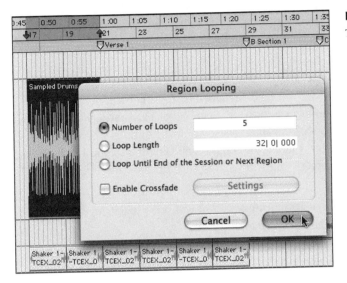

**Figure 6.12**
The Region Looping dialog box.

9. *Enter* 5 in the **Number of Loops** box and *select* OK. The Sampled Drums region now has a total of five iterations. Notice the Loop Arrow icon in the bottom-right corner of each iteration (see Figure 6.13).

10. *Select* the **Mute** switch on the **Sampled Drums** track to un-mute it, and then *hit* the **spacebar** to audition the new drums.

11. *Select* **Command+S** (Mac) or **Ctrl+S** (PC) to save.

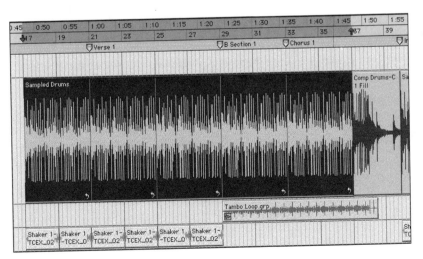

**Figure 6.13**
The looped Sampled Drums region created by the Region Looping dialog box. Notice the Loop Arrow icon in the bottom-right corner of each iteration.

167

The Loop Arrow icon indicates that these regions are Iterations. Iterations in consecutive order are connected to each other as a singular group. In that respect, they differ from duplicated or repeated regions in that they are not independent regions. This icon serves a dual purpose when editing iterations, which we will explore later in this section. But, before you go there, let's explore a few additional options for creating loop iterations.

### Exercise 6.2.2 Loop Length Options

When looping regions, the number of repeats will be determined by their musical necessity in the song. To state it more simply, it's a production decision. Some loops exist throughout a whole song; others appear only in certain sections of the song. There are three options when creating a region loop to help make the process easier: Number of Loops, Loop Length, or Loop Until the End of Session or Next Region. In the next exercise, you will go over each of these three methods and how they can be best employed.

1. *Select* Ex 6.2.2 from the **Memory Locations** window. You will see a highlighted Sampled Drums region at the beginning of the Verse 2 marker.

2. *Hit Option+Command+L* (Mac) or *Ctrl+Alt+L* (PC) to open the **Region Looping** dialog box.

3. *Enter* 4 in the **Number of Loops** box and *click* on **OK**. You have now created a region loop with four iterations. Easy!

4. *Select* the **Sampled Drums** region at the beginning of the **Solo** marker by *clicking* once with the **Grabber** tool, and *hit* the **right arrow** key on your keyboard to center the selected region on the screen.

5. *Hit Option+Command+L* (Mac) or *Ctrl+Alt+L* (PC) to open the **Region Looping** dialog box.

6. *Select* **Loop Length** as the method of copy and *enter* 100000 in the **Loop Length** box. *Click* **OK**. You have now copied the Sampled Drums loop for 10 bars. Because the Sampled Drums loop is four bars in length, the Region Loop feature will create 2-1/2 iterations in order to fill the 10-bar requirement. Even though it is half the length, this iteration is still part of the original loop and will follow all group activity (see Figure 6.14).

7. Now *select* the B Section 3 marker from the **Memory Locations** window and *hit* the **right arrow** key on your keyboard to center the display for the final loop section.

8. *Click* once on the **Sampled Drums** region at the beginning of the **Bridge** section with the **Grabber** tool to select it.

9. *Hit Option+Command+L* (Mac) or *Ctrl+Alt+L* (PC) to open the **Region Looping** dialog box one last time.

10. *Select* the **Loop Until End of the Session or Next Region** option and *select* **OK**. The area up to the next region will now be filled in with the Sampled Drums loop.

11. *Press Command+S* (Mac) or *Ctrl+S* (PC) to save.

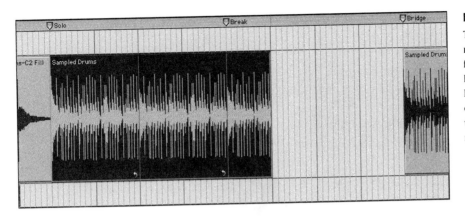

**Figure 6.14**
The newly created
10-bar loop length
for the Sampled
Drums loop.
Notice the half loop
created at the end
to fill the 10-bar
requirement.

As you can see, all of the three options for creating loop sections have a purpose. Each newly created loop now has its own freshly pressed set of iterations. If you decide that you want to edit any of the region loops that you have just created, you will need to take a look at the next exercise because you ain't in Kansas anymore....

### Exercise 6.2.3 Editing Loop Iterations: Part 1

There are two basic ways to edit a looped region. You can edit a loop and its iterations as a group, or you can edit the iteration's individual regions. Although the Edit tools perform the same basic functions that they do when used with regular regions, the way the region loop will react to each tool might surprise you at first. Once you have absorbed the logic of iterations, however, it will all start to make perfect sense. In the following exercise, you will look at each of the Edit tools and how they can be applied to loop iterations as a group.

1. *Select* Ex 6.2.3 from the **Memory Locations** window.

2. Open the Regions list by *hitting* the **double-arrow** at the bottom-right of the **Edit** window.

3. *Locate* the **Tambo Loop** region and *click/drag* it onto the **Tambo Loop** track to start at the beginning of the **B section 3** marker.

4. *Hit Option+Command+L* (Mac) or *Ctrl+Alt+L* (PC) to open the **Region Looping** dialog box.

5. *Select* **Number of Loops**, *enter* the number 4, and *click* **OK**. Your Edit window display should look like Figure 6.15.

   When a Region loop is created, it acts as a singular region, much like a Region group. Because the Smart tool is the main tool for all your region editing needs, you will need to see how it acts when working with Region loops. As you will see, it will act in a very similar manner when used with Region loops as it does with standard regions.

6. *Place* your **Selector** tool anywhere on the second **Tambo Loop** iteration and *click/drag* to the right. You have now created a selection area, just like a normal region.

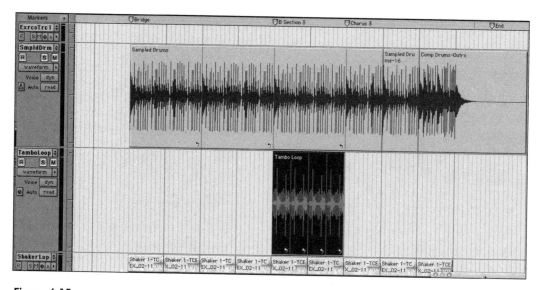

**Figure 6.15**

The Tambo Loop region placed at the B Section 3 marker on the Tambo Loop track and looped four times.

7. *Click* once with the **Grabber** tool on any **Tambo Loop** iterations, and you have selected all the Tambo Loop iterations.

8. Now *click/drag* with the **Grabber** tool and move the **Tambo Loop** to the left so that it starts at bar **83|000**. Verify your Start Time location in the Event Edit Area.

9. *Use* the **Trim** tool on the first **Tambo Loop** iteration and *click/drag* to the left until the region boundary starts at bar **77|000**. Notice how the Trim tool automatically creates more iterations.

10. *Use* the **Trim** tool on the last **Tambo Loop** iteration and *click/drag* to the right until the region boundary ends at bar **97|000**.

11. Find the Fade In tool at the top-left corner of the **Tambo Loop** iterations and *click/drag* to the right until you have created a two-bar fade-in. The final product should now look like Figure 6.16.

12. *Select Command+S* (Mac) or *Ctrl+S* (PC) to save.

The loop iterations as a unit act almost exactly as a single normal audio region would. The obvious exception is the ability to extend your loop iterations as far as you want with the Trim tool. A normal audio region, of course, would be limited to the length of the source audio file. Crossfades work much in the same manner, except they must be abutted to another audio region, Region loop, or Region group. Now that you have seen how Region loops can be edited as a whole group, it's time to look at editing the iterations independently.

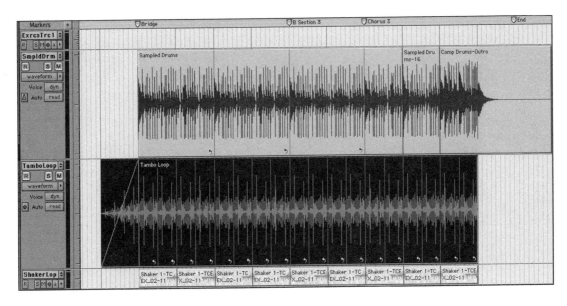

**Figure 6.16**
The two-bar fade-in performed on the first two Tambo Loop iterations.

## *Exercise 6.2.4 Editing Loop Iterations: Part 2*

The second way to edit Region loops is to edit the individual Region loop iterations. The loop iterations can be edited independently by selecting the tool you want to use and placing it over the small Region Loop icon. Each tool must be selected individually in the Tools section of the Edit window in order to work with the individual loop iterations. Because the Smart tool selects its tool based on the cursor position within the region, it will only serve to edit a set of iterations as shown in the previous exercise. In this exercise, you will explore a few possibilities for editing Region loop iterations independently.

1. *Select* **Ex 6.2.4** from the **Memory Locations** window. You are now back to the Sampled Drums at the Solo section of the song. To start, you will extend the loop iterations further into the Breakdown section with the Grabber tool.

2. *Select* the **Grabber** tool by *hitting Command+4* (Mac) or *Ctrl+4* (PC).

3. *Place* the **Grabber** tool over the **small Region Loop icon** in the lower-right corner of the second **Sampled Drums** iteration until it turns into a Loop icon and *click* once. You have now selected the individual iteration (see Figure 6.17).

4. *Hit* the **Delete** key (Mac) or **Backspace** key (PC) to delete the individual iteration.

5. Now *move* the **Grabber** tool over the **Region Loop icon** of the first **Sampled Drums** iteration until you see the **Loop** icon and *double-click*. You have now opened up the Region Loop dialog box.

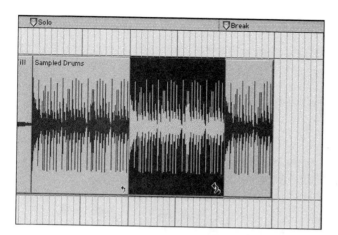

**Figure 6.17**

The Loop icon appears when the Grabber tool is moved over the Region Loop icon.

6. **Select** Number of Loops and *enter* the number **4**. *Click* on **OK** to add the iterations.

7. Switch to the **Selector** tool by *hitting Command+3* (Mac) or *Ctrl+3* (PC).

8. **Place** the **Selector** tool over the **Region Loop icon** of the last iteration you created, and you will see both the Selector tool and the Loop icon appear together (see Figure 6.18).

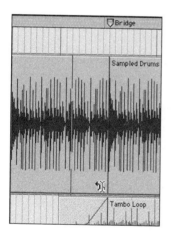

**Figure 6.18**

The Selector icon together with the Loop icon when the Selector tool is moved over the Region Loop icon.

9. *Click/drag* to the **left**, and you will select individual whole iterations as you drag across them. The Selector tool will be limited, however, to the members of that Region loop.

10. Finally, *select* B Section 3 from the **Memory Locations** window and *hit* the **right arrow** key on your keyboard to center the display on the end section of the song.

11. Now switch to the **Trim** tool by *hitting Command+2* (Mac) or *Ctrl+2* (PC).

12. *Place* the **Trim** tool over the **Region Loop icon** of the first iteration, starting at the **Bridge** section, until you see both the Trim tool and the Loop icon appear together. If you move the tool to the left along the bottom of the iteration, you will see that it changes its trim direction as the normal Trim tool would on an audio region (see Figure 6.19).

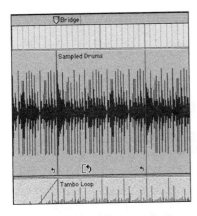

**Figure 6.19**
The Trim icon together with the Loop icon when the
Trim tool is moved to the bottom of the Region loop iteration.

13. *Move* the **Trim** icon back to the lower-right of the first **Sampled Drums** Region loop iteration at the **Bridge** section and *click/drag* to the **left** until the iteration length is half its normal size. *Release* the **mouse button**. Notice how the Region loop iterations, although half the length, still fill the same total bar count.

14. *Hit* the **spacebar** to audition and *select Command+S* (Mac) or *Ctrl+S* (PC) to save.

The ability to edit the individual Region loop iterations or the Region loop as a whole allows for many new editing possibilities. Occasionally, however, you might run into situations where you need to dissolve your Region loops. In such a situation, you need to unloop.

### Exercise 6.2.5 Unlooping Regions

If the whole Region loop editing thing has got you tied up in knots, or if you need to perform an editing task that is not allowed by the loop iterations, you might find that you need to unloop your iterations. When a Region loop is unlooped, you are given the choice to remove all iterations except for the first whole iteration, or to flatten them. Flattening a Region loop will turn the iterations into individual regions that can be edited without affecting their former bunkmates. Because the loop iterations are essentially a group of iterations, the Ungroup function in the Region menu will perform the same function as selecting Unloop and Flatten. The following exercise will clarify these options.

1. *Select* Ex 6.2.5 from the **Memory Locations** window. You will see the Acoustic Gtr_Vs Loop Region loop highlighted. In this exercise you will need to dissolve the Acoustic Guitar Region loop in the intro of the song. The Piano sample in the intro rubs with the second chord of the Acoustic Guitar. You will replace that section with a new Acoustic Guitar loop.

2. Select the **Smart** tool by *hitting Command+7* (Mac) or *Ctrl+7* (PC).

3. With the **Acoustic Gtr_Vs Loop** Region loop highlighted, *select* **Unloop** from the **Region** menu. You will be presented with the Unloop Regions dialog box, as shown in Figure 6.20.

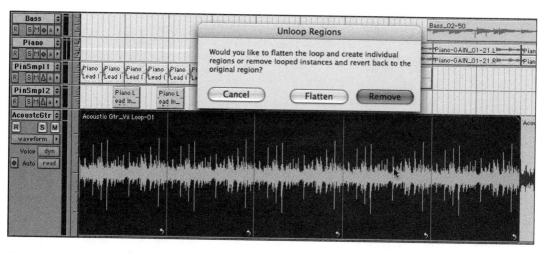

**Figure 6.20**
The Unloop Regions dialog box.

4. *Select* **Remove**. You will be left with only the first full iteration. The region no longer has a Region loop icon in the lower-right corner. It is now a standard audio region.

5. *Select Command+Z* (Mac) or *Ctrl+Z* (PC) to undo the Unloop function. The iterations will return.

6. Now *select* **Unloop** from the **Region** menu once more, and then *select* **Flatten** from the **Unloop Regions** dialog box. The selection of the Flatten function will result in the iterations being turned into separate standard audio regions. Notice that Region loop icon is no longer in the bottom-right corner of the region, and the region name now appears in each region.

7. *Double-click* with the **Selector** tool on the second **Acoustic Gtr Vs Loop** region to select it.

8. *Hit Shift+Return* (Mac) or *Shift+Enter* (PC) to select the region before it.

9. *Hit* the **Delete** key (Mac) or **Backspace** key (PC) to remove the selected regions.

10. Now open the **Regions list** by *clicking* once on the **double-arrow** at the bottom-right of the Edit window display, and *click/drag* the **Acoustic Gtr_Intro Loop** onto the **Acoustic Gtr** track at bar 11000.

11. *Press Option+Command+L* (Mac) or *Ctrl+Alt+L* (PC) and *enter 4* in the **Number of Loops** box. *Click* **OK**. The result will look like Figure 6.21.

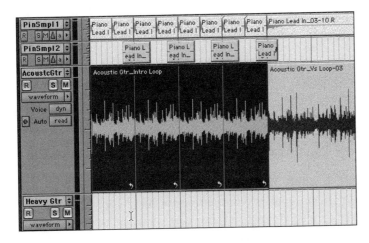

**Figure 6.21**

The new Acoustic Gtr Intro
Loop regions looped four times.

12. **Hit** the **Return** key (Mac) or the **Backspace** key (PC) to move the play cursor to the beginning of the session. **Hit** the **spacebar** to audition the edit.

13. **Select Command+S** (Mac) or **Ctrl+S** (PC) to save.

To this point in Chapter 6, you have uncovered the basics of good loop editing habits and the many ways they can be copied and pasted throughout a song. You expanded on these abilities with the Region looping feature, and the many ways Region loops can be manipulated and edited to achieve the desired result. Any tasks that cannot be performed with loop iterations can be unlooped to allow for all the normal region editing techniques discussed up to this chapter.

In the second half of this chapter, you will take the editing techniques you have learned up to this point and apply them in a more "musical" fashion. Dealing with the tempo and timing of a performance is an issue that no editor can avoid. Over-editing can render a performance lifeless, and not editing at all may leave a performance inconsistent and unfocused. In the following section, you will learn how best to deal with these issues.

# Tempo and Timing (Beat Detective)

With all the editing features available in Pro Tools that you have uncovered so far, it is hard to imagine how one could not accomplish any edit he or she desired if a little effort and creativity were thrown into the mix. It is human nature, however, to always want more than what is currently offered by a system once you become familiar enough with the way it works. It is this human nature that keeps the evolution process of nondestructive editing systems, such as Pro Tools, moving forward. All philosophical statements aside, everything you have done up to this point has involved a fixed tempo with regions mostly locked to mathematically defined grid lines. When you encounter or create music that is free of these rigid foundations, many of the editing features available soon become ineffective or limited in their capabilities. This section of the book will break

175

down the methods used to adapt the editing tools and features of Pro Tools to the tempo and timing variations that can make music so magical, and editing those performances such a nightmare.

To start, you will break down the way Pro Tools deals with tempo and timing issues and the basic logical design and flow of the software. By using many of these simplified tools, you will see how one can adapt tempo and timing issues on a smaller scale. Once you have assimilated this knowledge, Beat Detective will be much easier to understand. Beat Detective is really an amalgamation of many of these smaller tools combined and adapted with more sophisticated features.

## Tempo and Timing Issues

Many of the difficulties in editing audio are mainly derived from the fact that, in order to edit audio well, you must be one part musician, one part engineer, one part producer, and one part consumer. Every time an edit is performed or an arrangement is changed, you need to judge the musical content, perform the technical act, decide whether you have achieved the best result, and finally, sit back and judge it as if you have never heard it before in your life. Sybil would have been a great Pro Tools engineer!

Of course, the difficulty in presenting tempo and timing issues as technical skills is that tempo and timing are quite often more a matter of taste. With the practical examples given, I will try to present scenarios that will involve as many of these ways of interpreting audio as is practical. The focus of this section will be primarily on adapting a performance to tempo changes while preserving the groove or feel (timing). You will start with the basic editing features that allow this type of work to be performed, take careful note of the limitations, and build a foundation for the more advanced work with Beat Detective.

### Exercise 6.3.1 Tick- and Sample-Based Tracks

Anyone who has dealt with any kind of sequencing will tell you a simple fact about MIDI. It is tempo-based. This is not an earth-shattering realization, but a very important fact for us here. Because MIDI is tempo-based, when you change the tempo of your sequencer, everything will get compressed or expanded to adjust to the new tempo change without changing the pitch. Historically, the problem with audio was that changing the tempo had always necessitated a change in pitch. In other words, you didn't have a choice! In the analog tape world, once a track was recorded, the only way to change the tempo was to re-record or change the tape speed. This was called *varispeed*. To this day, varispeed still exists in Pro Tools|HD systems; changing the tempo in effect just changes the sample frequency and thus also changes the pitch. To change the tempo without changing the pitch in real time over the course of many tracks is, as of the writing of this book, not feasible because it would require too much processing power to perform practically in real time and not negatively affect the sound quality. As a result, all time compression/expansion processing needed to be done offline. Once the file is processed, it can be inserted into the new tempo grid on the correct bar number and mapped evenly to the tempo change.

To sum this up more practically, the majority of the existence of audio recording in digital audio workstations has always been *time-based*. In other words, if an audio file was recorded at 30 seconds, it would remain at 30 seconds regardless of any change in tempo. It may be at bar 15 at one tempo and at bar 14 beat 2 tick 231 at another tempo, but it would still be at 30 seconds. The bottom line was, once an audio track was recorded, you were pretty much stuck at that tempo. Otherwise, you would have to face hours of painstaking editing work, re-record everything at the new tempo, suffer the artifacts of time compression/expansion processing or varispeed the song and just deal with the change in pitch.

To deal with this issue, Pro Tools added a feature that allows audio tracks to be tick-based or sample-based. An audio track may be set to a tick- or sample-based configuration at any time. If the track is set to tick-based, an audio region that starts on bar 15 will stay at bar 15 when the tempo is changed. If it is sample-based, the region will remain at its clock time location to the exact sample, and ignore any change in tempo. It is important to note here that this, by no means, solves all our problems. When set to tick-based, a change in tempo will not time compress or expand the content of an audio region. As always, an example may best serve our cause.

1. ***Select* Ex 6.3.1** from the **Memory Locations** window. You will see two identical Sampled Drums regions. Notice that both regions start at bar 115I000 and also fall exactly on 5:42 clock time. The difference between the two tracks is a little icon in the Track Name section of the track display. The icon is located directly to the left of the Auto selection. A click/hold will result in a pop-up window just like the one in Figure 6.22.

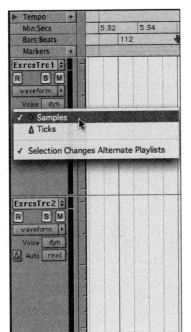

**Figure 6.22**

The sample- or tick-based pop-up window selector.

The icon on each track will display either the Tick or Sample icon so that you are aware at all times of its selection. A sample-based track will have a small blue clock displayed. A tick-based track will have small green metronome displayed.

2. *Click* once on the small **+ sign** at the right of the Tempo button in the **Timeline** bar, as shown in Figure 6.23. This will result in a Tempo Change dialog box. The Location number will default to the play cursor position, which was selected with the Ex 6.3.1 Memory Location.

**Figure 6.23**

The cursor over the Add Tempo Change button and the resultant pop-up window.

3. *Enter* **90.0000** in the **BPM** box and *click* **OK**. Notice how the top region remains at its clock time of 5:42 because it is set to sample-based. The bottom region remains on bar 115|000 because it is set to tick-based. The region length, however, does not change.

4. *Hold* the **Option** key (Mac) or the **Alt** key (PC) and *click* once on the **Tempo Change** marker in the **Timeline** bar at bar 113 to delete it. The regions will, once again, both start at bar 115 and at a clock time of 5:42.

If you are adapting a region to a tempo change and you want the region to follow, then set your track to be tick-based. If you are adapting a tempo to line up with a performance or if the audio is not tempo-related, then you want it to be sample-based so that the region does not move with the tempo changes.

With the concept of adapting audio regions to tempo changes, two companies forged a path that changed the way people worked with audio, particularly loops. The advent of tick-based tracks by Pro Tools is a result of the work of these two companies and the success of their products. The next exercise will look at what they have done and how Pro Tools has adapted to this way of working.

### Exercise 6.3.2 Using ACID and REX Loops

ACID files, created by Sony Media Software, and REX files, created by Propellerhead Software, were designed for applications that work specifically with loop-based audio. The wonderful thing about these applications is the ease with which a loop can be adapted in real time to tempo changes without inordinate amounts of processing power. ACID and REX file loops actually store tempo information within the data file itself. This allows them the unique ability to adapt to tempo changes created within the editing application.

The way this is accomplished is by simply cutting up the data into rhythmic segments called *slices.* The host application then quantizes or grids these slices to the new session's tempo so they will play back in time. Because the original file contains tempo information, it will know where to place the slices musically in order to preserve the original timing of the loop. Pro Tools now supports such activity. When a REX or ACID file is imported into Pro Tools, it is converted into a Region group, and the individual slices are converted to audio files and regions. Once converted and placed on a tick-based track, it is adapted to the session tempo. The following exercise will take you through this process.

Before you begin this exercise you must first download the ACID an REX loops from the course website. Visit www.courseptr.com/downloads, type in the name of this book, my name or the ISBN number and download the files. Place them in the folder along with the other files for this chapter

1. *Select* Ex 6.3.2 from the **Memory Locations** window. The Edit window will now display a blank track labeled ACID_REX Loops.

2. *Open* the **Workspace** window by *selecting* **Workspace** from the **Window** menu. *Locate* the ACID and REX files folder you downloaded from the Course website and *double-click* on it to open into a separate window. You should see two loops—an ACID loop and a REX loop, as shown in Figure 6.24.

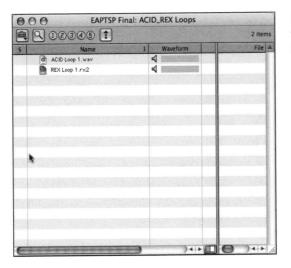

**Figure 6.24**

The ACID_REX Loops folder as displayed by the Pro Tools Workspace browser.

3. **Drag** this **display** over to the right of your screen to allow you to see the Edit window display as much as possible. Close the **Main Workspace** window if it is in the way by *clicking* once on the **red circle** at the top-left corner. Your display should look like Figure 6.25.

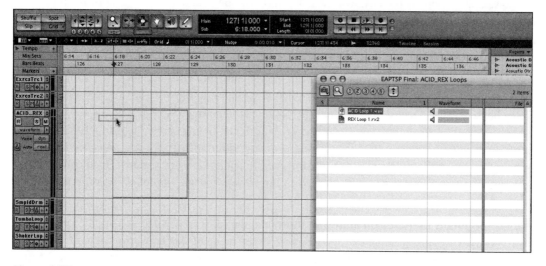

**Figure 6.25**

The Workspace browser window over the Edit window. The ACID Loop 1 region is being dragged onto the Edit window display.

4. *Click/drag* the **ACID Loop 1** file from the **Workspace** window to the **Edit** window display and *drop* it on the **ACID_REX Loops** track at bar **1271000**, as shown in Figure 6.25. Once dropped, the file will resize itself automatically to the session tempo. If you have trouble with the Workspace browser, you might find it easier to drag/drop the regions from your Mac Finder or Windows Explorer window.

5. Now *click/drag* the **REX Loop 1** file from the **Workspace** window to the **Edit** window display and *drop* it on the **ACID_REX Loops** track at bar **1301000**. Once dropped, the REX file will also resize itself automatically to the session tempo.

   It is important to note that the only reason the loop will resize itself to the session tempo is because the track is set to tick-based, not sample-based. The displayed region will look exactly like a Region group because it is, in fact, a Region group! As you might recall, a Region loop can contain many smaller regions beneath it, which is also the case here.

6. **Select** the **REX Loop 1** Region group and then *hit Option+Command+U* (Mac) or *Ctrl+Alt+U* (PC) to ungroup the region. The result will reveal a series of regions that make up the REX file loop. As noted at the beginning of this exercise, ACID and REX files contain slices that will line up automatically to their specific musical locations in the bar to the specified tempo. When imported into Pro Tools, the slices will become regions and will then be contained as a Region group.

7. Zoom in by *hitting Command+]* (Mac) or *Ctrl+]* (PC) twice.

8. *Click* once on the **small + sign** to the right of the **Tempo** button in the **Timeline** bar and *enter* **75.0000** into the **Tempo Change** dialog box. *Click* **OK**. Notice how the region automatically adapts to the new tempo change. The difference in length can be seen in the selection area, which remains the same.

9. *Click* once with the **Selector** tool before the **REX Loop 1** region and *hit* the **spacebar** to audition.

10. *Hold* the **Option** key (Mac) or **Alt** key (PC) and *click* once on the **Tempo Change** marker in the **Timeline bar** at bar **130** to delete the tempo change. The REX loop will once again resize back to the session tempo.

11. *Hit* the **spacebar** once again to audition the REX loop at the session tempo.

This basic tempo-adapting principle of edited regions on tick-based tracks may be performed in Pro Tools as well. In the following exercises, you will look at some of the ways you can separate and conform regions to the session tempo.

### Exercise 6.3.3 Separate Regions at Transients

The Separate Regions at Transients function is a quick and simple feature that creates region separation points at transient hits. Once the file is separated, the individual regions may be adapted to the session tempo or to tempo changes when placed on a tick-based track.

1. *Select* **Ex 6.3.3** from the **Memory Locations** window. You will see a selected Tambo Loop region on the Exercise track.

2. *Click/hold* on the **Edit** menu and *select* **Separate Region/At Transients**, as shown in Figure 6.26. You will be presented with a Pre Separate Amount dialog box. The purpose of this box is to leave a cushion at the beginning of each transient peak. This is sometimes necessary to protect against clipping the attack of a sound that does not exhibit a sharp transient attack, such as a bass or a vocal.

3. *Leave* the **Pre Separate Amount** at **0 mSec** and *click* **OK**. The result of this edit will leave you with a series of region separations at the transient hits of the Tambo Loop.

4. Upon close examination, you will notice that the fifth Tambo hit has an extra region separation that is not associated with a specific hit. When this happens, it must be removed separately. *Hit* the **Tab** key (Mac or PC) five times to cue the cursor up to the false separation and *hit* **Command+H** (Mac) or **Ctrl+H** (PC) to heal the separation.

Verifying your separation points is very important. The reasoning will become even more obvious once you start conforming these separations to grid lines. If the region separation points are not in their proper places, you might have false regions that interfere with the proper ones.

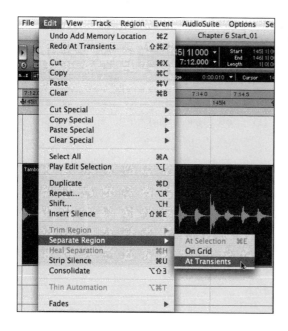

**Figure 6.26**
The Separate Region/At Transients feature selected from the Edit menu.

5. Now *place* the **cursor** just before the first **Tambo Loop** region separation and *click* once with the **Selector** tool. Because you are in Grid mode, the play cursor will be flashing at the head of the first region, bar 145l0000.

6. *Click* once on the small + **sign** to the right of the Tempo button in the **Timeline** bar. *Enter* **85.0000** into the **Tempo Change** dialog box and *click* OK. Because the tempo has increased, notice how the regions will overlap each other to adapt to the new tempo, just as the REX and ACID files did (see Figure 6.27).

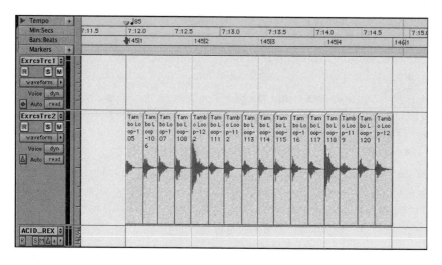

**Figure 6.27**
The Tambo Loop conformed to the faster tempo. Notice the folds at the top-left corner of each region, indicating a region overlap.

7. *Hit* the **spacebar** to audition the Tambo Loop at the faster tempo.

8. *Click* once on the small **+ sign** to the right of the Tempo button once again, enter **75.0000** into the **Tempo Change** dialog box, and *click* **OK**. Now the regions separate, leaving a space in between.

9. *Hit* the **spacebar** to audition the Tambo Loop at the slower tempo.

At this point you could create a Region group that would adapt to any tempo change when placed on a tick-based track. But before you do that, you will need to look at a few other features that may help you deal with some constancy issues. Quantizing regions is up next.

### Exercise 6.3.4 Quantize to Grid

Once regions are created on a track, they can be adapted to Grid lines on the Edit window display by selecting Quantize to Grid. The grid resolution will determine where selected regions will be moved. So set your grid resolution carefully! If you need to adapt to sixteenth-note triplets, then you must set your grid resolution to sixteenth-note triplets. A little music theory knowledge will be helpful when using this feature. The following exercise will allow you to adapt this very important concept into your Pro Tools editing knowledge base.

1. *Select* Ex 6.3.4 from the **Memory Locations** window. You are right where you left off in the last exercise. To start, you will need to select a finer grid resolution than quarter notes. Because the Tambo Loop part is a sixteenth-note rhythm, this might be a good place to start.

2. *Click* once on the small **down arrow** next to the **Grid** value display directly below the **Main Counter** and *select* **sixteenth notes** (see Figure 6.28).

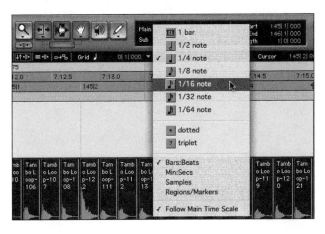

**Figure 6.28**
The grid resolution is set to sixteenth notes.

3. Next you will need to select all of the Tambo Loop regions. *Click* with the **Selector** tool just before the first **Tambo Loop** region and *drag* to the right until all the regions are selected.

4. *Click* on the **Region** menu and *select* **Quantize to Grid**. All the selected regions will now move their region start to the nearest grid line.

5. *Hit* the **spacebar** to audition the quantized Tambo Loop.

Now that you have quantized your regions, you might have been left with gaps between your regions that may create clicking or popping issues. The next exercise will show you how to deal with this problem in a quick and easy manner.

### Exercise 6.3.5 Trim to Fill (Gaps)

Trim Region Start to Fill Selection or Trim Region End to Fill Selection are features that fill the gaps that may be created when quantizing or adapting regions to a new tempo. The difference between the Start to Fill and End to Fill is simple. Imagine using your Trim tool, grabbing the start of a region, and moving it to the left until you reached the previous region boundary. This is Trim Region Start to Fill Selection. If you were to use the Trim tool at the end of a region and trim to the right up to the start of the next region boundary, this would be Trim Region End to Fill Selection. The audio material being edited will determine which feature will best suit the task. When editing separated percussive loops that are slowed down in tempo, it is typical that the Region Start to Fill Selection is used. The reason for this is simple. If you edit the end of a region to the next region boundary, you will be exposing the next hit early, and thus you will end up with a double hit or a flam.

1. *Select* **Ex 6.3.5** from the **Memory Locations** window. The all-too-familiar Tambo Loop will rear its head once again because you have not finished your work yet.

   Tucked away deep in the Edit menu is a feature called Trim Region. Once it is clicked on, a variety of options will come up to allow region-trimming tasks to be automated over a selected range of regions (see Figure 6.29).

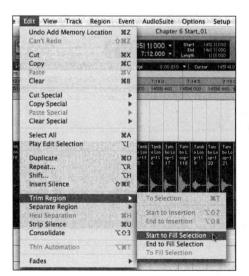

**Figure 6.29**

The options for the Trim Region selection in the Edit menu.

2. From the **Edit** menu *select* **Trim Region / Start to Fill Selection** and view the results in the Edit window. Notice how the region starts are trimmed back to the ends of the previous regions. The amount by which you can get away with doing this will vary depending on the degree of tempo change and the complexity of the material being trimmed.

3. *Hit* the **spacebar** to audition the Trim to Filled Tambo Loop.

### *Exercise 6.3.6 Identify Beat and Bar | Beat Markers*

Identify Beat is a quick, one-stop operation for extracting average tempo information from a region. Identify Beat is basically a tempo calculator that compares the number of beats against the selection length and calculates an average tempo. The accuracy of the tempo calculation is subject to the accuracy of the selection area, the identification of an exact beat count, and the consistency of the tempo within the selection area. When all are in good order, Identify Beat is a valuable tool for quickly setting a session's tempo to that of your region.

1. *Select* **Ex 6.3.6** from the **Memory Locations** window. You will see a selected Sampled Drums loop region that is four bars in length. A quick comparison of the grid marks will tell you that the loop is at a different tempo than the session. In this scenario you will need to adapt the session tempo to that of the selected region.

2. *Select* **Identify Beat** from the **Event** menu. A pop-up menu will open. It is the Add Bar | Beat Markers dialog box. In this box you will enter the necessary information that will allow the Identify Beat feature to generate an average tempo for the selection (see Figure 6.30).

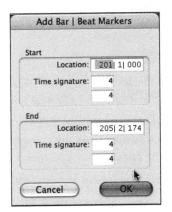

**Figure 6.30**

The Add Bar|Beat Markers dialog box.

The entry times are critical for accurate tempo calculation. The selection area Start and End Location times will automatically be filled in with the selection of the Identify Beat command. The issue, of course, is that these times are calculated based off of the *current* session tempo. With that in mind, it is best to place the region start exactly on the downbeat of a bar if possible.

Once the selected region's start time is exactly on a bar, then the rest is math. If the selection area is four bars long *musically*, then add four bars to the Start Location number and enter that value into the End Location field. Remember, because the region is at a different tempo than the session, all of your visual *length* cues on the Edit window are invalid.

Because the vast majority of modern music maintains a 4/4 time signature, it might be easy to overlook the Time Signature field and assume that Pro Tools knows what is going on musically. So whenever you happen across a waltz or one of those pieces in 7/8, make sure you remember to enter that value in the Time Signature field.

3. *Enter 2051000* into the **End Location** field.

4. *Click* **OK** on the **Add Bar | Beat Markers** dialog box and watch the grid lines lock to your region boundaries, as shown in Figure 6.31. A new tempo of 74.4993 BPM is created to reflect the selection area against the entered data.

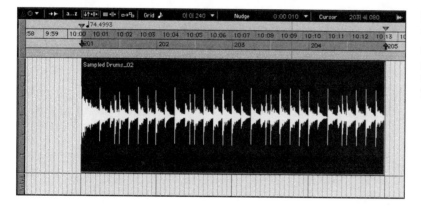

**Figure 6.31**

The result of a correctly executed Identify Beat command. Notice the newly calculated tempo in the Tempo bar.

If the tempo within the selection varies, you can adapt for this by inserting Bar | Beat markers. The process for creating Bar | Beat markers is similar to the Identify Beat command except that you are not creating a selection area, but rather just an insertion point.

5. To make the process a little easier, *click* once on the small **down arrow** next to the **Grid** value display directly below the **Main Counter** and above the Timeline bar and *select* **?** **note**.

6. Now *click* once on the **Sampled Drums** region with the **Selector** tool at bar **2031000**.

7. *Hit Command+]* (Mac) or *Ctrl+]* (PC) 10 times to zoom in to the new cursor position.

8. *Hold* the **Command** key (Mac) or **Ctrl** key (PC) and *click* once with the **Selector** tool, as close as you can to the beginning of the transient peak, as shown in Figure 6.32.

9. *Hit Command+I* (Mac) or *Ctrl+I* (PC) to open the **Add Bar | Beat Markers** dialog box. This is the shortcut for the Identify Beat command as well as the Bar | Beat marker generation. They are, in fact, one and the same.

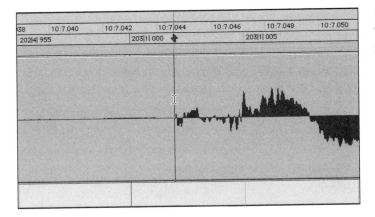

**Figure 6.32**

The Selector tool creating an insertion point at the head of the transient peak.

10. *Enter 2031000* in the **Location Field** and *click* OK. A new tempo marker will be created.

11. Now, *hit Command+[* (Mac) or *Ctrl+[* (PC) 10 times to zoom out for an overview of the region and tempo changes. As you can see, there now is a tempo change two bars into the selection region. If you really wanted to go crazy with this feature, you could map out the tempo changes bar by bar, beat by beat using this method.

In this scenario, one could tempo map a couple of bars that would follow the swing or groove of a drum loop and then copy and paste the loop with those tempo changes throughout the song. All future editing work in Grid mode would then lock to the swing or groove of the loop.

I'm sure at this point you are ready to explode with a laundry list of "what if I wanted to do [fill in the blank]." I have purposely not expressed any of the limitations of any of the editing features discussed in this section because they are specifically meant to be simple for simple scenarios.

For example, the Separate Regions at Transients feature does not offer a threshold to help prevent false separations. The Quantize to Grid feature does not offer a percentage value to vary the degree of quantization. The Identify Beat feature will only calculate an average tempo, and thus requires you to manually enter tempo changes within the selection area for a truly accurate mapping. All these shortcomings, of course, eventually lead to a solution for all these issues. That solution is Beat Detective. The remainder of this chapter will deal with the extensive capabilities of this invaluable tool for dealing with tempo and timing issues.

## Beat Detective Basics

In October of 2004, Pro Tools made an announcement that completely changed the world of editing audio for LE users. The announcement was the inclusion of Beat Detective in their version 6.7 software. If there is such a thing as a Holy Grail in the world of nondestructive editing, then Beat Detective must be it. For years, nondestructive editing was only really practical for songs that were cut to a click track or programmed with a sequencer. Although it was certainly possible to edit songs that were cut without a click track, many of the editing features that were designed specifically for editing to grids and defined tempo maps were rendered almost entirely useless.

The two problems commonly faced when dealing with live performances were adapting the performance to an existing tempo map or defining a tempo map from the live performance. In either case, the work had to be done manually, bar by bar, beat by beat—a long, grueling, and tedious process, to say the least! Beat Detective broke down those barriers by allowing one to adapt and automate those tasks that would typically take hours to perform one at a time.

### Exercise 6.4.1 Creating a Selection

For Beat Detective to work properly, an accurately defined Selection area must first be created. It is this Selection area that sets the stage for all future calculations. The Detection and Operation sections of the Beat Detective window will only work accurately if the Selection area is properly set up. This exercise will focus on the Selection section of the Beat Detective window.

1. **Select** Ex 6.4.1 from the **Memory Locations** window.

2. **Open** the **Beat Detective** window by **selecting** Beat Detective from the **Event** menu (see Figure 6.33).

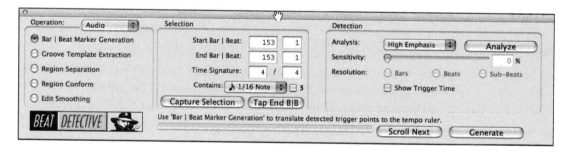

**Figure 6.33**

The Beat Detective window.

The Selection area is located at the center of the Beat Detective display. Regardless of the selected operation, the Selection section of the Beat Detective window will remain the same. The Selection section requires the entry of information relevant to the Selection area in the Edit window. The Start Bar | Beat, End Bar | Beat, and Time Signature areas operate identically to the Identify Beat window. The Contains selector will give Beat Detective information about the rhythmic content of the Selection area.

Whenever you are capturing a selection in this area, it is important to note what rhythmical values are contained within the Selection area. For example, if the selection contains sixteenth notes, then you should select sixteenth notes from the Contains selector. If the selection contains triplets or swung notes, then selecting the box between the Contains selector and the 3 will let Beat Detective know that triplets or swung notes are contained in the Selection area.

The way this area is set will depend on one basic factor: Is the content of the Selection area the same as the session tempo or at a different tempo? The following two examples will clarify the way the Selection section may be used in either scenario.

When the Selection area is the same as the session tempo, the easiest way to set up the Selection section of the Beat Detective window is with the Capture Selection feature.

3.  *Click* once on the **Sampled Drums_03** region with the **Grabber** tool.

4.  From the **Selection** section of the **Beat Detective** window, *click* once on the **Capture Selection** button. The selection start and end times are automatically entered into the Start Bar | Beat and End Bar | Beat fields.

    As long as the Contains field is accurate to the content of the Selection area, you are finished with the Selection section of the Beat Detective window!

    The second scenario involves defining the length of a Selection area whose content is *not* at the session tempo. When working in this situation, it is important to remember that the End Bar | Beat value will not be the same as the grid markings or bar numbers in the Edit window, but rather the bar number as defined by the *musical content* of the selection. There are two basic ways to define the length of a selection area.

5.  *Hit Command+[* (Mac) or *Ctrl+[* (PC) once to zoom out.

6.  *Click* once on the **Sampled Drums_02** region with the **Grabber** tool and *hit* the **right arrow** to move the selected region into the display area.

    If you are not sure of the selection length, the Tap End BB will help define the total number of beats. The concept of this feature is to calculate the length of a selection area by clicking on the Tap End B | B button in time with the Selection area while it is in play. The rate of the taps versus the Selection area length will determine the End Bar | Beat value. It is most important that you tap in time with the music and not concern yourself with starting exactly on the start of the region. The calculation is based on the rate of the taps, not what bar numbers they represent in the Selection area.

7.  Before you begin, you must enter the **Start Bar | Beat** value. *Enter* bar **159** and *hit* the **Return** key (Mac) or **Enter** key (PC).

8.  *Hit* the **spacebar** to play the region and *click* on the **Tap End B | B** button in time with the song until the **End Bar | Beat** value finds a value of **165|1** (see Figure 6.34).

189

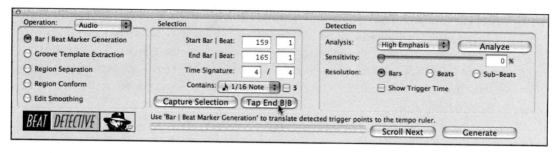

**Figure 6.34**

The correct End Bar | Beat value using the Tap End B | B button.

The accuracy of this feature is entirely dependent on the accuracy and consistency of your tapping. This might be helpful when you are dealing with long selection areas of undefined length.

The second method is simple. If you happen to know the exact length of your selection area in bars and beats, then you can enter those values into the Start Bar | Beat and End Bar | Beat fields manually. If the selection area starts on a bar other than bar 1 beat 1, it will be important to enter that exact bar number in the Start Bar | Beat field. Otherwise, if you are attempting to extract a tempo map, you will end up renumbering your bar numbers inadvertently.

Although it is a common practice to select the operation before defining the selection area, it will not change the way Beat Detective functions. The reason you defined the selection area first is that it is a natural extension from the Identify Beat exercise. In addition, the Operation and Detection windows are inextricably interconnected. To understand more about the capabilities of Beat Detective, you will need to understand the Operation section of Beat Detective.

### Selecting the Operation

Beat Detective offers a variety of unique editing features for all your tempo and timing needs. The Operation section of the Beat Detective window is where you select the function that best suits your needs. Beat Detective can be used on MIDI or audio data to perform a variety of automated editing tasks. The choice of Audio or MIDI is selected at the top of the Operation section of the Beat Detective window. For the purposes of this book, you will concentrate solely on the audio selection (see Figure 6.35).

With audio selected as the option, you have five available operations at your fingertips. The first two selections, Bar | Beat Marker Generation and Groove Template Extraction, are used to extract tempo or groove information from a selection area. The latter three allow you to separate and adapt selected regions to tempo maps and groove templates. In short, you are either extracting information from a selection or adapting information to a selection.

**Figure 6.35**
The audio/MIDI selection and the Operations section of the Beat Detective window.

The Bar|Beat Marker Generation feature will typically be used to generate tempo change information from material that was not performed to a click track. The changes in tempo can be tracked measure by measure, beat by beat, or sub-beat by sub-beat. Each selection will give you greater degrees of tempo variation and will be more accurate to the original performance. If the tempo extraction is being used to smooth out or create a consistency with the tempo across the whole song, then mapping measure by measure might be a better start point.

Groove template extraction is used to create a template by which other regions may be conformed. Groove is a magical mix of rhythmical content that creates a sense of movement or flow. It captures listeners and draws them into a song, makes their head move, their feet tap in time, or their body sway. It gets people out of their chairs and onto the dance floor before they are consciously aware of what they are doing. Because groove is such an important part of music, much effort has been put into capturing these variations of rhythm for later use. Without getting into a whole new chapter on what groove is, it is sufficient to say that it very rarely falls exactly on your comfy little mathematical bar and beat lines. This relative timing to the beat can be mapped and stored for later use. The concept of the Groove Template feature is that the groove information can be extracted from the audio and then used to adapt to later performances.

The last three selections also fall into a similar category. Region Separation, Region Conform, and Edit Smoothing are usually used together and typically in that exact order. Region Separation is essentially a more sophisticated version of the Separate Regions at Transients feature. The additional selections of the Generate section of Beat Detective will greatly enhance its accuracy and help limit the number of false triggers.

Region Conform is a process of quantizing or mapping regions to a tempo map or groove template. What's left over after the separation and conforming is a series of regions that, as a result of the conforming, may have gaps that cause audible clicks or pops. Edit Smoothing provides the tools to spackle up those gaps with batch selection Fill and Crossfade tools.

Once an operation is selected, a variety of parameters in the Detection section of the Beat Detective window will appear. The parameters for this section will vary depending on the selected operation. The next exercise will detail what these features are and how they are used.

## Tempo Extraction and Groove Templates

There are many occasions in which a performance containing drastic tempo changes will lose its dramatic effect if quantized to a strict tempo. It may also be that the way a performance swings, pushes, or pulls the beat has a life of its own and is worth mapping as a template to clean up other sections that are not quite as "groovy." It is precisely for occasions such as these that understanding the power of Beat Detective's Bar | Beat Marker Generation and Groove Template Extraction features will be an invaluable resource.

The following exercises will illustrate the process of extracting tempo information and creating groove templates.

### Exercise 6.5.1 Bar | Beat Marker Generation

The Detection area of the Beat Detective window will change depending on the selection in the Operation section of the Beat Detective window. Once an operation is selected, the parameters that arise will allow you to adapt Beat Detective to your audio or MIDI selection area and achieve the desired result. Let's break them down one by one.

1. *Select* Ex 6.5.1 from the **Memory Locations** window. You will see a four-bar drum loop region.

2. *Select* **Beat Detective** from the **Event** menu.

3. *Enter* 172  1 in the **Start Bar | Beat** box and 176  1 in the **End Bar | Beat** box. *Hit* **Return** (Mac) or **Enter** (PC).

4. *Verify* that the **Time Signature** is set to **4/4** and the **Contains** parameter is set to **1/16 Note**.

5. *Select* **Bar | Beat Marker Generation** from the **Operation** section of the **Beat Detective** window. Whether Bar | Beat Marker Generation, Groove Template Extraction, or Region Separation is selected, the following parameters will become available in the Detection section, as shown in Figure 6.36.

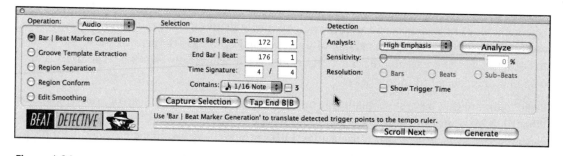

**Figure 6.36**

The parameters of the Detection section of the Beat Detective window when Bar | Beat Marker Generation is selected.

The Analysis parameter of the Detection section will help Beat Detective accurately define and generate accurate Bar | Beat markers for your Bar | Beat markings or groove templates. There are two selections available—High Emphasis and Low Emphasis (see Figure 6.37).

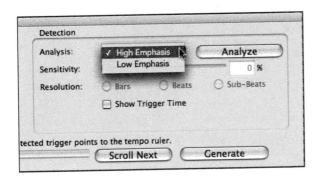

**Figure 6.37**
The Analysis parameter options.

If the majority of the material to be analyzed is percussive in nature and has a good amount of high-frequency content, then High Emphasis should be your selection. Most high-frequency drum and percussion material is best analyzed with High Emphasis. If the selection area content has a majority of low-frequency content, such as bass guitars, kick drums, and low frequency–based percussion instruments, then Low Emphasis is the better selection. When percussion or drums are mixed with high- and low-frequency elements, it is usually best to analyze both ways to see which form of analysis works best.

6. *Select* **High Emphasis** as the **Analysis** setting and *select* the **Analyze** button. The parameters directly below the Analysis selector will now be available for editing. First up, the Sensitivity setting.

The Sensitivity setting operates as a threshold to determine the Bar | Beat markings or groove template Beat Triggers. It is usually set to 0% and then moved upward until the Beat Triggers look correct on the selected region. The number and placement of those Beat Triggers will be determined by the Resolution setting. If you are attempting to generate Bar | Beat Markers to extract tempo information from the selected material, then the resolution should be set to bars or beats. If you are looking to generate a groove template, then Sub-Beats is your choice because you will be trying to capture the push, pull, or swing of a performance, which is contained in the sub-beat information.

7. *Select* **Bars** as the **Resolution** and *move* the **Sensitivity** slider to the right until four yellow lines appear across the region. The first of those lines will reside at the beginning of the selection area and is sometimes hard to see. These lines are called *Beat Triggers*, and they show bar delineations. If you select the Show Trigger Time box, the mapped Bar | Beat time will be displayed in addition to the Beat Triggers (see Figure 6.38).

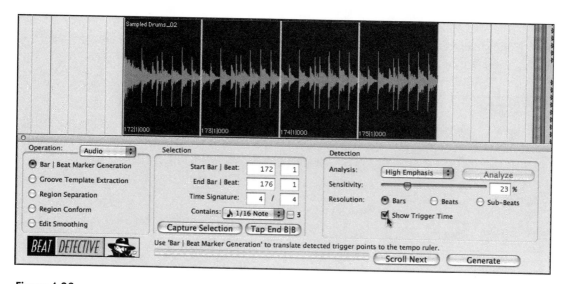

**Figure 6.38**

Generated Beat Triggers with the Resolution set to Bars. The trigger times are displayed at each Beat Trigger.

8. Now *select* **Beats** as the **Resolution** and *move* the **Sensitivity** slider to the right until **Beat Triggers** are displayed for each beat. Notice how the Beat Trigger lines are thinner for the beats than they are for the bars.

9. Finally, *select* **Sub-Beats** as a **Resolution** and *move* the **Sensitivity** slider up to 52%. A *sub-beat* is any rhythmical value that is smaller than quarter notes. Notice how each individual transient peak now has a Beat Trigger. Notice how the Beat Trigger lines for sub-beats are narrower than the Beat Trigger lines for the beats.

This is very simple example of proper Beat Trigger detection. If the selection area is properly defined, the beat triggers are usually generated properly. If the rhythmic content has greater inconsistencies within the selection area, however, then you may have difficulty getting properly defined Beat Triggers. When this problem arises, you may need to edit them manually. Even when the Beat Triggers seem to be generated easily, as in the preceding example, it is worth a closer look to verify that they are placed exactly on the transient peak. The next exercise will run you through a little Beat Trigger editing boot camp.

## Exercise 6.5.2 Editing Beat Triggers

Editing Beat Triggers is usually the one part of the Beat Detective process that scares people away the most. There are all these little yellow lines all over the place, and one false move can undo everything. I know, I can hear you! The sooner you dive into this process, however, the more satisfactory all of your Beat Detective work will be.

When Beat Triggers are missing, falsely generated, or not precisely placed by Beat Detective, it might be necessary to get your hands a little dirty and dig those suckers out one by one. The importance of verifying the accuracy of your Beat Triggers should not be underestimated. Accurate Beat Triggers will make your Tempo Mapping or Groove Template Extraction operations better and, by default, all your future editing better. This modest investment of your time and energy will pay dividends all the way to the finished product by making the rest of your work less complicated. The following exercise will take you through the process of deleting, adding, moving, promoting, and redefining Beat Triggers.

1. *Select* Ex 6.5.2 from the **Memory Locations** window. You will see a four-bar drum loop region.

2. *Select* **Bar | Beat Marker Generation** from the **Operations** section.

3. *Set* the **Analysis** to **High Emphasis** and *select* **Analyze**.

4. *Select* **Sub-Beats** as the **Resolution** and *move* the **Sensitivity** slider up to **68%**. This will create a series of extra Beat Triggers that do not serve a purpose. It is not uncommon for extra Beat Triggers to be generated when you are trying to generate valid Beat Triggers elsewhere in the selection.

5. *Select Command+]* (Mac) or *Ctrl+]* (PC) four times to zoom in to the beginning of the selection area.

6. *Hold* the **Option** key (Mac) or the **Alt** key (PC) and *move* the **cursor** over the first sub-beat. *Click* once on the **Beat Trigger** (see Figure 6.39).

   Occasionally, a properly created Beat Trigger will not fall exactly on a transient peak. When this occurs, the placement of the Beat Trigger can be manually moved into the correct position.

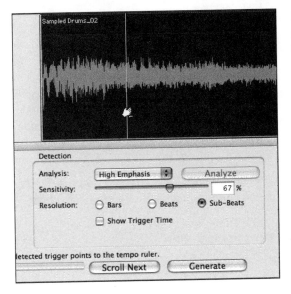

**Figure 6.39**
A false Beat Trigger being selected for deletion.
Notice the small minus sign next to the hand cursor.

7. **Select Command+]** (Mac) or **Ctrl+]** (PC) three times to zoom in, and then *click* once on the **Scroll Next** button at the bottom of the **Beat Detective** window. The screen display will move over to the next Beat Trigger. Holding the Option key (Mac) or Alt key (PC) when clicking on the Scroll Next button will move you to the previous Beat Trigger.

8. **Click/drag** the displayed **Beat Trigger** and move it left or right. Try to line it as close to the transient peak as possible, and *release*. You have now manually lined up a Beat Trigger.

9. **Select** Ex 6.5.2 from the **Memory Locations** window once again. This will clear the Beat Triggers.

10. **Set** the **Sensitivity** to 0% and *select* **Analyze** in the **Detection** section.

11. **Select** Beats as the **Resolution**.

12. **Raise** the **Sensitivity** setting to read **31%**. You can click in the value box and enter the percentage manually if desired. You will notice that one of the Beat Triggers is missing for beat 2 of the first measure of the selection. Occasionally, it is easier to add a missing trigger than it is to delete all of the extra false Beat Triggers that may be generated by the detection process.

13. **Select Command+]** (Mac) or **Ctrl+]** (PC) three times to zoom in.

14. **Move** the **hand cursor** over the second transient peak and *click* once to generate a **Beat Trigger** (see Figure 6.40).

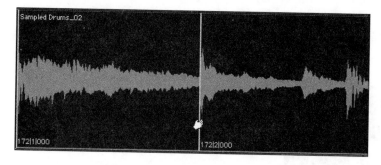

**Figure 6.40**

A Beat Trigger is added with a single click.

To prevent a Beat Trigger from being affected by the Sensitivity setting, it can be promoted. When a Beat Trigger is promoted, any Sensitivity setting other than a setting of 0% will not remove the Beat Trigger. A Beat Trigger can be promoted by Command+clicking (Mac) or Ctrl+clicking (PC) on the Beat Trigger.

15. **Command+click** (Mac) or **Ctrl+click** (PC) on the newly created **Beat Trigger** to promote it. Notice the small up arrow that appears inside the hand to indicate that the selected Beat Trigger will be promoted.

16. **Select Command+[** (Mac) or **Ctrl+[** (PC) four times to zoom out.

17. *Lower* the **Sensitivity** setting to 1%. Notice that all the Beat Triggers disappear except for the Promoted Beat Trigger. This is particularly handy when the sensitivity setting causes the number of false Beat Triggers to outnumber the missing Beat Triggers in a selection.

Now that you have gone through the process of creating and editing Beat Triggers, it's time to put them to a more practical use. A Beat Trigger on its own is only a setup so that an operation may be performed. Those operations are Generating Bar | Beat Markers, Extracting Groove Template, or performing Region Separation. In the next exercise, you will look at how to extract a tempo map from your beat markers.

## Exercise 6.5.2 Extracting a Tempo Map

When editing a live performance in Pro Tools it is often very helpful to extract a tempo map to allow for ease of editing when using Grid mode and tick-based tracks. Because live performances, even when cut with a click track, will drift in and out of time, it may be helpful to map out those variations so that any future work will have something to grab on to. Depending on the variations in tempo or the degree of editing work you are expecting to do, the Resolution setting in the Detection area will either be set to Bars or to Beats. Bars will give you more general tempo swings, and Beats will give you a new tempo for each beat. In the following exercise, you will lay out a short tempo map to give you some insight to the process.

1. *Select* Ex 6.5.3 from the **Memory Locations** window. This will clear the Beat Triggers.
2. *Select* Bar | Beat Marker Generation from the **Operation** section of the **Beat Detective** window.
3. *Enter* 172 1 in the **Start Bar | Beat** box and 176 1 in the **End Bar | Beat** box. *Hit* **Return** (Mac) or **Enter** (PC).
4. *Verify* that the **Time Signature** is set to 4/4 and the **Contains** parameter is set to 1/16 **Note**.
5. *Set* the **Analysis** to **High Emphasis** and *select* **Analyze**.
6. *Set* the **Resolution** to **Beats** and the **Sensitivity** setting to 52%. At this point it would normally be necessary to carefully view each Beat Trigger to verify that all are accounted for and are correctly placed. Because you have covered this process in a previous exercise, you will not go through it again here.
7. *Click* on the **Generate** button at the bottom of the **Beat Detective** window.

    You will be presented with a Realign Session dialog box. The selection here will determine what happens to regions on tick-based tracks that occur after the selection area. Because you will be changing the tempo, selecting Preserve Tick Position will make regions on tick-based tracks maintain their Bar | Beat tick location but will move them from their sample location. If you choose to Preserve Sample Position, regions on tick-based tracks will maintain their sample location but move from their Bar | Beat tick location.

What it all boils down to is this: If you are generating a tempo map section by section, from the beginning, select Preserve Sample Position. If you are mapping a new tempo grid that will follow throughout the remainder of the song, then select Preserve Tick Position. This way, your subsequent regions will stay on their Bar | Beat tick locations. This is especially true if you are dealing with REX and ACID loops that will adapt instantly to the new tempo settings (see Figure 6.41).

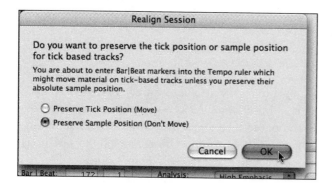

**Figure 6.41**

The Realign Session dialog box.

8. **Select Preserve Sample Position (Don't Move)** and **click** OK. You will now see a series of tempo changes in the Tempo bar for each beat. You have officially mapped a tempo for each beat.

9. **Hit Command+Z** (Mac) or **Ctrl+Z** (PC) once to undo the Bar | Beat Marker Generation. This will set you up for the next exercise.

Should you find a section of a performance that has a great feel to it, it might be worth storing this feel to be used in other sections of the song that don't quite feel as good. This concept is called *groove templates*, and extracting them is the focus of the next exercise.

## Exercise 6.5.4 Extracting a Groove Template

Groove templates have been around for quite some time in MIDI sequencing programs. Many of them were purely mathematically created swing variations that made eighth or sixteenth notes sound more like triplets. As technology developed, the ability to generate your own templates came to the forefront and opened up a whole new level of creative tools. When dealing with audio, however, this has never been such an easy matter. Adapting audio to a template must inherently involve a lot of additional editing work to smooth out the artifacts left by moving regions around. When the material is close enough in feel to be adapted, then the work can be done with a minimum amount of effort and artifacts. The creation of a groove template, therefore, must also be done with careful consideration. The next exercise will explain.

1. **Select** Ex 6.5.4 from the **Memory Locations** window. This will clear the Beat Triggers.

2. *Select* **Groove Template Extraction** from the **Operation** section of the **Beat Detective** window.

3. *Enter* 172 1 in the **Start Bar | Beat** box and 176 1 in the **End Bar | Beat** box. *Hit* **Return** (Mac) or **Enter** (PC).

4. *Verify* that the **Time Signature** is set to **4/4** and the **Contains** parameter is set to **1/16 Note**.

5. *Set* the **Analysis** to **High Emphasis** and *select* **Analyze**.

6. *Select* **Sub-Beats** as a **Resolution** and *set* the **Sensitivity** to **52%**.

7. *Click* on the **Extract** button. Carefully note that each transient hit is indeed accounted for.

8. *Click* on the **Extract** button. You will be presented with the Extract Groove Template dialog box, as shown in Figure 6.42.

**Figure 6.42**

The Extract Groove Template dialog box.

From this box you can Save to Groove Clipboard or Save to Disk. Once the template is stored in the Clipboard, it will be available for immediate use but not stored on disk. This option may be better if the template is unique or only usable for the current editing task. Save To Disk will store the groove template for later use.

9. *Select* **Save to Disk** and *name* the **groove template** "Sometimes Beat." It will be stored in the Grooves folder.

The processes of Bar | Beat Marker Generation and Groove Template Extraction are identical except for the very end. The Bar | Beat Marker Generation operation will remap the tempo of the session, and therefore each grid mark will reflect a direct connection to the source region. This method is most often used when there is no click or steady tempo source at the time of the performance. Groove Template Extraction is better used for sessions that maintain a steady tempo. The template will force regions to relative positions around the existing steady grid marks. This will require less editing work when moving regions to and from different sections of the song.

Of course, once you have a map or a tempo grid to adapt your regions to, Beat Detective will aid in the process of separating and conforming those regions to the new tempo map or groove template. In the next section, you will look at the equally powerful process of separating and conforming regions.

## Separating and Conforming Regions with Beat Detective

One of the most popular uses of Beat Detective is to separate audio regions into individual segments that can be adapted or quantized to a tempo map or grid. This work can range from tightening up a live drum performance that is a little loose to creating a completely different performance by extracting the main elements and completely reorganizing them. The process usually involves three main steps: Extract or separate the individual elements, adapt or quantize them to a tempo map, and smooth over the edit transitions to make it sound like it really happened that way!

The following exercises will break down this process step by step to help you understand more clearly each phase of the work.

### Exercise 6.6.1 Region Separation

Region Separation is the first stage of a three-step process to adapt regions to existing tempo maps or groove templates. The process involves the exact same parameters set forth with Bar|Beat Marker Generation or Groove Template Extraction. The only difference is that the regions will be adapting to a tempo or groove, not creating one.

1. *Select* Ex 6.6.1 from the **Memory Locations** window. This will clear the Beat Triggers.

2. If it is not already open, *select* Beat Detective from the **Event** menu.

3. *Select* Region Separation from the **Operation** section of the **Beat Detective** window.

4. *Enter* 185 1 in the **Start BarBeat** box and 189 1 in the **End Bar | Beat** box. *Hit* **Return** (Mac) or **Enter** (PC).

5. *Verify* that the **Time Signature** is set to **4/4** and the **Contains** parameter is set to **1/16 Note**.

6. *Set* the **Analysis** to **High Emphasis** and *select* **Analyze**.

7. *Set* the **Resolution** to **Sub-Beats** and the **Sensitivity** setting to **52%**. Remember, this Sensitivity setting works only for this particular region and would normally need to be carefully adjusted to set the correct Beat Triggers.

8. Now, *click* on the **Separate** button. You have now created a new region at each Beat Trigger location (see Figure 6.43).

9. *Hit Command+S* (Mac) or *Ctrl+S* (PC) to save.

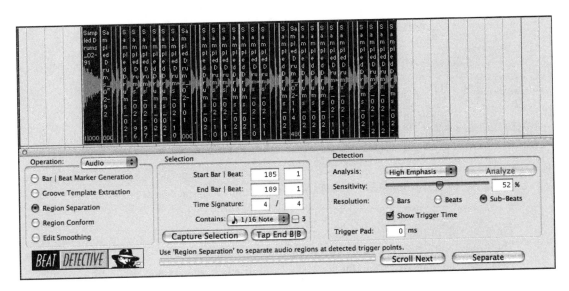

**Figure 6.43**
The region separations created by the Region Separation operation.

Once the regions are separated, they can be conformed to a new tempo map or groove template. It is critically important that the Beat Triggers are accurate so that any future work will be consistent in the way it responds when conformed. In the following exercise, you will finally get to conform this silly beat so you can use it in the song.

### Exercise 6.6.2 Region Conform

Conforming regions to a grid can actually be a fun and creative process. Unlike the Bar | Beat Marker Generation, Groove Template Extraction, and Region Separation operations, region conforming opens up a whole new palette of controls that will allow you to set just how much you want to conform by and what way to do it. Conforming can sometimes be made out to be a rigid, sterilizing, mathematical process that squeezes the life out of your music. On the flip side, it can also be a way of stabilizing a rhythm pattern for a song that relies on the consistency of that rhythm to drive the track. When taken to extremes, it can also create new patterns that did not previously exist.

The following exercise will explain the parameters that make this an incredibly valuable tool.

1. *Select* Ex 6.6.2 from the **Memory Locations** window.

2. *Select* **Region Conform** from the **Operation** section of the **Beat Detective** window. The Detection section will now become a Conform section and display a whole new set of parameters to adjust (see Figure 6.44).

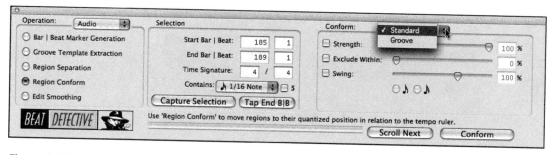

**Figure 6.44**

The Conform section of the Beat Detective window when the Region Conform operation is selected.

From the top of the Conform section, you can select Standard or Groove as your method. The Groove selection will bring you straight to the Grooves folder to select a groove template. The Standard selection will allow you to adapt your region separations to the session's tempo map.

The Strength setting will determine how aggressively Beat Detective will conform the regions. A setting of 100% will move the selected regions exactly to their assigned beat or sub-beat. A setting of 0% will preserve the original feel.

The Exclude setting will set a threshold for which regions will be moved. A lower percentage setting will only conform regions that are far away from their assigned beat or sub-beat. This is great way to fix inconsistencies in a performance without destroying the feel. A higher percentage will conform all selected regions.

The Swing setting will determine how far an eighth or sixteenth note will move toward its triplet counterpart. A setting of 0% will leave the regions unaffected. A setting of 100% will move the selected regions exactly to the triplet note counterpart. A setting of 150% will move the selected regions to the next sixteenth note value after the triplet when set to eighth notes.

To get a feel for the parameter settings and what they do, let's experiment with a couple of different Swing settings.

3.  *Select* **Standard** as the **Conform** method and *click* on the **Strength** and **Swing** boxes. *Set* the **Strength** to **100%** and the **Swing** to **0%**. *Select* the **Sixteenth** note icon, as displayed in Figure 6.45.

4.  Once you have verified your settings with Figure 6.45, *select* **Conform**. All of the regions will now adapt to the session tempo using the Swing and the Strength settings.

5.  *Hit* the **spacebar** to play the selection. Notice how the feel is very mechanical.

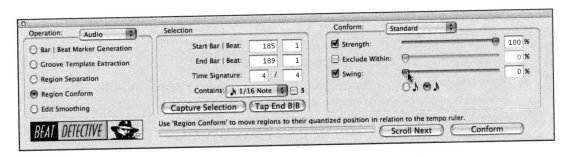

**Figure 6.45**
The settings for the Conform section of the Beat Detective window.

6. *Hit Command+Z* (Mac) or *Ctrl+Z* (PC) once to undo the conform. It is important to undo your previous conform before moving on to a new setting; otherwise, the settings will be based on something that has already been moved. This can leave you with unanticipated and inaccurate results, or it can leave you with something really cool!

7. Now *set* the **Swing** to 75%. And *click* on the **Conform** button once again and *hit* the **space-bar** to play the selection. Notice how the feel has a swing to it. As the regions move farther away from their original place, gaps will start to appear.

8. *Hit Command+Z* (Mac) or *Ctrl+Z* (PC) once to undo the conform, *set* the **Swing** to 150%, and *click* on the **Conform** button one last time.

9. *Hit* the **spacebar** to play the selection. At this setting, you are changing the rhythm pattern by moving the swing past the triplet and all the way to the next sixteenth note. You will find some noticeable gaps and artifacts. This, of course, will require a bit of smoothing to make it work.

10. *Hit Command+S* (Mac) or *Ctrl+S* (PC) to save.

Whenever a region is conformed with extreme parameters, such as you have just done, the artifacts created will needed to be smoothed out. Even when the parameter settings in the Conform section are fairly mild, you will find the need to fix and fill up your edits. Edit Smoothing offers just exactly these tools. In the following exercise, you will smooth out the edits on this drum loop so you can use it someplace in the song.

### Exercise 6.6.3 Edit Smoothing
Edit Smoothing is the final Beat Detective feature, but hardly the least important. Where most of the other tools in Beat Detective are used to hammer out tempos, templates, or separation and conforming functions, Edit Smoothing is more like applying that glossy finish to cover up all the more aggressive heavy work. The features offered in this operation are simple but effective.

Edit Smoothing consolidates the features of Trim Region Start to Fill and Batch Crossfades. In the following exercise, you will apply both in one fell swoop.

1. *Select* Ex 6.6.3 from the **Memory Locations** window.

2. *Select* **Edit Smoothing** in the **Operation** section of the **Beat Detective** window. The Conform section now turns into the Smoothing section (see Figure 6.46). Fill Gaps will simply fill the empty areas created by the Conform operation by editing region starts backward to fill the gaps. The Fill and Crossfade feature will add a crossfade value of defined length to all region separations.

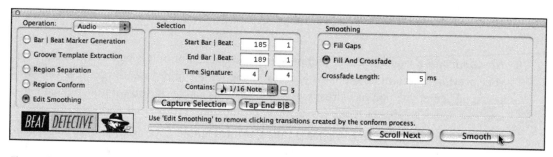

**Figure 6.46**

The Smoothing section of the Beat Detective window when the Edit Smoothing operation is selected.

3. *Select* **Fill and Crossfade** and *enter* a crossfade **Length** of **5ms**.

4. *Click* on the **Smooth** button to enable the settings.

5. *Hit* the **spacebar** to play the selection. As you can hear, you have altered the rhythmic feel of the drum beat. In this case, it's because of the extreme manner with which you adjusted the regions using the Region Conform operation.

   With all of the individual regions conformed and smoothed out, it's time to verify your loop length and create a Region group.

6. If they are not already selected, select all the regions in your new drum pattern by *clicking* once on the **first region** with the **Grabber** tool and, while holding the **Shift** key, *selecting* the **last region** by *clicking* on it with the **Grabber** tool.

   A quick look at the Event Edit area next to the Main Counter will tell you that the length is a little longer than exactly four bars. In this case, it might be easier to create a Region group first and edit it, rather than zooming in.

7. *Press Option+Command+G* (Mac) or *Ctrl+Alt+G* (PC) to create a new Region group.

8. Using **Grid** mode, *find* the **Trim** tool at the far right of the Region group and *click* once to reset the region length to exactly four bars.

9.  If not already selected, select Loop Playback by *hitting Shift+Command+L* (Mac) or *Shift+Ctrl+L* (PC) on your keyboard.

10. *Hit* the **spacebar** to play and verify the loop. Once verified, *hit* the **spacebar** again to stop playback.

11. *Double-click* on the **Region group** with the **Grabber** tool to **rename** it "Breakdown Drums." Now that you have created a little breakdown section drum beat, let's place it into the track.

12. *Hit Command+C* (Mac) or *Ctrl+C* (PC) to place the Region loop in the paste buffer.

13. Close the Beat Detective window by *clicking* once on the **small circle** at the top-left corner.

14. *Select* Ex 6.6.4 from the **Memory Locations** window. You will now see the drums for the Breakdown section prominently displayed. As you can see, the drum regions in the Solo and Breakdown sections are part of a Region loop.

15. *Click* once on **any iteration** with the **Grabber** tool to select them all.

16. *Hit Option+Command+U* (Mac) or *Ctrl+Alt+U* (PC) to ungroup the Region loops.

17. Now select the first Sampled Drums region of the **Breakdown** section by *double-clicking* once with the **Selector** tool.

18. *Hit Command+V* (Mac) or *Ctrl+V* (PC) to paste the Breakdown Drums Region group at the beginning of the Breakdown section, as shown in Figure 6.47.

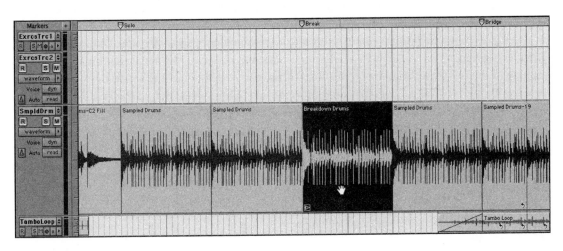

**Figure 6.47**
The newly pasted Breakdown Drums Region loop at the beginning of the Breakdown section.

19. Now *press Command+D* (Mac) or *Ctrl+D* (PC) to duplicate the Breakdown Drums region and fill out the Breakdown section with the new drum loop.

20. *Click* anywhere before the **Breakdown** section with the **Selector** tool to move the play cursor, and *hit* the **spacebar** to audition the new Breakdown Drums.

21. *Hit Command+S* (Mac) or *Ctrl+S* (PC) to save.

22. *Hit* the **Return** key (Mac) or the **Enter** key (PC) to return to the top of the song and *hit* the **spacebar** to take in all of your work.

I think it is clear from this small sampling of Beat Detective that it is without a doubt one of the most powerful tools offered in Pro Tools. The ability to create tempo maps and groove templates, or to simply separate and conform regions to an existing tempo or groove template is an incredibly valuable production tool. The difficulty in presenting a tool such as Beat Detective is that the subject matter could easily cover a whole book's worth of material on its own.

I have presented Beat Detective from the perspective of the LE user so that all readers will be able to benefit from the design, function, and features. But, Beat Detective for HD users adds the additional capabilities of multitrack usage. This has an obvious advantage for editing live drum performances that are recorded to multiple tracks. This is allowed through a feature called *Collection mode*. By selecting individual tracks at a time, the Detection parameters can be adjusted uniquely to each track so that a minimum number of false triggers are generated. Once created and edited, clicking on the Collection Mode button will allow the Beat Triggers to be added to a collection of the other detected drum tracks. To deal with this multitrack issue in LE, it is sometimes advisable to create a mono mix with the Bounce to Disk function. Import the mix of your drums back into your session and generate your tempo maps or groove templates from the mono drum mix. If you need to separate and conform, you can still do so on the mono drum mix track. Then add it to a Track Edit group with all your individual drum tracks and duplicate the separations manually by tabbing to the region separations on the mono drum mix and applying the separations to the live drums with the Separate Region command. It might take a bit longer, but a little creative thought using all of the editing features you have learned so far will get you a long way.

## Tips for Beat Detective Bliss

Because Beat Detective encompasses so many additional bits of knowledge and procedures to follow for effective operation, I have compiled a list of things to keep in mind when working with it. Many of the items on this list are bullet points from the content of the "Tempo and Timing (Beat Detective)" section of this chapter.

- **Work with small selections.** Working with small selection areas will make your workload easier and will allow you to find the parameter settings that work best faster. Once you have developed a working formula, you can adapt it to larger selections without getting overwhelmed.

- **Define accurate selection areas.** Beat Detective works most accurately when the selection area is defined accurately. This is most apparent when defining Beat Triggers.

- **Carefully define and edit your Beat Triggers.** Don't assume that they are all perfectly placed. Zoom in to sample accuracy. If necessary, place them one by one with the Scroll Next button.

- **Use the Show Trigger Time option when editing Beat Triggers to help you know exactly what you are editing when zoomed in.**

- **If your system is running slow with Beat Detective, consider upgrading your RAM or lowering the levels of the Undo History in the Preferences menu.** Beat Detective can create an extraordinary amount of edits in a short period of time that can eat up your RAM very quickly. If each level of undo contains all of these edits, you might be eating up too much of your RAM and CPU power to run your session efficiently.

- **When creating tempo maps, it is best to set your audio tracks to be sample-based so that subsequent regions do not move around while you are entering tempo data.**

- **When extracting groove templates, make sure there are no Bar | Beat markers contained within the selection area.** The Beat markers will compromise the accuracy of the extraction.

- **Use the Trigger Pad selection when editing material with softer transients to prevent clipping of those regions.** Sync Points will be created to preserve the region timing and placement.

- **When conforming regions, experiment with the Strength, Exclude Within, and Swing parameters to get the feel you are looking for.** Remember to undo your previous conform before trying the new settings.

- **Consolidate your regions into a single audio file when you are done with your smoothing process.** When there are a large number of edits with crossfades, consolidating will take a great load off of your RAM and CPU power, as well as leave you with a readymade backup of your editing work should disaster strike.

Congratulations!!! If you've made this far, you've finished the book and hopefully enjoyed it as well. Maybe in the process you learned a thing or two about editing audio in Pro Tools. The most difficult part about writing this book was not what to put in the book, but rather, what to leave out. Fully understanding the editing capabilities of Pro Tools requires years of work, and there is no greater teacher than experience. The only way I ever learned a new software program was to give myself a project to work on with it. Having little or no experience with Pro Tools more than 10 years ago, I took on a whole album production project and used Pro Tools as the recording and editing platform. I didn't sleep very much for the four-month period it took to complete the project, but I learned more about Pro Tools than I ever would have just fiddling around with it in my spare time.

The genesis of this book stems entirely from my own experience as an engineer, as well as through all the students I've tortured over the years. It is really their feedback, from the many variations of this theme I conjured up, that culminated in the book you are reading today. What I really hoped to accomplish with this book was to give the reader a good, solid foundation into the Pro Tools editing system by giving practical examples and a song as a platform. I hope I have represented that desire well. I look forward to receiving your feedback on this book so that the next one will be even better. I can be reached at mpwhite3d@gmail.com.

Thank you!

# Index

# License Agreement/Notice of Limited Warranty

By opening the sealed disc container in this book, you agree to the following terms and conditions. If, upon reading the following license agreement and notice of limited warranty, you cannot agree to the terms and conditions set forth, return the unused book with unopened disc to the place where you purchased it for a refund.

## License:

The enclosed software is copyrighted by the copyright holder(s) indicated on the software disc. You are licensed to copy the software onto a single computer for use by a single user and to a backup disc. You may not reproduce, make copies, or distribute copies or rent or lease the software in whole or in part, except with written permission of the copyright holder(s). You may transfer the enclosed disc only together with this license, and only if you destroy all other copies of the software and the transferee agrees to the terms of the license. You may not decompile, reverse assemble, or reverse engineer the software.

## Notice of Limited Warranty:

The enclosed disc is warranted by Thomson Course Technology PTR to be free of physical defects in materials and workmanship for a period of sixty (60) days from end user's purchase of the book/disc combination. During the sixty-day term of the limited warranty, Thomson Course Technology PTR will provide a replacement disc upon the return of a defective disc.

## Limited Liability:

THE SOLE REMEDY FOR BREACH OF THIS LIMITED WARRANTY SHALL CONSIST ENTIRELY OF REPLACEMENT OF THE DEFECTIVE DISC. IN NO EVENT SHALL THOMSON COURSE TECHNOLOGY PTR OR THE AUTHOR BE LIABLE FOR ANY OTHER DAMAGES, INCLUDING LOSS OR CORRUPTION OF DATA, CHANGES IN THE FUNCTIONAL CHARACTERISTICS OF THE HARDWARE OR OPERATING SYSTEM, DELETERIOUS INTERACTION WITH OTHER SOFTWARE, OR ANY OTHER SPECIAL, INCIDENTAL, OR CONSEQUENTIAL DAMAGES THAT MAY ARISE, EVEN IF THOMSON COURSE TECHNOLOGY PTR AND/OR THE AUTHOR HAS PREVIOUSLY BEEN NOTIFIED THAT THE POSSIBILITY OF SUCH DAMAGES EXISTS.

## Disclaimer of Warranties:

THOMSON COURSE TECHNOLOGY PTR AND THE AUTHOR SPECIFICALLY DISCLAIM ANY AND ALL OTHER WARRANTIES, EITHER EXPRESS OR IMPLIED, INCLUDING WARRANTIES OF MERCHANTABILITY, SUITABILITY TO A PARTICULAR TASK OR PURPOSE, OR FREEDOM FROM ERRORS. SOME STATES DO NOT ALLOW FOR EXCLUSION OF IMPLIED WARRANTIES OR LIMITATION OF INCIDENTAL OR CONSEQUENTIAL DAMAGES, SO THESE LIMITATIONS MIGHT NOT APPLY TO YOU.

## Other:

This Agreement is governed by the laws of the State of Massachusetts without regard to choice of law principles. The United Convention of Contracts for the International Sale of Goods is specifically disclaimed. This Agreement constitutes the entire agreement between you and Thomson Course Technology PTR regarding use of the software.